Teaching 1: Classroom Management

Wesley C. Becker

Professor of Special Education   University of Oregon

Siegfried Engelmann

Professor of Special Education   University of Oregon

Don R. Thomas

Director, Minnesota Learning Center   Brainerd State Hospital

A Modular Revision of
Teaching: A Course in Applied Psychology

 SCIENCE RESEARCH ASSOCIATES, INC.
Chicago, Palo Alto, Toronto, Henley-on-Thames, Sydney, Paris, Stuttgart
A Subsidiary of IBM

To Sidney W. Bijou
He saw the future and led us to it.

© 1975, Science Research Associates, Inc. All rights reserved.
Printed in the United States of America.
Library of Congress Catalog Card Number: 74-31012
Library of Congress Cataloging in Publication Data
Becker, Wesley C   1928–
    Teaching—a modular revision of Teaching.

    Includes bibliographical references and indexes.
    CONTENTS: 1. Classroom management.
    1. Educational psychology. I. Engelmann,
Siegfried, joint author. II. Thomas, Donald R.,
joint author. III. Title.
LB1051.B2985   1975   370.15   74-31012
ISBN 0-574-18025-7 (v. 1)

This is a revised, three-part edition of
Teaching: A Course in Applied Psychology, © 1971.

contents

preface

New technologies of teaching are being fashioned from the growing knowledge of the events that influence learning. This course aims to teach principles underlying new teaching technologies, and at the same time to teach experienced and future teachers *what they need to do* to be better teachers. Our primary goal is to improve the practice of teaching rather than to enable the student to talk about various theories of learning.

In designing this course, we have attempted to use the principles we are trying to teach. Our field tests have convinced us that the student who approaches these materials with at least a modest level of diligence will come away with new skills that will be of value throughout his or her professional career. Many of you, we hope, will come away from this course as better persons because you will have learned how to help others become more capable and loving persons.

This modular edition of *Teaching: A Course in Applied Psychology* has been completely revised, updated, reorganized, and extended to cover the topic of *evaluation*. By means of new unit sections called "Broadening Your Perspective," the text becomes more completely self-sufficient. The student receives a broad exposure to the experimental literature without having to read a lot of technical jargon or spending many hours in the library.

This programed course is presented in three volumes. Volume 1 focuses on the use of behavior principles in *classroom management*. It deals with principles and procedures underlying effective social development and the use of positive motivational methods with children and young adults.

Volume 1 is a behavior-modification primer. Some teachers view behavior modification as simply a bag of tricks to get children to behave and make the teacher's life less troublesome. This is far from the case. Behavior modification is effective education. It is the systematic use of learning principles to accomplish our goals for children. From the beginning of this venture, we wish to emphasize that the primary goal of teaching is the induction of knowledge and skills that will enable a person to achieve a fuller life in our society. Even though this text at times focuses on the elimination of problem behavior, keep in mind that teaching is still the primary goal.

Volume 2 in this series shifts to an analysis of *instruction*. It concerns itself with the essential components of effective instruction, with the requirements for teaching a general case, with strategies for instructional programing, and with applications of these ideas to teaching concepts, operations, and intelligent problem-solving skills. There is also a concern with the problems of remedial and special instruction.

In Volume 3, the problem of *evaluation* for and by the classroom teacher is examined with the goal of improving the teacher's skills in selection of programs and procedures, in placing and monitoring students, and in evaluating whether the instructional goals are in fact met. Basic statistical concepts helpful in evaluation are introduced and taught as needed through programed practice. Diagnostic, criterion-referenced, and norm-referenced testing are examined. The traditional concepts of aptitude and ability are re-examined. A logic for program evaluation is provided.

It is the intent of the authors to provide the teacher, through these three volumes, with a modern, up-to-date knowledge of, as Sidney Bijou put it, "What psychology has to offer education now."

We wish to give special thanks to Jeanne Schultz for her careful and dedicated work in preparing this revised manuscript.

to the instructor: course organization

This course is designed to operate without lectures. Films might be added at various times, and demonstrations can be provided. Occasional lectures in special areas might be helpful, especially on the first unit. The *Instructor's Manual* that accompanies this text (which may be obtained at no cost to you) makes it possible for the instructor to use a variety of procedures. The following suggestions are teaching formats that have been found effective.

Self-Paced Progress

Each student reads a unit, does the exercises, checks his own exercises, goes over the discussion questions, and then is checked out by another student who has already passed that unit. In conducting the checkout, the examining student uses the *Instructor's Manual* as a source of questions and criteria for acceptable responses. Tests are taken as scheduled and projects are turned in for evaluation by the instructor.

Leader-Paced Progress, Students as Group Leaders

In this course format, each student reads the assigned unit, completes his exercises and checks them, and prepares for the group session, being sure he can answer each of the discussion questions. At the group session, each student is asked to write out answers to two of the questions selected by the instructor. Papers are turned in for credit. Then the instructor appoints one-fourth of the class to be group leaders for that session. Small groups of four are formed. Each group leader then uses the *Instructor's Manual* to take the other three students through the objects of the unit. The leader asks questions from the manual and the students take turns answering. The leader and the group members help when there are mistakes or omissions.

Leader-Paced Progress, Former Students as Group Leaders

In this format there is an instructor or group leader for each ten students. The students do a lesson, complete the exercises, and check their answers prior to the group discussion session. The group leaders have the only available *Instructor's Manuals.* At the group sessions, group members are asked in turn to respond to questions. The whole group writes answers to two questions each session, or takes a ten-minute quiz at each lecture session. Remedial assignments are made when performance is not adequate.

Each of these course organization formats attempts to provide appropriate consequences for appropriate study behavior and thereby increase the chances of each student being successful in mastering the objectives of the course. Whatever procedures are used in your course, keep in mind that *knowing* is not *doing.* Aim for changes in what students do as well as what they say.

to the student: how to use this text

Our experience suggests that the student will gain the most from this text if he follows these steps:

1 Read a unit.
2 Do the self-test. If you miss 0 or 1 item, skip the programed practice exercise and do the other exercises and discussion questions. If you make more than one error, do the section called programed practice.
3 When an item gives you trouble, return to the text to study the problem in context.
4 Calculate the percentage of items correct and record it for each programed practice exercise.
5 If a score on a programed practice exercise is above 90 percent, go on to the discussion questions and other exercises. If a score is much below 90 percent, review the unit before going on to the discussion questions.
6 When answering the discussion questions, be prepared to give your answers orally or in writing. The questions serve as a basis for discussion in the group sessions.

Projects to provide practice in the use of some procedures are provided with units 2, 4, 7, and 11. Be guided by the instructor's requirements in planning and executing projects.

Acknowledgments

From *Issues in the Analysis of Behavior* by Richard W. Malott, Dale A. General, and Vivian B. Snapper. Copyright © 1973, by Behaviordelia, Inc. Used by permission of Behaviordelia.

From "Application of Behavioral Principles to Classroom Settings" by David Phillips, in *An Empirical Basis for Change in Education*, W. C. Becker (ed.), Science Research Associates, 1971. Reprinted by permission of the author.

From "The Lincoln Elementary School Projects: Some Results of an In-Service Training Course in Behavioral Psychology" by W. Scott Wood, in *Behavior Modification Monographs*, Vol. 1, No. 2, Roger Ulrich (ed.), Behavior Development Corporation.

From C. Madsen, W. Becker, D. Thomas, L. Koser and E. Plager, "An Analysis of the Reinforcing Function of 'Sit Down' Commands," in Ronald K. Parker (ed.), *Readings in Educational Psychology*. © Copyright 1968 by Allyn and Bacon, Inc., Boston. Reprinted with permission.

From "The Contingent Use of Teacher Attention and Praise in Reducing Classroom Behavior Problems" by W. Becker, C. Madsen, C. Arnold, and D. Thomas, in *The Journal of Special Education*, Vol. 1, No. 3, 1967. © 1967, Buttonwood Farms, Inc.

From "How Behavior Modification Principles Have Affected My Teaching," a term paper by Constance Carlson. Reprinted by permission of the author.

From "Prompting a Consumer Behavior for Pollution Control" by E. Geller, J. Farris, and D. Post, in *Journal of Applied Behavior Analysis*, Vol. 6, 1973.

From "The Organization of Day-Care Environments: Required *vs* Optional Activities" by L. Doke and T. Risley, in Journal of *Applied Behavior Analysis*, Vol. 5, 1972.

From *Handwriting with Write and See* by B. F. Skinner and S. Krakower, Lyons and Carnahan, 1968.

From "Use of Positive Reinforcement in Conditioning Attentive Behavior" by H. M. Walker and N. K. Buckley, in *Journal of Applied Behavior Analysis*, Vol. 1, 1968.

From *Token Reinforcement Techniques: Classroom Applications for the Hard-to-Teach Child* by H. M. Walker and N. K. Buckley, E-B Press, 1974.

From "Fixed-Interval Work Habits of Congress" by P. Weisberg and P. B. Waldrop, in *Journal of Applied Behavior Analysis*, Vol. 5, 1972.

From *Distar*™ *Library Series* by Siegfried Engelmann and Elaine C. Bruner. © 1971, Science Research Associates, Inc. Reprinted by permission of the publisher.

From "Behavior Modification of an Adjustment Class: A Token Reinforcement Program" by K. D. O'Leary and W. C. Becker, in *Exceptional Children*, No. 34, 1967.

From "Achievement Place: Token Reinforcement Procedures in a Home-Style Rehabilitation Setting for Pre-delinquent Boys" by Elery Phillips, in *Journal of Applied Behavior Analysis*, Vol. 1, 1968.

From "The Home Point System: Token Reinforcement Procedures for Application by Parents of Children with Behavior Problems" by E. R. Christopherson, C. M. Arnold, D. W. Hill, and H. R. Quilitich, in *Journal of Applied Behavioral Analysis*, Vol. 5, 1972.

From "A Programmed System of Instruction" by F. Keller, in Behavior Modification Monographs, Vol. 1, No. 2, 1970, Roger Ulrich (ed.), Behavior Development Corporation.

From *Corrective Reading Program: Student Materials* by S. Engelmann, W. Becker, L. Carnine, L. Meyers, J. Becker, and G. Johnson, E-B Press, 1973.

From "Effective Behavior Change at the Anne Arundel Learning Center Through Minimum Contact Interventions" by S. Cohen, J. Keyworth, and I. Kleiner, Jr., in *Volume Three: Control of Human Behavior, Behavior Modification in Education*, Scott, Foresman.

From "Effect of Contingent and Non-Contingent Social Reinforcement on the Cooperative Play of a Preschool Child" by B. Hart et al., in *Journal of Applied Behavior Analysis*, Vol. 1, No. 1, 1968.

From "The Modification of a Child's Enuresis: Some Response-Response Relationships" by V. Nordquist, in *Journal of Applied Behavior Analysis*, Vol. 4, 1971.

From "Freedom and Responsibility in an Elementary School" by C. Salzberg, in *Behavior Analysis and Education*, Univ. of Kansas, 1972.

From "Open Classrooms: Supporters of Applied Behavior Analysis" by M. McNeil, in *Behavior Analysis and Education*, Univ. of Kansas, 1972.

From "Operant-Interpersonal Treatment for Martial Discord" by R. Stuart, in *Journal of Consulting & Clinical Psychology*, 33, 1969, American Psychology Association.

unit 1

Human Concerns and a Science of Behavior

objectives

When first exposed to an experimental analysis of behavior, students frequently have many questions. We have found that once these are answered, many find a new hope for humanity in the study of behavior. We hope you will too. The main objective of this unit is to get you, the student, to the point where you will want to give the behavioral approach a chance to prove its value.

When you complete this unit you should be able to—

1 Point out some of the essential characteristics of a behavioral approach to the study of man.
2 Discuss the issue of humanistic values and scientific methods.
3 Discuss the issues of control, determinism, freedom of choice, and responsibility.
4 Discuss the bribery issue.
5 Identify several kinds of false explanations of behavior.
6 Explain some implications of modern behavioral technology for teaching.

lesson

The behavioral psychologist assumes that we can make more reasonable decisions about ourselves if we know the causes of behavior. This requires the use of methods that will keep us from deception. Central to research methods in behavioral psychology are: (a) the reliable observation of some behavior (*dependent variable*), (b) introduction of a change (called the *independent variable*), and (c) observation of the effects of the change on the dependent behavior. With carefully chosen procedures, we can learn what leads to what. For example, to learn about classroom management procedures, we might count how often the students get out of their seats when they are supposed to be studying (dependent variable). We then have the teacher increase the frequency of critical comments about their out-of-seat behavior (independent variable) and find that the students get out of their seats even *more*. Well, that procedure produced an effect, but not one we were looking for. So we try again. Next, we have the teacher praise sitting and working, and we find out that there is less getting out of seats. We are beginning to learn some procedures for classroom management and some causes of behavior.

The good teacher uses procedures very much like those of the behavioral scientist. Before teaching in a particular area, he first finds out what the students can do (dependent variable); then he teaches (independent variable); and finally he tests to find the effects of the teaching on the students. The good teacher, like the behavioral scientist, remains open to data from the students and adjusts procedures accordingly.

Natural Lawfulness

When we find again and again that a change in an independent variable leads to a change in a dependent variable, we have a basis for a generalization. For example, we might observe that teachers' praise can be used to increase completion of assignments. We might go on to observe many other situations in which some consequence increases a wide variety of behaviors. From these observations, we can generalize. First we *define* as reinforcers those consequences that increase a behavior. (Other consequences might decrease it or have no effect at all.) Then we note that the law applies only to voluntary responses (technically we call these *operant responses*) and not to reflexive reactions. Now we can state a general law of reinforcement: Operant responses have the potential of being strengthened by consequences (called reinforcers).

The law specifies:

1	A dependent variable	Operant behavior
2	An independent variable and a procedure for using it	Reinforcers presented *after* the operant behaviors
3	An effect	Operant behavior strengthened

Most of us are convinced that there is lawfulness in the physical world. The sun rises predictably; A-bombs explode on signal; and ice melts at 32° F. That *behavior* is lawful is sometimes quite obvious. After a day on a hot desert with no water, people will drink. In different learning environments around the world, we can see remarkable consistencies in language, dress, gesture, and patterns of relating. For example, Russians speak Russian, not Italian. The more we as scientists investigate the environmental conditions that control learning (behavior change), the more convinced we are that *all learning follows lawful processes*, which can be known. This is equivalent to saying that behavior is determined by causes. It does not mean that we know enough about the variables affecting a given individual at a given point in time to precisely predict his or her every behavior. It simply means that they are potentially knowable.

After millions of corroborating observations, the initial assumption that behavior is determined has assumed the status of an empirical law: All behavioral events have causes. This same lawfulness is also found in the rest of the physical world.

Humanistic Values and Behavior Science

As with many fields of study, behavioral psychology has its controversies and critics. One goal of this unit is to deal with some of these issues. Foremost in criticizing behavioral approaches are those who identify themselves with modern humanism. Historically, humanists have been concerned with the problems of people, here and now, rather than in some afterlife that might be. It was the early humanist movement that helped to create the Renaissance and foster the development of modern science. Humanists are still concerned for the individual. They value such qualities as self-determination, self-knowledge, personal responsibility, individuality, diversity, and openness. But some humanists today oppose making human behavior the object of scientific study because they feel that such study of man as seen from the outside will somehow destroy what they value in man as seen from the inside. This argument seems to contradict their concern with self-knowledge. Also, to become mature involves developing a more objective frame of reference about oneself.

When we examine the values held by most behaviorally oriented professionals, we find that they also must be called humanists. They are concerned with helping others as individuals find solutions to their here-and-now problems. The major difference seems to be not in the *values* held but in the *methods of knowing* considered acceptable. The humanists today who oppose behaviorism usually conceptualize behavior from an internal frame of reference, in terms of feelings, thoughts, and goals, rather than from an external one, in terms of the environmental variables that affect behavior.

The behavioral scientist insists on dealing with observations that can be verified by others. For example, value terms like concern, self-determination, and openness are not sufficiently specific for the behaviorist. He would first have to ask, "What do you mean by openness; that is, how does this value affect your behavior?" In the process, the value terms are given some observable action equivalents. For example:

Concern	"I will volunteer as a classroom aide working with disadvantaged children."
Self-determination	"I carefully listen to both sides of an argument and make my own decision about what is right."
Self-knowledge	"When I do a job for others, like giving a lecture, I ask for feedback on my performance. I try to know how I affect others."
Personal Responsibility	"I consider the potential effects of what I do on others. I do not do things that might be harmful to others."
Individuality	"I support the right to be different."
Diversity	"I do not accept the proposal that there is only one right way to do something. I support the search for many 'right' ways to solve people's problems."
Openness	"I let others know what I am thinking and feeling. I encourage others to talk to me."

Many people may have the same actions in mind when they use a particular value term, or they may not. One person's concern may not be another's. The behaviorist would seek to clarify such terms before studying their role in human behavior. But it does not mean that his values are different. It only means that the terms are not acceptable in a science of behavior until they have been defined in terms of observables. The issue is one of methods, not value differences.

The Problem of Control

The idea that behavior is lawful (determinism) gives many students fits. They don't like the idea of being controlled. In fact, they don't believe that they are controlled. This problem involves the concepts *determinism, indeterminism, control,* and *freedom of choice.* We will begin with determinism and control.

If we agree that behavior is lawful, we have accepted the assumption that behavior is *determined* (controlled) by causes. These causes are environmental events, called stimuli. Thus, to the behavioral scientist, it is correct to say that behavior is controlled by stimulus events. But this is not the kind of control that we personally find upsetting. We are content when we can do what we have found is rewarding for us. The fact that we have learned to do things in a determined world poses no problem; it is when someone tries to *prevent us* from doing what we have learned to do that we get upset. We object to *social* controls, usually in the form of threat or force.

But social control need not be aversive. In fact we are all social controllers to the extent that we teach each other. Much of what each of us does determines how others behave. Parents teach children, children teach parents, husbands teach wives, wives teach husbands, caring people teach each other. In a very real sense we are each responsible for what others learn—how they learn to behave with us. We have the power to make others better people. With a knowledge of behavior principles we can facilitate what we value in people and their social systems.

Some students decide that the only tolerable position is "I just won't use my behavior to influence others at all." We contend that this is not a responsible alternative. The real choice open to each of us is not *whether* we influence others, but *how* we influence them. To passively withdraw from others is to give the influence to those who may not be as noble or kind as you, like negligent parents who leave their child's learning to the consequences provided by other kids on the street. The responsible course of action is to learn to use the principles of behavior to help others reach their objectives and to learn to manage our own lives more effectively. We are the controllers of each other. Let's learn to do it in positive ways.

...JUST MINDING MY OWN BUSINESS

The Problem of Indeterminism

Indeterminism is a belief that some events are not caused. They just happen unpredictably, or randomly. It is an assertion that the empirical law, determinism, is not true. What is the evidence? Don't games of chance involve random, uncaused events? The answer is "no." As the operators of gambling establishments know, the outcomes are very predictable. The actions of slot machines or dice are caused and lawful. But multiple causes are operating on any individual event so that they are not predictable under specific circumstances; only the long range trend is predictable. However, each individual event could be predicted if the multiple causal factors were systematically controlled in their own operation.

The most frequently cited argument against determinism is based on Heisenberg's *Principle of Indeterminancy*. This title gives the impression that some things are uncaused, but Heisenberg was only pointing to a measurement problem in subatomic physics. He said that you cannot measure both position and velocity of a subatomic particle at the same time because the process itself changes what you are measuring. The following quote from Malott discusses the issue:

> Heisenberg stated the principle in reference to the science of physics. He said that in the case of certain subatomic particles it is impossible to determine both position and velocity simultaneously. The reason for this is that the photon of light, by means of which the observation is made possible, itself exerts an effect on the particle. Heisenberg used the word "determine" to mean *measure*. If you try to measure one aspect of the particle, the measuring process may affect that particle so that another aspect can no longer be accurately measured. For example, you cannot measure velocity and location at the same time. The antideterminists have grabbed at the principle like "drowning men grabbing at straws." They have interpreted his word "determine" to mean *cause*, citing Heisenberg as having argued against determinism. They might make a statement like the following: if certain factors in physics are indeterminate (uncaused), then how can the behavioral sciences, where the variables are more difficult to define, more complex and harder to isolate, hope to discover the operation of deterministic laws?
>
> Since this antideterministic argument is based on misinterpretation of the Heisenberg Principle, we cannot accept the suggestion that it adds credence to the antideterministic point of view.[1]

The Problems of Free Will and Responsibility

In the history of philosophy, the concept of free will has had two features: (1) it refers to the behavior of making choices without being hampered, and (2) it involves an assumption that choices are not caused by physical or divine events. The problem that arises is this: If all behavior is determined, then man cannot have a free will. If man does not have a free will, how can he be held responsible for his actions?

As we know them today, the facts of the matter are these: (1) man does make choices at times without being coerced by others, but (2) this choice behavior is determined by natural events or causes. Where then does that leave responsibility? To unravel this historic confusion, let us consider the distinction between *laws of nature* and *laws of state*, or natural laws and social laws.[2]

NATURAL LAWS	SOCIAL LAWS
DESCRIBE WHAT LEADS TO WHAT. EVENTS ARE DETERMINED OR THEY ARE NOT.	PRESCRIBE WHAT SHOULD BE. THERE IS COERCION OR FREEDOM OF CHOICE.

Natural laws describe the way we understand things to be in nature. For example, water boils when heated to 212° F. at sea level. As some wag put it, "Nature doesn't violate her own laws," and being part of nature, neither do we. Natural laws are true whether we like them or not, whether we know them or not. The current evidence supports the position that all natural events have causes (are determined).

Social laws, on the other hand, prescribe what people should do and the consequences for a failure to follow the prescription. People make them and they can change them. They are not true, but only potentially useful to us. All explicit or implicit contracts and agreements have a similar prescribing function. These obligations of people to each other define a social system, and *it is within these obligations that freedom and responsibility exist, not in nature*.

Freedom of choice is an issue that arises in the context of human agreements. Some social systems allow more opportunities for uncoerced choice than others. In fact we are probably now at a point in history when we could begin to experimentally examine alternative political-social structures in terms of their facilitation of choice, individuality, closeness, and so forth. Keep in mind that what we do in a choice situation is determined by our learning history. Behavior is lawful, and this includes choice behavior. What we are suggesting is that we can design alternative systems where there is a greater opportunity to make choices in accordance with our individual learning histories, and where coerciveness is minimized.

With this background, we can now deal with the issue of *responsibility*. Legal responsibility does not exist independently of contracts, both explicit and implicit, and laws of states. Legal responsibility can be *assumed* (for example, by entering into a marriage contract) or *assigned* by laws of state (such as parents being responsible for their children). The fact that legal responsibility is assumed or assigned does not make a person act responsibly. The contract or law simply specifies the penalties for the failure to live up to a responsibility, or the rewards for doing so. People become law-abiding if they are taught to be so. The current knowledge from behavior science can in fact be used to teach children to be more responsible citizens.

But what about personal, rather than legal, responsibility? It is an *assumed* responsibility based on an *implicit* contract with others to take care of each other. It is assumed because of an understanding of our mutual dependence on each other for important human satisfactions—such as love, affection, sharing, giving, safety, and nourishment. We are our brothers' keepers.

The Problem of Predestination

A confusion sometimes arises between determinism and predestination. Both ideas assert that events are caused. Predestination, however, asserts that some powerful being (like God) has prearranged all worldly events. As a result there is nothing we can do about anything (fatalism). Determinism, on the other hand, offers the hope that, with a better knowledge of how things work, we can build a better mouse trap or a better world. We can control the environment that controls us.

The Problem of Simplicity

It is not at all uncommon to find modern behavior theory characterized as too simplistic to deal with the complexities of human cognitive processes. Some critics say that concept formation, problem-solving behavior, and operational thought are not covered by stimulus-response theories and that stimulus-response association theories are appropriate only for understanding simple habits and reflexes. Such a position is fundamentally incorrect. It reflects the confusion of some early behavioristic models of learning processes, which are now more than fifty years old, with modern behaviorism. The position shows its proponent to be uninformed about modern behavior theory.

It is true that early behaviorists placed a great emphasis on stimulus-response connections. In modern behavior theory, such a model is primarily used to describe reflexive actions, such as sneezing in the presence of pepper, salivating when food is placed in the mouth, or an increase in heart rate when a sudden-intense stimulus occurs. Reflexive actions like these, which involve the smooth muscle system and glands, are called *respondent behaviors* in modern behavior theory. They account for only a small share of human behavior, albeit an important one (for example, they provide a basis for understanding many aspects of emotional behavior). Respondent behavior responds to the environment.

As you will see, modern behavior theory effectively deals with behaviors that we normally refer to as intelligent or voluntary behavior. As noted earlier, this is technically called *operant behavior*. Operant behavior operates on the environment. In volume 2 of this text, we analyze how differential reinforcement and other principles can be used to teach concepts and operations. This analysis then provides the basis for understanding what problem-solving behavior is about. With a simple extension, "thinking" becomes the problem-solving behavior that we do in our heads through manipulation of words and symbols, rather than through operating physically on the environment.

Operant behavior classes are basically the same as Piaget's mental operations except that operant behavior classes are overt and mental operations are covert. For example, the operant class *adding* is at first adding members to a physical group (an overt operation). When these operations are carried out symbolically through a chain of words and pictures in our heads, we have a mental operation. Modern behavior theory may be easy to understand, but it is not restricted to simple or trivial aspects of human behavior.

The Problem of Bribery

Essential to the analysis of operant behavior is the principle that reinforcers and punishers control (cause) the learning. Using this principle, we recommend that teachers use reinforcers, which in some cases might be candy, toys, or even money. It is at this point that the question of bribery arises. It is common folklore among parents and teachers that bribery is bad. "You should not bribe children." This dictum is taken to mean that it is bad to use *any concrete rewards under any circumstances* with children. This position is again based on a misunderstanding. In the 1930s a number of child psychologists rightly pointed out that the use of rewards under some circumstances is *bribery* and should be avoided. Consider this example: Billy did not clean up his room, which is an assigned responsibility, and his mother said, "Look, Billy, clean up your room, and I'll give you a quarter." Later mother found that Billy did not help with the dishes either, as he was expected to, and mother said, "Look, Billy, dry the dishes, and you can earn a dime." Before too long mother had taught Billy not to complete his responsibilities because that is what mother rewards. *This is bribery.* It involves a misuse of rewards and teaches irresponsible behavior. However, mother could have used rewards differently to teach responsible behaviors. She could have worked out *ahead of time* a chart system, so Billy could earn stars daily for keeping his room clean and helping with the dishes. Then on Saturday, his allowance would be determined by the number of stars earned. In this way, rewards would be used responsibly to help Billy learn to keep his part of an agreement with his parents. If using rewards of any kind in any way is bribery, then we all had better stop accepting our paychecks and work for free.

False Explanations for Behavior

History is full of false explanations for behavior. As recently as 1692 people were executed as witches in this country and as late as 1782 in Switzerland. Devils, gods, and ghosts have carried a big load in the accounting for behavior in the past. Unfortunately, there are continuing misconceptions cloaked in the guise of scientific explanations to bedevil the teacher.

The Medical Model

One of these is the attempt to understand behavior problems using an analogy based on organic disease processes. Using the scientific principle "Treat causes, not symptoms," the medical/disease analogy leads one to look within the "personality" for "conflicts" that are the presumed causes. For example, Tony is constantly on the move, never sitting still, and therefore not getting his work done. Every so often the teacher tells Tony, sometimes angrily, to get back in his seat. When he is in his seat, she attends to other problems. His teacher suspects he is "hyperactive" and has some kind of home-related conflict or brain injury. She refers Tony to a psychologist who confirms her concerns: "The test results suggest that Tony may have a minimal brain damage. He showed several word-reversals and introduced a number of distortions in copying geometric figures. He also appears to have a conflict with authority. On a projective test he created several stories in which a boy was getting into trouble and being punished by an old woman. Tony should be given play therapy." Well, either there is no play therapist available to see Tony, and the teacher is right back where she started; or Tony goes into play therapy, and his teacher sees no change in the classroom.

A behavioral psychologist would take a different approach. A behavioral learning model leads directly to an examination of the environmental conditions that function to produce and maintain the problem behavior. Behavior is learned and maintained by consequences. So what are the consequences maintaining Tony's out-of-seat behavior? When Tony is in his seat, the teacher ignores him and probably punishes him with an assignment he cannot do. When he is out of his seat, the teacher is more likely to respond to him, and so are the other children. If we change the attention Tony gets from his teacher and find exercises at a level he can succeed with, he might stay in his seat more. Actually, this procedure was tried, and it worked. Tony's teacher started giving him attention and praise when he was working and ignoring him if he left his seat. She found study problems he could do and told him to ask her for help when he needed it. Three weeks later, his teacher wondered why she ever thought he was a behavior problem. He needed extra help in learning, but he could do it when the teacher set the scene right.

Circular Explanations

Early psychologies explained behavior in terms of needs, instincts, ego forces, and the like. These often lead to circular explanations. Common lay explanations for behavior also include this error in logic. Here are some examples:

"Why does man build bridges?"   (Behavioral effect)
"He has a construction need."   (Pseudo cause)
"How do you know that?"   (Investigation)
"See how he builds bridges."   (Because the cause is another version of the observed behavior, the explanation is circular.)

"Why is he so suspicious and jealous?" (Behavioral effect)
"He's paranoid." (Pseudo cause)
"How do you know that?" (Investigation)
"See how suspicious and jealous he is." (Circular reason)

"Why can't he learn to read?" (Behavioral effect)
"He has a learning disability." (Pseudo cause)
"How do you know that?" (Investigation)
"See, he can't read." (Circular reason)

The logical structure of a circular explanation is *A is A*: he does it because he does it. However, this structure is hidden by a label for the behavior to be explained. He doesn't read because he has a *learning disability*. But investigation shows that the only information available is that he doesn't read because he doesn't read. No independent variable or cause is specified.

In the following examples, a cause is specified.

Independent Variable (Cause)	*Dependent Variable (Effect)*
Rivers that hinder food-gathering	Builds bridges
Poor reading instruction	Can't read
No reinforcement for sitting and working	Stays out of seat (called hyperactive)
Reinforcement for schoolwork	Does well in school

Purposeful Explanations

Another common error is to assert that something is done *in order to get something*. Something that has not yet happened cannot cause an occurrence. This is a logical impossibility, because cause, like time, runs only forward. Causes must precede their effects. As we shall see in unit 3, when we assert that consequences control what is learned, we mean they affect the *future probability* of behavior. They do not control the response in the first instance. There is nothing wrong with using purposeful statements as shorthand accounts for our actions. The statements are quite understandable and useful in communication. But they are not true statements of causes.

Teacher Responsibility

We wish to mention one final set of misconceptions commonly held about learning and teaching today, namely, learning is the student's responsibility. If there is a technology of teaching that can be used by any teacher to effectively teach children, then we can no longer excuse teaching failures because of the *student's* home background, the *student's* low IQ, or the *student's* poor motivation. We can no longer accept the proposition that rate of learning is solely a function of the student, or that learning is the student's responsibility. We cannot accept the statement: "I can't teach him if he doesn't want to learn." It is time to recognize that the teacher is responsible for whether or not the students progress in learning. The teacher is responsible if there is systematic knowledge that can be used to do the job, and if the teacher contracts to do it.

The Design of a Better World

As you learn about the principles of behavior, you will develop skills important in teaching children and adults alike. You will also develop skills that will make you a more effective person in dealing with an ever-changing world. And, you will begin to develop skills that can be useful in the design of a better world for all. In a democratic society, for example, we are searching for ways to give each member a fuller voice in major decisions. It is possible that with a better knowledge of the laws of behavior, we will be able to design systems of government and law that are more responsive to the needs of each of us. As long as we hold ultimate control with our ballots over the system that governs us, this dream has a chance of coming true.

summary

In this opening unit we have discussed the scientific approach to the study of learning processes and tried to face some common misunderstandings and questions students may have about it.

When the behavioral scientist talks about causes, he means that environmental events (independent variables) can produce changes in behavior (dependent variables). Scientific laws are statements of relationships between independent and dependent variables, between causes and effects. They are statements of what leads to what. It has become quite clear that human behavior follows lawful processes just as the rest of the physical world does. When the scientist uses the word *control,* it is simply another name for a cause. In popular usage, control often means coercion, and usually we don't like it. We are afraid that knowledge of how behavior works will be used to harm others. Actually, this knowledge can make us more effective in our efforts to help others.

We see no inherent conflict between humanistic values and scientific methods, although we grant that not all scientists have shown adequate concern for their "subjects." We believe that better knowledge of human behavior can be used to more effectively meet human needs.

Determinism is another expression of the statement that behavior is lawful or predictable. Indeterminism refers to the converse condition, namely, randomness or unpredictability. The attempt to cite Heisenberg's *Principle of Indeterminacy* to support an antideterministic position is found lacking, since it is based on a misinterpretation of the Heisenberg Principle. Heisenberg was talking about a measurement problem, not the absence of causality.

Philosophically, free will implies that the choices are not caused. Because of the current knowledge that natural law governs behavior, we cannot accept the notion of uncaused behavior. Behaviorally, free will refers to making choices without being coerced. The problems of freedom of choice and responsibility arise in social settings. Some social systems allow more freedom of choice than others. Responsibility exists in terms of agreements people make with each other. Laws of state assign or permit various legal responsibilities. Personal responsibility is *assumed* through an implicit contract with others to be mutually supporting.

Accusations that behavior theory is too simplistic to handle the complexities of human cognition are usually based on knowledge of early behaviorism and ignorance of modern behavior theory.

The bribery issue confuses the misuse of reinforcers (given following misbehavior) with the use of all reinforcers. Only under certain conditions can rewards be considered bribes.

Several false explanations for behavior were discussed. By looking within the "personality," the medical model misses entirely the environmental events responsible for what we do. Although sounding like causal statements, circular explanations contain no independent variable and, in reality, say nothing. That we do things for a purpose has to be logically incorrect, since causality runs only forward like time.

Explanations of student behavior that place the blame (cause) for teaching failures on the students are no longer acceptable. The teacher is responsible. Present knowledge of behavior can be used to help you learn to become an effective teacher. It can also be used to help you better manage your own life and to contribute to a better world.

self-test

This section provides you with a check of your understanding of the material in this unit. Cover the answers on the left with a marker. Read each item and write in your answer. Then check the answer by moving your marker down one step. If you get nine or ten answers right, we suggest you skip the Programed Practice and go on to the discussion questions. If you make more than one error, do the Programed Practice, study the text to correct mistakes, and then go on. The self-test begins at the top of the next page.

1 causes

2 independent

3 generalization

4 determined

5 caused

6 uncaused,
   random, chance

7 measure

8 uncoerced,
   freedom of

9 independent

10 not happened

1 The scientist believes that man can make more reasonable decisions about himself and others if the _____ of behavior are known.

2 A basic method in science is the careful measurement of some dependent variable, the introduction of a change procedure (_____ variable), and the measurement of the effects of this change on the dependent variable.

3 When we find again and again that a change in an independent variable leads to a consistent change in a dependent variable, we have a basis for a _____ or law (of nature).

4 To say that behavior follows lawful processes is to say that behavior is _____ by causes.

5 When the scientist talks about control of behavior, he simply means that behavior is _____ by environmental events.

6 Indeterminism refers to _____ events.

7 Heisenberg used the word "determine" to mean _____.

8 Some social systems allow more opportunities for _____ choice than others.

9 The trouble with a circular explanation is that there is no _____ variable or cause specified.

10 Purposeful explanations make the error of asserting that something that has _____ _____ can be the cause of something that has happened.

NUMBER RIGHT _____

exercise 1 programed practice

Cover the answers on the left with your marker. Read each item, and write in your answer. Then check the answer by moving your marker down one step. Accept your answers if the meaning is the same as that given. If you are not sure about the material covered, return to the text.

1 The scientist believes that man can make more reasonable decisions about himself and others if the _____ of behavior are known.

2 To know about the causes of behavior requires that we use _____ that will answer our questions.

1 causes

3 Common to these scientific methods are careful _____ of some behavior (dependent variable), introduction of a change (_____ variable), and observation of the effects of the change on the _____ variable.

2 methods

3 observations;
   independent;
   dependent

4 There should be no _____ conflict between personal values and the use of scientifically sound methods for knowing.

5 When we find again and again that a change in an independent variable leads to a change in a dependent variable, we have a basis for _____

4 inherent

or a law of nature.

5 generalization

6 Most of us are convinced that there is _____ in the physical world.

6 lawfulness

7 Most people don't like the idea of being _____.

8 Several misunderstandings may be involved here. When the scientist talks about control, he means that behavior is _____ by environmental

7 controlled

events. This is equivalent to saying that "behavior is _____."

8 caused;
   lawful

9 When we as individuals talk about "being controlled," we mean being

_____ by others (or man-made laws) to do what we do not want to.

10 This latter kind of control might best be called _____ control in

contrast to the natural control talked about in science.

11 We can use the principles of behavior to help others reach _____

objectives. We can use them to learn to manage _____

_____ lives more effectively.

12 It remains possible that a better knowledge of the _____

_____ _____ will enable us to design systems of govern-

ment and law that are more responsive to our needs (values or goals).

13 Indeterminism refers to _____ or uncaused events.

14 Many who have rejected behavioral determinism have used (misused)

Heisenberg's *Principle of* _____ to justify their position.

15 Heisenberg used the word "determine" to mean _____. If you try to

measure one aspect of a particle, the measuring process may affect that parti-

cle so that another aspect can no longer be accurately measured.

16 Since indeterminacy in Heisenberg's Principle refers to a _____

problem, rather than noncausality, it can hardly be used to support an an-

tideterministic position.

17 Free will refers fundamentally to the behavior of making choices without

being hampered. It is equivalent to the term _____-_____-

_____.

---

9   forced

10   social

11   their; our own

12 laws of behavior

13   random

14   *Indeterminacy*

15   measure

16   measurement

17   freedom-of-
choice

18 Philosophically, free will also means that choices are not _____ by physical or divine events.

19 Current knowledge of behavior makes clear that choice behavior is _____. So the concept of free will as uncaused behavior must be discarded.

20 Natural laws _____ the way we understand things to be in nature—what leads to what.

21 Man-made laws, on the other hand, _____ what people should do and the consequences for a failure to follow the prescription.

22 All explicit or implicit _____ and agreements have a similar prescribing function.

23 Legal responsibility does not exist independently of _____ (explicit and implicit) and laws of states.

24 Legal responsibility can be _____ (for example, by entering into a marriage contract) or _____ (such as parents being responsible for their children) by laws of state.

25 The fact that legal responsibility is assumed or assigned does not make a person _____ responsibly. People become law abiding if they are _____ to be so.

26 The current knowledge from the scientific study of behavior can in fact be used to teach children to be more _____ citizens.

27 Personal responsibility is a responsibility assumed because of an under-

18 caused

19 determined

20 describe

21 prescribe

22 contracts

23 contracts

24 assumed;
assigned

25 act;
taught

26 responsible

standing of our _____ _____ on each other for important

human satisfactions.

28 Determinism offers us the _____ that with a better _____

of how things work, we can build a better world.

29 The medical model leads one to look within the _____ for conflicts

which are the presumed causes.

30 A behavioral learning model leads directly to an examination of the

_____ conditions that function to produce and maintain problem

behavior.

31 The logical structure of a circular explanation is _____ is

_____. No _____ variable or cause is specified.

32 Purposeful explanations err by asserting that something that has

_____ _____ can cause an occurrence. This is a logical

impossibility, since cause, like time, runs only in a _____ direction.

33 Early behaviorists placed a great emphasis on _____-

_____ connections in accounting for human behavior. In modern

behavior theory, such a model is primarily used to describe _____

actions.

34 Operant behavior _____ on the environment and includes intelli-

gent problem-solving behavior.

35 Bribery involves a _____ of rewards.

27 mutual
dependence

28 hope;
knowledge

29 personality

30 environmental

31 A; A;
independent

32 not happened;
forward

33 stimulus-
response;
reflexive

34 operates

35 misuse

36 If using rewards of any kind in any way is _____, then we all had better stop accepting our paychecks and work for free!

37 The teacher is _____ for the learning progress of the students. The teacher contracts to teach, and there is systematic _____ that can be used to get the job done.

36   bribery

37   responsible;
     knowledge,
     technique

discussion questions

1 Does the experimental study of behavior imply that people are responsible for each other?

2 Can scientific methods be used to support or enhance human values, to build a better world?

3 Define these terms:
a) cause
b) independent variable
c) dependent variable
d) control (in a scientific context)
e) determinism
f) indeterminism
g) free will
h) predestination

4 State the basis for the belief that behavior is lawful.

5 State the differences between natural control and social control.

6 State the fallacy in the position that the "Heisenberg principle of indeterminacy implies that some events are not caused."

7 Explain how "freedom of choice" can exist in a determined world.

8 Explain how laws of nature differ from laws of state.

9 Explain how a person can be responsible in a determined world.

10 Define a circular explanation, give an example, and contrast circular explanations with causal explanations.

11 Answer the charge that behavior theory is too simplistic.

12 Explain the fallacy in the "bribery issue."

13 State why the teacher should take responsibility for the success of each student.

unit 2

First Steps in the Analysis of Behavior

objectives

This unit is the first step toward making you a behavior analyst—that is, it provides you with the skills to experimentally determine the causes of behavior, which you might be interested in changing. The unit begins with important definitions and procedures relating environmental events (stimuli) to behavioral events. It is also concerned with skills for defining behavioral and stimulus events in ways that will permit you to gather data on their occurrence. In subsequent exercises, you will get practice in collecting such behavioral data.

   When you complete this unit you should be able to—

1 Distinguish between operant and respondent behavior and give examples of each.
2 Define the functions of eliciting stimuli, discriminative stimuli, and two kinds of consequent stimuli.
3 Discuss the difference between antecedent and consequent stimuli.
4 Discuss the difference between eliciting and discriminative stimuli.
5 State why trait labels and words referring to internal events are not useful in defining behavioral events.
6 Discriminate between behavior definitions that are objective and those that are not and begin to write your own.
7 Discriminate between discrete and continuous-stream behaviors and suggest methods for recording each.
8 Describe several behavior-change projects and state their common essential features.

20

lesson

Respondents and Operants

Modern behavior theory distinguishes between two classes of behavior, *respondent* and *operant*. Respondent behavior involves reactions of the smooth muscles and glands; it includes such reflexive reactions as sweating, salivating, secreting digestive juices, shivering, and the activation syndrome (secretion of adrenalin, increased blood sugar, increased heart rate, increased respiration rate). Operant behavior involves the striated muscular system (or the muscles that we normally talk about as under voluntary control). Behaviors such as talking, walking, eating, and problem solving are examples of operant behavior. Although currently there are some controversies about the distinction between operants and respondents, this distinction has proved to be very useful in applied work.

In the analysis of behavior, the environmental events that can be shown to influence responding are called *stimuli*. Respondent behavior is controlled by preceding stimuli. For example:

S	$\longrightarrow$	R
Preceding Stimulus	$\longrightarrow$	*Respondent Behavior*
Lemon juice in mouth	$\longrightarrow$	Salivation
Sudden loud noise	$\longrightarrow$	Startle reaction
Bright light in eye	$\longrightarrow$	Pupil contraction
Tap to knee	$\longrightarrow$	Knee jerk
Tactile stimulus to sex organs	$\longrightarrow$	Orgasm
Crushing of finger	$\longrightarrow$	Activation syndrome

In the case of respondent behavior, preceding stimuli are said to *elicit* (or cause) the response. Present the stimulus and you get the response.

In contrast, operant behavior is controlled by stimulus events that immediately follow the operant. Naturally, a following stimulus cannot cause the operant, but once an operant behavior occurs, *its future rate* depends upon its consequences. Consequent stimuli can have either a reinforcing or a punishing function (see unit 3).

A particular preceding stimulus can become the signal for an operant response if reinforcing consequences are provided only when the response occurs in the presence of that stimulus. The procedure of reinforcing right responses and not reinforcing wrong ones is called differential reinforcement. The basic sequence in operant learning has three steps.

$$S \longrightarrow R \longrightarrow S$$

Teacher Presents Preceding Stimulus (Signal)	Child Responds	Teacher Presents Following Stimulus (Consequence)
The teacher presents a red truck and asks, "What color is this truck?"	"Blue."	"No. It is red."
The teacher presents a red ball and asks, "What color is this ball?"	"Red."	"Yes. It is red. Good!"
The teacher presents a red pencil and asks, "What color is this pencil?"	"Red."	"Yes. It is red. You got it." She pats him on the head.

After many examples have been presented, the child will say "red" only when a red object is shown. The operant response ("red") will be under the control of the stimulus property called redness.

Thus, both respondents and operants can be controlled by preceding stimuli, but there is a difference in the nature of the control. The respondent reflex is caused by an appropriate preceding stimulus. Technically, the preceding stimulus is said to have an *eliciting function*. In the case of an operant, we would be hard put to say that the redness in the red ball caused the response "red." In fact, when we look at the learning history, we see that initially the red ball brought out no response. Only after many teaching examples in which positive and negative consequences were applied, did saying "red" to red stimuli occur. The *consequences* of the child's answers caused him to learn to name red-colored objects correctly. The red objects themselves only *set the occasion* where saying "red" would be reinforced. Technically, redness became a *discriminative stimulus* for saying "red." The child learned to discriminate (respond correctly to) red stimuli. In sum, preceding stimuli can have an eliciting function for respondent behavior and a discriminative function for operant behavior.

Thus far we have distinguished between two types of behavior and discussed the way antecedent and consequent stimuli relate to each. These distinctions may be diagramed as follows:

Model 1

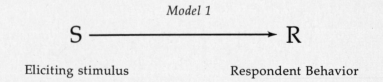

Eliciting stimulus   Respondent Behavior

Model 2

$$S \longrightarrow R \longrightarrow S$$

Discriminative Stimulus   Operant Response   Consequent Stimulus

Operant behavior usually involves a three-part contingency (discriminative stimulus, response, consequent stimulus). It is this behavioral model that is most important to the teacher. In fact, we will use the respondent model at only two other places in this text—in the analysis of conditioned reinforcers and conditioned emotional reactions. The operant model provides the basis for a model of teaching. Teaching is changing what children do or say (responses) under particular stimulus conditions. We make learning happen by systematically controlling stimuli that precede a child's response and those that follow it. The teacher basically uses discriminative stimuli and consequent stimuli to change behavior.

Defining Behavioral Events

A key problem in the scientific analysis of behavior is *defining behavior in such a way that another person can agree on its occurrence.* The problem is the same whether we are talking about social behavior, study behavior, or instructional objectives. Some ways of describing behavior are open to more interpretations than others. In general, when we restrict our descriptions or definitions to *observable behavior,* we can get more agreement than when we use trait labels or make inferences about internal events. Consider this episode between a teacher and Mr. Behavior.

Teacher: Johnny has a perceptual problem. That's why he can't read.
Mr. B.:   Is it serious? Should he see a doctor?
Teacher: Well, what I mean is that he gets the letters mixed up when he reads words.
Mr. B.:   Is it because he can't see?
Teacher: I don't think so. He can name all the letters. He can hit a ball. I don't mean that kind of perceptual problem. I mean he can't see the difference between words that are similar.
Mr. B.:   Can you give me some examples?
Teacher: Well, he calls *was* "saw," *left* "felt," and *bud* "dud."
Mr. B.:   I understand now. He doesn't always respond correctly to the words he is reading. Why don't you teach him to do it right?
Teacher: How can I if he has a perceptual problem?

Mr. Behavior decided not to pursue the problem further at this time.

This is another example of circular reasoning as well as an illustration of a problem in defining behavior. Certain behaviors have been labeled "perceptual problem" and then the label has been used to explain the behavior.

When we talk about behavior in terms of the labels we place on it, we are likely to infer different things. Both the teacher and Mr. B. could agree that Johnny called *was* "saw," *left* "felt," and *bud* "dud." This was observable behavior. They disagreed on what this meant for instruction. If they agreed on what the behavior problem was (the dependent variable), they could try various procedures (independent variables) to see what works in changing Johnny's reading. He might be given practice to help him learn the difficult discriminations.

Using *trait labels*, such as aggressive, smart, helpful, kind, diligent, honest, anxious, unmotivated, or stupid, for describing behavior leads to the same kind of problem encountered in saying that Johnny has a perceptual problem. Another observer is likely to want to know what you saw the child do before he will understand what you are talking about.

The use of terms that refer to *internal events* leads to a similar result. Suppose a teacher states as an objective in English Literature: "I want my students to *really understand* and *fully appreciate* Shakespeare by the end of this year." Different observers will have different ideas about what this means. Is it getting 80 percent on an objective test? Is it writing an essay analyzing the major themes in three of Shakespeare's plays? Is it giving an oral report on "My personal interpretation of *A Midsummer Night's Dream*"?

In stating educational objectives, verbs like *to know, to believe, to enjoy,* and *to understand* are open to many interpretations. They refer to internal events. Verbs like *to identify, to differentiate, to compare* and *to write* refer to external events (observables) and observers are more likely to agree on what they mean.

Feelings are another set of internal events that can give trouble. "He is feeling happy" is not observable; "He is smiling and singing" is. "He is afraid" is not observable; "He is hiding behind the chair" is. "He is angry" is not observable; "He is hitting Billy over the head with a stick" is.

Thus the first rule for defining behavioral events is to restrict the definition to observables. A good test of a behavior definition can be obtained by having two observers code the same behavior sequence to see if they get similar results. Dividing the number of agreements by the number of agreements plus disagreements, yields a measure (percentage) of agreement. In most cases, an agreement over 80 percent is acceptable.

Consider each of the following examples of definitions of behavior:

Behavior Class	*Definition*
On-task	Listening to, looking at, or answering teacher; reading to self, writing out an assignment, and so forth. (In a given twenty-second time interval, On-task is checked only if looking away from teacher or work occurs for less than four seconds.)

Gross Motor Behavior	Getting out of seat, standing up, running, hopping, skipping, jumping, walking around, rocking in chair, moving chair to neighbor, putting knees on chair.
Disturbing Others	Grabbing objects or work, knocking neighbor's books off desk, destroying another's property, pushing with desk.
Blurting Out	Verbalizing aloud to self, classmates, or teacher without first having been called on by teacher. (Do not count "whispered" conversations with other children.)
Polite Behavior	In obtaining teacher's attention or requesting materials or help, using such words as "please," "thank you," "may I." Making requests in a quiet manner; acknowledging when help is received.
Spontaneous Speech	Speaking when not preceded by a question or prompted from teacher or peer.
Tantrum Behavior (1)	Any crying, whining, or sobbing.
Tantrum Behavior (2)	The occurrence of any of these: loud crying, kicking, or throwing himself or objects about.
Work Completion	Completing assigned page with all errors corrected.

There are many ways behavior classes can be defined. While there are some general guidelines, in most cases the particular objectives with a particular child will determine your definitions. For example, one child's tantrum behavior might have an entirely different set of behaviors associated with it than tantrum behavior for another. A group of behaviors may be placed together because they have some common form, such as spontaneous speech and blurting out, or some common function, such as on-task, work completion, and disturbing others. What you focus on depends on what you want to demonstrate or change. As long as you stay with observables and can get another observer to agree with you, you are on solid ground.

Defining Stimulus Events

Defining stimulus events based on physical objects poses no special problem as long as we use physical dimensions to talk about them, such as space, time, size, color, and speed. Consequent events, such as points, stars, tokens, candy, or toys, can be readily described in physical terms; so can antecedent stimulus events, such as a light coming on, or the teacher pointing to the letter k.

On the other hand, when the stimuli involve the social behavior of the teacher or other children, we face the same problems as are encountered in defining response classes. In fact, we are again defining responses of the teacher, which function as stimulus events for the child. Consider the following examples:

Stimulus Class	*Definition*
Attention from Teacher	Touching, standing near (within two feet) facing a child, talking to or assisting him.
Positive Physical Contact	Embracing, kissing, patting on head, holding arm, taking hand, allowing a child to sit on lap.
Praise	Verbal comments such as "That's good," "Fine job," "I like your work."
Physical Restraint	Holding a child in place so he cannot move, pulling him into the hall, grabbing, pushing, shaking.
Questions	Asking any member of the class a question.

Selection of a Recording Method

In selecting a method of recording, it is important to distinguish between behaviors that can be counted (discrete behaviors) and those that cannot (continuous-stream behaviors). You can count: how many words a child reads per minute; the number of arithmetic problems he completes in ten minutes; how often the teacher praises a child; and the number of times one child hits another. But you cannot readily count attention behaviors or on-task behaviors.

If a behavior can be counted, then it can be recorded with a wrist counter (like those used to keep score in golf), with marks on a paper, or by scoring a child's worksheet. You also need to keep track of the length of time the behavior was observed. With this information, you can convert your observations into a rate measure indicating frequency per minute or per hour. Figure 2.1 shows a recording sheet. Each time the teacher praised (P) or criticized (C) the child, P or C was recorded. In this example, the rate of praise was .5 times per minute.

For continuous-stream behaviors, like on-task behavior, it is necessary to devise a measure based on observation intervals. The observer uses a clipboard to which is taped a watch with a second hand and a recording sheet like that in figure 2.1 For each ten-second interval (each box on the recording sheet), the observer records T for on-task or —— for off-task. Then the number of intervals in which on-task occurs is counted and divided by the total number of intervals to give a percentage. For example, in figure 2.1, the child was on-task 67 percent of the time intervals.

The use of the observation interval procedure is also advisable when you are trying to record more than three different behaviors. A code symbol is devised for each behavior class. If the behavior occurs in the ten-second interval, the symbol is placed in the appropriate box. Most observers, without extensive training, can learn to rate about eight behaviors at once using this method. If more than one behavior class is rated at the same time, be sure to define your classes so that they *do not overlap* each other. For example, in most cases off-task would include out-of-seat behavior, so an observation system would not use both of these classes.

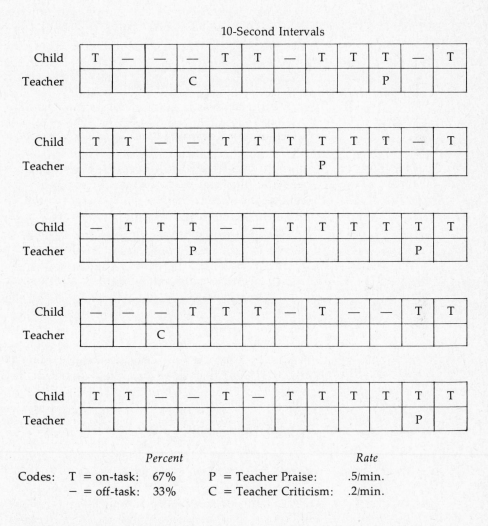

10-Second Intervals

Child	T	—	—	—	T	T	—	T	T	T	—	T
Teacher				C						P		

Child	T	T	—	—	T	T	T	T	T	T	—	T
Teacher								P				

Child	—	T	T	T	—	—	T	T	T	T	T	T
Teacher				P							P	

Child	—	—	—	T	T	T	—	T	—	—	T	T
Teacher			C									

Child	T	T	—	—	T	—	T	T	T	T	T	T
Teacher										P		

	Percent			*Rate*
Codes:	T = on-task:	67%	P = Teacher Praise:	.5/min.
	— = off-task:	33%	C = Teacher Criticism:	.2/min.

Figure 2.1 Sample observation record form for ten-minute total observation

Some Examples of Behavior-Change Studies by Teachers

The following studies were designed and carried out by teachers learning about behavior modification methods. The reports were written as part of their class assignments. They illustrate different recording methods and will give you some ideas of how these procedures can be useful to you.

Classroom Project in Behavior Modification
by Judy Wieting

Target Behavior: To decrease blurting out.

Recording Procedure Used: My observer recorded the number of "blurts" (undesirable verbalizations) occurring within thirty-minute periods each day for thirteen days.

Procedures Used to Modify the Behavior: I ignored any comments which were blurted out. I praised hand raising and talking only when called on.

My subject was Louis, nine years old, a second grader.

Those verbalizations by Louis which I considered to be undersirable, i.e., blurting out behavior, were comments which he made aloud to himself, classmates, or the teacher without having first been called on. I did not count as "blurts" whispered conversations with a neighbor; but, rather, only his random remarks, often only one or two words, which were audible to all in the room.

During the four-day baseline period, I continued to treat Louis as I had all year. I felt it would render the results of the experiment invalid if I instituted any of the behavior modification procedures before baseline data had been gathered. Therefore, I at times reminded Louis, either privately or in front of the class, not to talk without being called on. On occasion I responded to Louis' blurts, especially when he had given a comment or answer that I had been seeking. Therefore, on Day 5, when the time came to begin extinction of Louis' blurting out behavior, I had to discipline myself to be sure that at all times I ignored his blurts and gave attention only to the desired behavior.

On the first of the nine experimental days (Day 5), I posted a chart in the front of the room, enumerating the following three rules:

1 Raise your hand if you wish to talk.
2 Wait to be called on.
3 Listen while others talk.

I purposely listed as few rules as possible while still managing to cover the essentials. I felt that the task might seem easier to master if it did not involve numerous rules.

The entire class read the rules together and discussed each rule, being careful to follow the rules during our discussion. Louis seemed especially anxious to please me and had his hand up constantly. On this first day and for a few days following, I called on Louis every time he raised his hand and as soon as possible after he raised it. After Day 7, I found that by stressing rules 2 and 3, I could lengthen the interval between the time Louis raised his hand and the time I called on him, and still maintain the reduction of blurts.

At first I praised Louis's slightest hand-raising movement. However, not much shaping was required. Louis was eager to receive positive attention. I praised Louis (and others) whenever they applied the rules, and referred to the rules in my reinforcing comments. Aside from the usual "goods" I used such comments as, "I called on _____ because he had his hand up" or "I like the way _____ always listens while others are talking." Whenever possible I named Louis in the comments. I praised good raisers, good waiters, and good listeners. In regards to the effectiveness of vicarious reinforcement on Louis, I found that it worked best if I could praise someone for an incompatible behavior at the *exact* moment when Louis was blurting out.

The whole class cooperated, too, by not responding to any comments blurted out by classmates. For example, during show and tell, if a classmate had a comment or question, the "shower" would not acknowledge it unless he had first called on that classmate. We recited the rules each morning, and when necessary or applicable, we reviewed the reasons for the rules and evaluated our class progress.

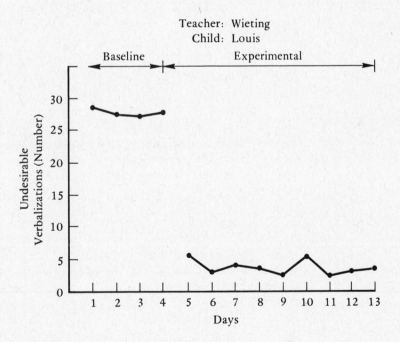

Figure 2.2 Modification of undesired verbalizations

Results of the Experiment: I feel that I learned and accomplished much through this first project. Not only was my target behavior realized, proving to me the effectiveness of the ignore-and-praise combination, but fringe benefits were gained also. I became accustomed to giving praise freely and sincerely. And I am training myself not to acknowledge deviant behavior by means of any verbal, facial, or physical response. Although my primary goal was to stop Louis's blurting out and to get him to raise his hand if he wished to speak, good listening habits for the whole class resulted from this experiment. Toward the end of the thirteen days, after the basics of raising-hand-to-talk had been mastered, I pursued the skills further by branching off into connecting areas. All children learned to listen while classmates or teachers were talking. If a comment was made which repeated what another had just finished saying, I ignored it. I employed such questions as "What do you think of what _____ said?" or "Please tell me what _____ just said."

The graph vividly illustrates the results of my application of principles of behavior modification. By ignoring the undesirable behavior and giving positive reinforcement to behaviors compatible with it, the blurting out behavior was drastically reduced from a high frequency of occurrence. Perhaps over a longer period of time, the blurting out behavior can be totally extinguished.[1]

A Project in Behavior Modification

by Anne Manton

The subject for this project was an eight year old fourth-grade boy. He and a third-grade girl come daily to my room for forty minutes of Type A tutoring in arithmetic.*

The behavior to be modified was the *utterance of words or noises not relevant to the arithmetic tasks assigned.* Acceptable verbalization, as defined for the observer, was questions about work or saying answers and problems aloud. Unacceptable verbalization was grunts and various other guttural sounds, giggles, whistles, sobbing, humming, and comments such as "goodie" and "yah." Target behavior was silence or acceptable verbalization 80 percent of the time.

The observer sat behind the subject. She observed for ten seconds, then recorded for ten seconds using a stop watch and clip board. Data were gathered for thirty minutes each day.

Five days of baseline observation were done during which time I continued my previous practice of ignoring the deviant behavior of the subject. On the sixth day the experimental program was initiated. Both children were given copies of a chart (figure 2.3). The three rules were discussed with them. It was explained that for each five minutes they followed the rules, an X would be placed in the box on the clock representing that time interval, and

*Type A is a term used to designate children diagnosed as socially maladjusted.

these points could be used to earn rewards. The reinforcers were then shown to them and consisted of things they had suggested, such as play dough, darts, a toy truck, a ring, coloring books, a doll, and candy. A chart showing the points needed to earn each reward was included.

On the third day of the experimental period I began to give additional points for work completed. They could earn two points for a perfect paper and one point for not more than two errors. A point was also given for five correct responses to flash cards. These points were recorded in the boxes to the left of the clock. Each day the points were totaled and the children chose whether to use them or save them for a reward that required more points.

The graph (figure 2.4) shows the effect of the experimental program on the child. As his deviant behavior decreased his time on task increased and his work output increased from one-half paper to two or three papers completed daily.[1]

RULES

1 No talking unless it is about arithmetic.
2 Sit in seats unless asked to come to board.
3 Raise hands in group discussions.

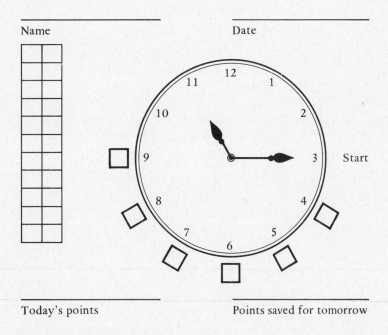

Figure 2.3 Rules and chart for implementing a reinforcement program

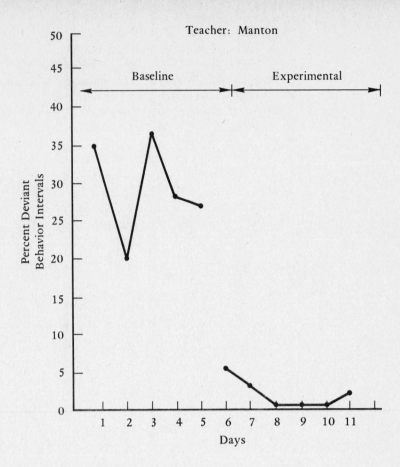

Figure 2.4 Change in deviant behavior

How to Begin a Class Promptly

by Jill Stiltner

Problem

The children in my class had some difficulty in settling down when they came into the classroom. Frequently many were still out of their seats when the last bell rang. I decided to attempt to change this situation by arranging things a little differently in the classroom.

Method

I began by simply counting the number of children not in their seats at the last bell both at the beginning of the morning and afternoon school sessions. In my class of 21, frequently as many as half of the children were not seated at the last bell. I kept this record without letting the children know that I was doing it for a total of eight days. On the ninth day, I told the children what I was doing and what would happen to them if they were not in their seats when the last bell rang. The punishment was that each child who was not in his seat would miss five minutes of Physical Education time. He would go to the Physical Education class but would have to remain standing at the back of the room for five minutes before he could enter into the games. I issued this warning both on the ninth and tenth day, with no appreciable effect on their behavior. On the eleventh day, the contingency went into effect.

Results and Discussion

As you can see by the graph, the number of children out of their seats at the last bell has decreased considerably. This has proven to be an effective way to lessen the confusion and increase the instruction time at the beginning of school.[2]

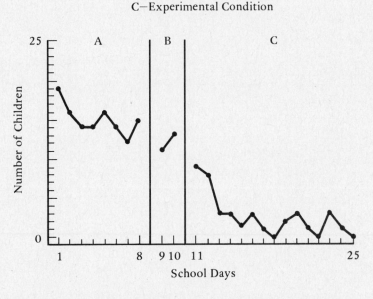

A—Baseline   B—Warning Period
C—Experimental Condition

Figure 2.5 Number of children who failed to be seated by the final bell

summary

There are two functionally different classes of behavior—respondent and operant. Respondent behavior involves the reflexive action of the smooth muscles and glands. Operant behavior involves the striated muscle system, or what we normally call the voluntary muscles. Respondents are controlled by preceding stimuli called eliciting stimuli. Operants are controlled by following stimuli, which are called reinforcing stimuli and punishing stimuli.

In the model of respondent behavior (S → R), a preceding stimulus elicits a response. Operant responses can be brought under the control of preceding stimuli by the use of differential reinforcement. If an operant response is reinforced in the presence of one stimulus and not others, it will tend to occur more often when that stimulus is presented. A preceding stimulus that influences the occurrence of an operant is called a discriminative stimulus. It sets the occasion in which an operant response is more likely to be reinforced (or lead to the avoidance of punishment). The operant model is S → R → S; here the consequences of behavior are very important. Teachers are mostly concerned with operant behavior.

In learning to use behavior principles to help others reach their objectives, the first step is to learn how to define behavioral events (operant behaviors) and stimulus events in objective terms. The key is to keep the definitions or descriptive examples restricted to what you can see—observables. What is he doing? What is she saying? The focus of a behavioral event is on the performance itself. Trait labels, such as intelligent, aggressive, or retarded, are to be avoided. Also avoid referring to internal events, such as feelings, motives, knowledge, and thoughts.

A good test of a behavioral definition is to have two observers use it to code a sequence of behavior and see if they come up with similar results. A percentage of agreement can be computed by dividing the number of agreements by the number of agreements plus disagreements.

Stimulus events can be readily defined by descriptive language when they deal with physical events. When the stimulus events for one person involve the behavior of another (for example, teacher's praise), then apply the same rules used in defining behavioral events.

In selecting methods for recording behavioral events, first decide whether the behavior can be counted meaningfully. If it can, count the number of times it occurs in a unit of time to get the behavior rate. If the behavior is continuous (or of widely varying durations), use a time-interval method. For a given time interval, simply record whether or not it occurs; then use as your measure the percent of time intervals in which it occurs.

The final part of this lesson presented three behavior-change studies designed and carried out by teachers learning about behavior modification. The basic steps common to these studies are defining a target behavior, determining a measurement procedure, determining a change procedure, executing the change, and recording the progress on a graph to see if the procedure worked. Before too long you will be able to do studies like these!

self-test

This section provides you with a check of your understanding of the material presented in this unit. Cover the answers on the left with a marker. Read each item and write your answer. Then check it by moving your marker down one step. If you get nine or ten answers right, we suggest you skip the Programed Practice and go on to the next exercise. If you make more than one error, do the Programed Practice, go back to the text to correct any mistakes, then do the next exercise.

1   smooth

2   operant

3   preceding

4   eliciting

5   discriminative

6   consequent

7   observable

8   behavior

1   Respondent behavior involves reactions of the _____ muscles and glands.

2   Such behaviors as talking, walking, eating, and problem solving are examples of _____ behavior.

3   Respondent behavior can be shown to be controlled by _____ stimuli.

4   The preceding stimulus that controls a respondent is said to have an _____ function.

5   The preceding stimulus that controls an operant is said to have a _____ function.

6   The teacher basically uses discriminative stimuli and _____ stimuli to change child behavior.

7   When we restrict descriptions or definitions to _____ behavior, we can get more agreement than when we use trait labels or make inferences about internal events.

8   When stimulus events to be defined involve social _____ , we face the same problems as are encountered in defining response classes.

9 In selecting a method of recording, it is important to distinguish between behaviors that can be _____ (discrete behaviors) and those that cannot (continuous-stream behaviors).

10 For continuous-stream behaviors, like on-task behavior, it is necessary to devise a measure based on observation _____.

NUMBER RIGHT _____

9 counted

10 intervals

exercise 1 programed practice

Cover the answers on the left with your marker. Read each item and write in your answer. Then check the answer by moving your marker down one step. Accept your answers if the meaning is the same as that given. When you are not sure about the material covered, return to the text.

1 Modern behavior theory distinguishes between two classes of behavior, _____ and operant behavior.

2 Respondent behavior includes such _____ reactions as sweating, salivating, secreting digestive juices, shivering, and the "activation syndrome."

1 respondent

3 Respondent behavior involves reactions of the _____ muscles and _____. Operant behavior involves the _____ muscular system.

2 reflexive

4 Such behaviors as talking, walking, eating, and problem solving are examples of _____ behavior.

3 smooth; glands; striated

5 The environmental events that influence responding are called _____.

4 operant

5 stimuli

36   UNIT 2

6 Respondent behavior is controlled by ＿＿＿＿＿＿ stimuli.

7 In the case of respondent behavior, preceding stimuli are said to ＿＿＿＿＿＿ (or cause) the response.

8 Operant behavior can be shown to be controlled by stimulus events that immediately ＿＿＿＿＿＿ the operant. Once an operant behavior occurs, its ＿＿＿＿＿＿ rate depends upon its consequences.

9 Thus, consequent stimuli can have either a ＿＿＿＿＿＿ function or a ＿＿＿＿＿＿ function.

10 A particular ＿＿＿＿＿＿ stimulus can become the signal for an operant response if reinforcing consequences are provided only when the response occurs in the presence of that stimulus.

11 The basic sequence in operant learning has three steps: teacher presents ＿＿＿＿＿＿ stimulus ⟶ child responds ⟶ teacher presents ＿＿＿＿＿＿ stimulus.

12 The preceding stimulus that controls a respondent is said to have an ＿＿＿＿＿＿ function. The preceding stimulus that controls an operant is said to have a ＿＿＿＿＿＿ function.

13 The model of operant behavior has ＿＿＿＿＿＿ steps. (discriminative stimulus, response, consequent stimulus).

14 It is the ＿＿＿＿＿＿ model that provides the basis for a model of teaching.

15 Teaching is ＿＿＿＿＿＿ what children do or say (responses) under particular stimulus conditions.

---

6 preceding

7 elicit

8 follow; future

9 reinforcing; punishing

10 preceding

11 preceding; consequent

12 eliciting; discriminative

13 three

14 operant

15 changing

16 Basically, the teacher uses _____ stimuli and consequent stimuli to change child behavior.

17 A key problem in the scientific analysis of behavior is defining behavior in such a way that other people can _____ on its occurrence.

18 When we restrict our descriptions or definitions to _____ behavior we can get more agreement than when we use trait labels or make inferences about _____ events.

19 In stating educational _____, verbs like *to know, to believe, to enjoy,* and *to understand* are open to many interpretations. They refer to _____ events.

20 Verbs like *to identify, to differentiate, to compare,* and *to write* refer to _____ events (observables) and observers are more likely to agree on what they mean.

21 Feelings are another set of _____ events that can give trouble. "He is feeling happy" is not _____. "He is smiling and singing" is _____.

22 Thus the first rule for defining behavioral events is to restrict the definition to _____.

23 A good test of the adequacy of a behavioral definition can be obtained by having _____ observers code the same behavior sequence.

24 When stimulus events to be defined involve the social _____ of the teacher or other children, we face the same problems that we encounter in defining response classes.

16 discriminative

17 agree

18 observable;
    internal

19 objectives;
    internal

20 external

21 internal;
    observable;
    observable

22 observables

23 two

24 behavior

25 responses

26 counted;
    continuous

27 can

28 cannot

29 counted

30 intervals

31 recording

32 total

33 three

34 overlap

25 In fact, we are defining _____ of the teacher, which function as stimulus events for the child.

26 In selecting a method of recording, it is important to distinguish between behaviors that can be _____ (discrete behaviors) and those that cannot (_____-stream behaviors).

27 You _____ count the number of arithmetic problems completed in ten minutes.

28 You _____ count attention behaviors.

29 If a behavior can be _____, then it is possible to record the behavior with a wrist counter, with marks on a paper, or by scoring a child's worksheet.

30 For continuous-stream behaviors, like on-task behavior, it is necessary to devise a measure based on observation _____.

31 The observer uses a clipboard, a watch with a second hand, and a _____sheet.

32 Then the number of intervals in which a behavior occurs is counted and divided by the _____ number of intervals to give a percentage.

33 The use of the observation interval procedure is also advisable when you are trying to record more than _____ different behaviors.

34 Be sure to define your behavior classes so that they do not _____ each other.

exercise 2

Discrimination of Observables and Countables

A For each of the following, if the statement is restricted to observables, mark O in the blank. If the statement contains words referring to nonobservables, mark NON in the blank and underline the word(s) referring to nonobservables. As you work each problem, uncover the answers. The words you should have underlined are given in the answer box.

NON anger	1 _____	The target behavior was the number of anger responses made.
O	2 _____	To be counted as a smile, the outside edges of his mouth had to move upward.
NON know	3 _____	When he completes this unit, I want him to know every president this country has had.
NON concentrating thinking	4 _____	On-task behavior includes concentrating on his work and thinking only about the assigned problem.
O	5 _____	On-task behavior involves looking at his workbook, looking at the teacher when she is talking to him, and writing in his workbook.
NON perceptual see	6 _____	When I say that Jimmy has a perceptual problem, I mean he doesn't see the difference between *was* and *saw*.
O	7 _____	I am going to count the number of times Bill hits or pushes other children.
O	8 _____	I decided to count the number of children out of their seats when the last bell rang each morning.
NON hostile intended hurt	9 _____	Mrs. X counted the number of hostile statements made by Mary, that is, statements intended to hurt somebody.

O	(The word *friendly* refers generally to a feeling, but here it is defined in terms of verbal behaviors.)	**10** _____ The goal was to measure the number of friendly interactions in the class. For this task, friendly interactions were defined as verbal statements to another child containing words of praise about the other child, his dress, his work, and so forth.

B For each of the following observable behaviors, indicate whether it is a countable behavior (C) or one that requires an interval measurement procedure (I). Cover the answers with a marker until after you have responded.

C	**11** _____	Hitting another child
I	**12** _____	Working on-task
I	**13** _____	Being out of seat
C	**14** _____	Raising hand to be called on
C	**15** _____	Taking out a cigarette and lighting it
C	**16** _____	Spelling a word on a spelling test
I	**17** _____	Working on a self-study project
C	**18** _____	Asking questions
I	**19** _____	Studying for an examination
I	**20** _____	Riding a bike

exercise 3

Define these terms.

1 Operant behavior: _____

_____

2 Respondent behavior: _____

_____

3 Eliciting stimulus: _____

_____

4 Consequent stimulus: _____

_____

5 Discriminative stimulus: _____

_____

Answers for Exercise 3

Term	Essential Points
1. Operant behavior	a) involves the striated muscular system b) is controlled by consequent stimuli c) is equivalent to voluntary or intelligent behavior
2. Respondent behavior	a) involves the smooth muscles and glands b) is controlled by preceding stimuli (eliciting stimuli). c) is reflexive in nature
3. Eliciting stimulus	a) is a preceding stimulus b) controls respondent behavior (causes it)
4. Consequent stimulus	a) is a following stimulus b) controls operant behavior by increasing or decreasing its future occurrence.
5. Discriminative stimulus	a) is a preceding stimulus b) causes responses reinforced in its presence (and not reinforced in its absence) to occur more frequently when the stimulus is presented in the future, or alternatively, sets the occasion when making a certain response is likely to lead to reinforcement

exercise 4

A For each of the teacher studies reported in this chapter specify the following information.

Judy Wieting's study

1 Define the target behavior: _____

_____

2 Specify the measurement procedure: _____

_____

3 Specify the behavior-change procedure: _____

_____

4 Describe the outcome: _____

_____

B Anne Manton's study

1 Define the target behavior: _____

_____

2 Specify the measurement procedure: _____

_____

3 Specify the behavior-change procedure: _____

_____

4 Describe the outcome: _____

_____

C Jill Stiltner's study

1 Define the target behavior: _____

_____

2 Specify the measurement procedure: _____

_____

3 Specify the behavior-change procedure: _____

_____

4 Describe the outcome: _____

_____

discussion questions

Be prepared to answer these questions orally or in writing.

1 What is the difference between operant and respondent behavior?

2 Give three examples of an operant behavior.

3 Give three examples of respondent behavior.

4 Give examples of discriminative stimuli.

5 In what way are discriminative stimuli like eliciting stimuli, and how are they different?

6 How do consequent stimuli differ from eliciting and discriminative stimuli?

7 Give examples of two different kinds of consequent stimuli.

8 What is the difficulty with statements about people based on trait labels and internal events, when it comes to the scientific study of behavior?

9 Give examples of objective definitions of behavior.

10 Give examples of nonobjective definitions of behavior.

11 What are the characteristics of easily countable behavior?

12 How do you measure behaviors that are not easily counted?

13 Describe the essential steps common to the behavior-change projects by teachers reported in this unit.

Be prepared to discuss this issue.

14 Does the fact that internal events, such as feelings and thoughts, are not readily studied mean that they are not important?

project 1

Name _____

Date Due _____

Section _____

Defining and Counting Behavior

This is a one-week project. Your task is to define two separate target behaviors in different situations. One should be a discrete behavior and the other a continuous-stream behavior. You are to record the target behavior each day for five days. Each day you are to figure the *rate* of the discrete behavior and the *percentage of intervals* for the continuous-stream behavior. Then enter these measures on the graphs provided.

Part A. Countable Behavior

A behavior is countable if it has a clear-cut beginning and end, and each behavior cycle, takes about the same time. Examples: a smile, smoking a cigarette, doing a math problem, saying something nice to another, a kiss, eating a bit of food.

Steps to Take:

1 Define the behavior.
2 Find a way to count it.
3 Observe it each day for a ten-minute period.
4 Determine the daily rate by dividing the number of occurrences by the number of minutes observed (rate per minute).
5 Record the rate per minute on the chart. The horizontal axis is for days (1, 2, 3, 4, 5), and the vertical axis is for rate per minute. Label the vertical axis according to the range of rates you are dealing with. For example, if smiling occurs between .2 and .7 times a minute, the vertical axis might be labeled in tenths (.1, .2, .3, etc.). If smiling occurs between 1 and 7 times a minute, the vertical axis would be labeled in units (1, 2, 3, etc.).

Part B. Continuous-stream Behavior

A continuous-stream behavior is one that goes on and on without clear-cut behavior units. Examples: watching TV, working on-task, singing, hugging, attending.

Steps to Take:

1 Define the behavior.

2 Select a recording interval (10 seconds, 20 seconds, 30 seconds, etc.).

3 Prepare a recording sheet corresponding to your recording intervals (see figure 2.1).

4 Observe the behavior each day for a ten-minute period, using a clipboard, a watch with sweep hand, and a recording sheet. Improvise where you must. If possible, use a second observer to check on the reliability of your observations.

5 Determine the percentage of intervals the target behavior occurs each day. To do this, divide the intervals in which it occurs by the total intervals.

6 Record the percentage of interval data on the chart. The horizontal axis is again for days (1 to 5), the vertical axis for the percentage of intervals.

behavior a.

Define: _____

_____

Day-(date)	Number of Behaviors	Time Observed	Rate
1_____			
2_____			
3_____			
4_____			
5_____			

$$\text{Rate} = \frac{\text{Number of Behaviors}}{\text{Time Observed}} = \underline{\hspace{2cm}}$$

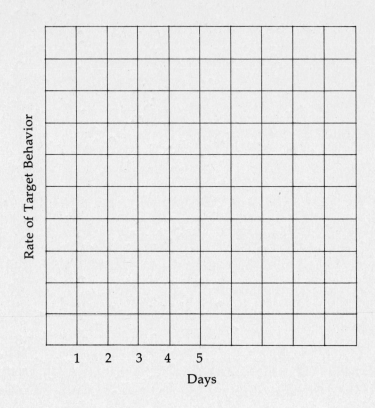

behavior b.

Define: _____

_____

Day	Intervals of Target Behavior	Total Intervals	Percentage of Intervals
1_____			
2_____			
3_____			
4_____			
5_____			

$$\text{Percentage of Intervals} = \frac{\text{Intervals Target Behavior}}{\text{Total Intervals}}$$

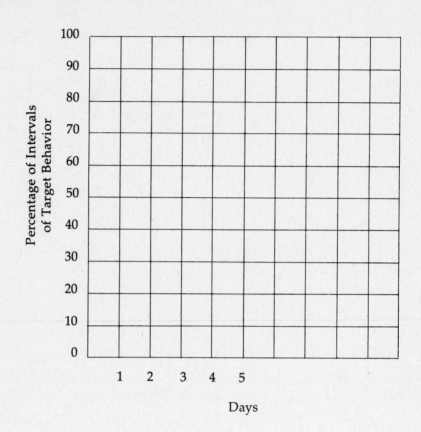

unit 3

Consequences: Basic Principles

objectives

When you complete this unit you should be able to—

1 Define and give an example of
   a) reinforcer   e) punishment
   b) punisher   f) time out
   c) extinction   g) response cost
   d) reinforcement h) negative reinforcer
2 Specify three main principles in using consequent stimuli to change behavior.
3 Analyze a behavior-change program and state which procedures are examples of which principles.
4 State three general rules that the teacher can use in changing problem behavior in the classroom.
5 Specify the difference between a reinforcer and reinforcement.
6 Specify the difference between positive and negative reinforcers.
7 Specify the difference between extinction and time out.
8 Describe some creative ways to use reinforcers and punishers.

lesson

Mother Changes Peter (and Mother)

Peter was a four-year-old boy. His mother was having great difficulty managing him and sought help. Peter often kicked objects or people, removed or tore his clothing, spoke rudely to people, hurt his younger sister, made

51

various threats, hit himself, and was easily angered. He demanded constant attention. He had been seen at a clinic and was found to have poor verbal skills. He was said to be very active and possibly brain-damaged.

Peter's behavior was observed in the home an hour a day for sixteen days. During an hour Peter showed from 25 to 112 instances of behavior objectionable to his mother. When he misbehaved, his mother would often attend to him and try to explain why he should not do so and so. At times she would try to interest him in some new activity by offering him toys or food. She would sometimes punish Peter by taking away a toy or misused object, but he was usually able to persuade her to return the item almost immediately. Occasionally he was placed on a chair for short periods of time as a punishment. Tantrum behavior usually followed such discipline. His mother responded with additional arguments, attempting to persuade him to stop.

Peter's behavior was changed by the following procedure. An observer in the home would cue his mother by raising one, two, or three fingers. One finger was raised when Peter showed an objectionable behavior. This meant she was to tell him to stop what he was doing (*a warning signal*). If he did not stop, two fingers were raised. This meant she was to immediately place him in his room and shut the door (*punishment*). He had to stay there until he was quiet for a short period. If he was playing in a nice way, three fingers were raised. This meant she was to go to him, give him attention, praise him, and be physically affectionate (*reinforcement*).

Peter's objectionable behavior dropped to near zero within a few days. Follow-up observations showed a continuing good interaction between him and his mother and an absence of the objectionable behavior. He was receiving more affection from his mother and approaching her in more affectionate ways. She was much more sure of herself, provided clear consequences for his behavior, and no longer gave in after starting a correction procedure.[1]

Peter's mother learned that by following his good behavior with attention and affection, and by consistently giving a mild punishment for objectionable behavior when a warning failed, his behavior changed dramatically. His mother was taught how to teach him to behave in a friendlier and more cooperative way. She learned that she had to consistently respond with positive reactions to behavior she wanted to strengthen.

A Teacher Learns to Manage Her Class

Observations on February 1: "Six children were in a reading group and fifteen were working on individual projects. The noise level for the entire classroom was extremely high and went higher just before recess. Some behavior noted included whistling, running around the room (five occasions), yelling at another child (many times), loud incessant talk, hitting each other in recess line. Mrs. E. would reestablish quiet by counting to ten after giving a threat."

Mrs. E. was a young teacher who had not been taught how to manage children. She attempted to control the children by shouting and scolding, but it would only slow down the unwanted behavior for a short time, and she would have to "get on them" again. Two boys in Mrs. E.'s class were studied closely.

Edward was six years nine months old and of average ability. His teacher described him as distractable, with poor attention and poor work habits. He did not comprehend what he read. He never finished assignments. He was often seen wandering about the room or turning in his seat. He made odd noises with his mouth. He was in speech therapy and was being seen by the social worker.

Elmer was two months older than Edward and was also of average intelligence. He apparently started out the school year working well, but got worse. He was described as nervous and very active. He would not work. He cried or threw a tantrum if his work was criticized. Observers thought Elmer might have brain damage, since he was so very active. He did not stay in one place or on any task very long.

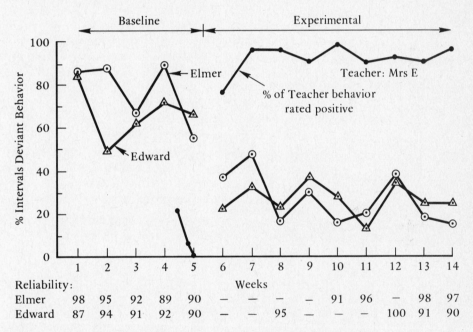

Figure 3.1 Changes in behavior for two children and their teacher

Figure 3.1 tells the story of the change in these two boys. You first need to understand that observers in the classroom were recording a variety of deviant behaviors shown by these boys using a twenty-second observation interval. Before attempting to change the situation, the boys were observed for five weeks (the baseline condition). Elmer was showing deviant behavior in nearly 80 percent of the observation intervals, and Edward was showing deviant behavior in over 60 percent of them. In figure 3.1, the vertical axis represents the percent of deviant behavior for the two boys. It also represents the percent of positive behavior shown by Mrs. E. If you will look carefully at the solid circles between week four and week five, you will see that Mrs. E. rarely used praise in the classroom.

Beginning in week six (the experimental condition), Mrs. E. was asked to follow these preocedures:

1 *Give clear signals.* Specify the desired behavior. Make your rules clear, so that the children will know what is expected of them. Repeat the rules as necessary.
2 *Ignore disruptive behavior.* Do not attend to the behavior you wish to weaken. Get involved with other children showing behavior you wish to strengthen. Praise a child showing behavior incompatible with the disruptive behavior. Play deaf and dumb.
3 *Praise the children for improvement in behavior.* Catch the children being good, rather than bad. Tell them what it is you like that they're doing. Award privileges to those showing good behavior. For example, say "You can lead the salute because you are paying attention so well."

Prior to week six, this teacher used very little praise. After week six, over 90 percent of her comments to children were positive rather than negative. Elmer and Edward changed greatly, as did the teacher and other members of the class. It took some time for the teacher to become comfortable in her new role of being a reinforcer for children, but the children responded to her new behavior whether she felt comfortable about it or not. The classroom became quieter; many members learned to work on-task for long periods of time. There was order and cooperation. The teacher found she had more time to teach now that she spent less time trying to control the children.[2]

The classroom referred to above is just one of many where significant improvement has resulted from changing the consequences of children's behavior. In a follow-up to this study it was found that just repeating rules was not effective in changing behavior in the classroom.[3] Only when praise was given for following the rules, and disruptive behavior was ignored, were results similar to those in figure 3.1 obtained.

Consequent Stimuli

Research on teaching has convincingly demonstrated that consequences (events following operant behavior) can either strengthen or weaken behavior. Those consequences that strengthen behavior are called *reinforcers* or *reinforcing stimuli*. The procedure involving the use of a reinforcing stimulus is called *reinforcement*. Those consequences that weaken classes of behavior are called *punishers* or *punishing stimuli*. The procedure involving the use of a punishing stimulus is called *punishment*. No longer following a behavior with a reinforcer can also weaken behavior. This procedure is called *extinction*. Which consequent events strengthen or weaken behavior is determined

JUST KEEP THINKING OF THAT FIRST PRIZE.

by investigation. Generally, those consequences we would label as rewards, or the stopping of painful events, have been found to strengthen the behavior they follow. Those consequences we would label as punishing or painful, or the stopping of rewarding events, have been found to weaken the behavior they follow.

In Mrs. E.'s class, praise was the main reinforcer used by the teacher to increase appropriate behavior. Ignoring disruptive behavior was an extinction procedure, because the teacher no longer followed disruptive behavior with attention (the reinforcer for such behavior.)

In the case of Peter, his appropriate behavior was reinforced by attention, praise, and physical contact. His objectionable behavior was punished by shutting him in his room if he did not comply. He was shut off from possible reinforcement for a period of time to punish his objectionable behavior. This kind of punishment is called *time out* (time out from reinforcement). Another kind of punishment procedure sometimes available to the parent or teacher is called *response cost*. Response cost involves taking away specified units of a reinforcer (like a fine) for each misbehavior. We will come back to the details of procedures for using punishment effectively in unit 13. In the meantime, we will focus on learning to use reinforcers to become more positive with others.

Positive Versus Negative Reinforcers

All reinforcers strengthen behavior. In some textbooks, reinforcers that involve *presenting* stimuli (such as giving a child candy) are called positive reinforcers, and reinforcers that involve *terminating* stimuli (buckling your seatbelt to turn off a raucous buzzer) are called negative reinforcers. This terminology is troublesome because negative reinforcers are easily confused with negative consequences or punishing stimuli. To avoid this confusion, we will simply talk about two kinds of reinforcing events—in one case a stimulus is turned on (music) or presented (food), and in the other case it is turned off (a noisy fan) or its effect is stopped (removing hand from a hot stove).

Extinction Versus Time Out

Since extinction and time out both involve withholding reinforcers, the procedures are sometimes confused. The difference is this: in time out, no reinforcers are given for any response; in extinction, responses other than those being extinguished may be reinforced. When Peter's mother used time out (placing him in his room until he was quiet for a few minutes), she was careful not to give any reinforcers to him during the period of punishment. When Mrs. E. ignored disruptive behavior, she was withholding a social reinforcer (attention) from that behavior. She was using extinction to eliminate problem behavior. At the same time, she was using reinforcement to strengthen on-task behavior.

summary

There are three main procedures for using consequent stimuli to modify operant behavior.

1 *Reinforcement.* Follow responses you wish to strengthen with reinforcing events. Reinforcing events can include both the presentation (positive reinforcers) and termination (negative reinforcers) of stimuli.
2 *Extinction.* Weaken undesired responses by stopping the reinforcement that keeps them going.
3 *Punishment.* Follow responses you wish to weaken with punishing events. Punishing events can include both the presentation of stimuli (generally called aversive stimuli) and the withholding of reinforcers. As explained in unit 13, punishing by withholding reinforcers (time-out and response-cost) is usually more effective.

broadening your perspective

In new learning, generalizations about the range of applications of new concepts and procedures are very much restricted by the examples to which the student is exposed. Therefore, from time to time we will try to broaden your perspective by presenting short summaries of research studies that might suggest unusual or creative applications of the basic principles we are learning about.

Music to Quiet the Restive Adolescent Soul

Four home economics classes in a junior high school had a problem of too much noise. In each class there were seventeen to nineteen girls, some of whom were considered to have serious behavior problems. An apparatus was installed that would automatically turn off radio music from a local popular station if the noise level in the room exceeded seventy-six decibels. The music would stay off until the noise level was back in the acceptable range for twenty seconds. Turning the music on was used to reinforce quieter behavior and turning it off (for twenty seconds or more) was used to punish noisy behavior. Without the music as a consequence, noise was above seventy-six decibels 23 percent of the time in one class and about 40 percent of the time in the other three. When music was used as a consequence, noise was above the criterion an average of 2.4, 0.3, 9.8, and 7.6 percent of time for each of the classes. Since these remarkable effects were produced by automatic equipment, the teacher was free for instructional activities.[4]

Reinforcing Integration

Most racial integration has been accomplished by enforcing compliance with the law through threat of loss of the federal dollar. Norma Hauserman and her colleagues suggest an alternative. They set up a procedure in a first-grade class to reinforce "sitting with a new friend at lunch each day." By doing this the children could earn tickets that could be exchanged for a candy treat at recess. There were seven blacks in the class of twenty-five. The effects of the reinforcement procedure were also tested during a free-play time that occurred right after lunch. The number of interracial interactions increased dramatically at lunch and during free play. To help get the process going, the teacher at first prompted "sitting with a new friend" for four days by playing the "new friend game" just before lunch. As they lined up for lunch she produced a hat and drew out papers that had pairs of names on them (different each day). The children whose names were together were encouraged to sit together for lunch and were reinforced if they did.[5]

Getting to the Plant on Time

The Ideal Standard Company in Mexico City had tried a number of procedures to increase the punctuality of its employees. Annual bonuses were given to those with the best attendence records. Repeated tardiness could be punished by a one-day suspension. If a person were more than ten minutes late his supervisor could send him home.

Tardiness was still occuring at a rate of 10 to 15 percent. Some behavioral psychologists tried to change this by using more immediate reinforcement. Each day the workers were on time, they received a note saying they had earned an extra two pesos (sixteen cents) for being on time. Thus they could earn ten extra pesos in a week. Tardiness dropped to 2 percent. A control group studied at the same time (for fifty weeks) actually increased in tardiness during the study.[6]

Peer Therapists

Most teachers have long suspected that some kids in the class have a lot to do with sustaining the problem behavior of others. Solomon and Wahler have demonstrated just that. They found that the peers of problem children attend to them exclusively when they are showing problem behaviors. They also have shown that if this peer attention is changed so that it occurs only for desirable behavior, the problem behavior will be reduced. In effect, the peers were able to serve as behavior therapists.

Five problem boys in a sixth-grade class were each paired with a nonproblem classmate who would later become his "therapist." During a baseline condition the five problem boys were showing problem behaviors in over 80 percent of the observation intervals. This produced a lot of attention from peers and seemed to reinforce the problem behavior. This possibility was tested by having the "therapist" assigned to each problem boy ignore misbehavior and respond positively to deisrable behavior. The "therapists" were trained in their jobs using videotapes to teach them to discriminate problem and desirable behavior. By the end of the first treatment period, problem behavior had dropped to an average of 28 percent. When peer attention was again given to the problem behavior, it rose again. During a second treatment period, problem behavior averaged 29 percent. These changes amounted to a 50 percent decrease. It should be noted that peers other than the "therapist" still responded to problem behavior and probably helped to keep some problem behavior going. However, the powerful influence of peers on each other is clearly demonstrated, along with a way to use this influence constructively.[7]

A Shocking Story About Smoking

Laboratory experiments show that punishment is very effective in weakening behavior. Powell and Azrin tried to see if punishment could be used in a self-management procedure to reduce smoking. A cigarette case was constructed to produce a shock through electrodes attached to the subject's shoulder. The wearer could not get a cigarette without taking a shock. The case automatically advanced a counter each time it was opened. Of twenty smokers asked to participate, six volunteered. Each participant recorded his or her smoking behavior for five days. Then the participants were required to read some literature on the health hazards associated with smoking and to continue recording when they smoked. The third step was to wear the apparatus for three days to get used to it. Finally, the shock was turned on. The experimenters increased the intensity periodically with the participants' permission. In a final stage, the shock was turned off again, but the apparatus was kept on. Of the six participants, two withdrew before shock began, and one quit after one day of shock.

No appreciable change in smoking occurred as a result of reading the health-hazard literature. Just wearing the apparatus had no effect. The amount of smoking decreased as the shock intensity was increased. The aim of the study was to increase the shock until smoking stopped. One participant did stop smoking while the apparatus was on. Smoking was reduced 30 percent and 70 percent for the other two. Both, however, refused to take a higher level of shock. When the shock was stopped, smoking returned to earlier high rates.

These findings indicate that the attempt to control smoking behavior with this special shock apparatus was not very successful. If we can *avoid* punishment, we are likely to do so. As we will see in unit 13, there are few conditions under which aversive stimulation, like spankings or shock, can be used effectively. For the most part, however, the use of reinforcers is the key to reducing undesired behaviors as well as strengthening desired ones. [8]

self-test

If you get nine or ten answers right, then we suggest you skip the Programed Practice and go on to the next exercise. If you make more than one error, do the Programed Practice, refer to the text to correct mistakes, and then do the next exercise.

1 The three key words for the procedures used by Mrs. E. were *specify*, *praise*,

and _____.

2 The procedure of withdrawing all reinforcers for a fixed period of time is

called _____ _____.

1 ignore

2 time out

3 The procedure of taking away some reinforcers (points, or whatever) for each misbehavior is called _____ _____.

4 Reinforcement that occurs because of the termination of an aversive stimulus is called _____ reinforcement.

5 Time out differs from extinction in that in time out no _____ are given for any response, while in extinction other responses than the class being extinguished may be reinforced.

6 Punishing events can include both the presentation of aversive stimuli and the _____ of reinforcers.

7 The clear signals or rules given by Mrs. E. are an example of (*circle one*): (a) reinforcing stimuli, (b) discriminative stimuli, (c) consequent stimuli, (d) punishing stimuli, (e) extinction.

8 For Peter, Elmer, and Edward (prior to the experimental change of procedures) attention from an adult appeared to _____ inappropriate behavior.

9 A rat presses a bar about four times an hour when it produces no effects except a clink and the bar movement. If the setup is changed and the rat receives a shock every time he presses the bar, he presses the bar 130 times an hour on the average. The shock stimulus was a _____ for bar pressing.

10 We can know if a consequent stimulus is a reinforcer or punisher only by examining its _____ on behavior.

NUMBER RIGHT _____

---

3 response cost

4 negative

5 reinforcers

6 withholding

7 (b)

8 reinforce, increase

9 reinforcer

10 effects

exercise 1 programed practice

Cover the answers on the left with a marker. Read each item and write in your answer. Then check the answer by moving your marker down one step. Accept your answer if the meaning is the same as that given. If you are not clear about the material covered, return to the text.

1 Peter's mother would try to divert him from objectionable behavior by offering him _____, _____, and access to other activities.

2 When Peter was punished, he frequently exhibited _____ behavior, to which his mother responded with additional arguments and attention.

3 We would expect Peter's behavior to change if the consequent events were changed. Therefore, if reinforcement for undesirable behavior was removed and reinforcement for desirable behavior was begun, we would expect an increase in _____ behavior.

4 The procedure used with Peter was, first, to have his mother _____ him when he showed an objectionable behavior; second, if he did not stop, he was to be placed in his room and the door shut; third, if he was playing in a nice way, his mother was to give him _____.

5 The result of these procedures was that Peter's _____ behavior dropped to near zero within a few days.

6 The children in Mrs. E.'s class were observed to run around the room, yell, talk loudly, and push and hit other children. The teacher's major means of keeping control was by _____ or scolding; this slowed down unwanted behavior for only a _____ time.

1 toys; food

2 tantrum

3 desirable

4 warn; praise, attention

5 objectionable, undesirable

6 shouting; short

7   50 to 90

8   specified

9   ignored

10 praised,
     rewarded

11 good

12 ignore

13 strengthen,
     increase

14 punishers,
     punishing
     stimuli

15 reinforcers,
     reinforcing
     stimuli

16 reinforcer,
     reinforcing
     stimulus

17 extinction

18 time out

19 response cost

---

7 Figure 3.1 shows that prior to a change in teacher behavior Edward and Elmer were spending approximately _____ percent of their time showing behavior incompatible with working and paying attention.

8 The teacher made her rules clear so that the children knew what they were supposed to do. She _____ the desired behavior.

9 She _____ disruptive behavior and thereby removed a source of reinforcment.

10 She also _____ the children for improvement in their behavior.

11 Using this procedure, you might say she was trying to "catch them being _____ rather than bad."

12 Thus the three key words for the procedures the teacher used would be *specify, praise,* and _____.

13 Research on teaching has demonstrated that consequent events can function to _____ or weaken responses.

14 Consequent events that weaken behavior are called _____.

15 Consequent events that strengthen behavior are called _____.

16 Behavior may also be weakened by no longer following it with a _____.

17 This procedure is called _____.

18 The procedure of withdrawing all reinforcers for a fixed period of time is called _____ _____.

19 The procedure of taking away some reinforcers (points, or whatever) for each misbehavior is called _____ _____.

20 negative

21 strengthen,
   increase

22 weaken,
   decrease

23 reinforcers

24 strengthen

25 reinforcement

26 punishing
   stimuli

27 withholding

28 extinction;
   reinforcer

29 reinforcing

30 (b)

20 Reinforcement that occurs because of the termination of an aversive stimulus is called _____ reinforcement.

21 Negative reinforcers, like positive reinforcers, also _____ behavior.

22 Negative reinforcers should not be confused with negative consequences (punishers), which function to _____ behavior.

23 Time out differs from extinction in that in time out no _____ are given for any response.

24 Follow responses you wish to _____ with reinforcing events.

25 Weaken undesired responses by stopping the _____ that is keeping them going.

26 Responses can also be weakened by following them with _____.

27 Punishing events can include both the presentation of aversive stimuli and the _____ of reinforcers.

28 Ignoring disruptive behavior is an example of the use of the procedure called _____, assuming that attention from the teacher in any form is a _____.

29 Attention, toys, and food usually act as _____ stimuli for small children.

30 A teacher decides she will weaken Jimmy's blurting out in class by not calling on him any time he blurts out. However, she will immediately call on him if he raises his hand. Blurting out has been placed on (circle one): (a) time out, (b) extinction.

31 The teacher said, "See how hard Billy's working," each time he stayed seated and busy with his reading for more than a minute. The amount of time Billy

worked on his own during the seatwork period increased from five to twenty minutes (out of thirty) within two weeks. The phrase, "See how hard Billy's working," was a _____ for working behavior.

32 When the music in the home economics classes was turned off because the girls were too loud, the function of withdrawing the music was to _____ the noise-making behavior.

33 In the integration study, the immediate reinforcers for sitting with new friends were _____ that could later be exchanged for _____.

34 The punctuality study in Mexico City gave _____ as the reinforcer.

35 Peers maintain a lot of problem behavior in the classroom through the _____ they give to it.

36 The attempt to control smoking through the use of shock is an example of the application of _____ in the attempt to weaken behavior.

31 reinforcer

32 punish

33 tickets; candy

34 money, pesos

35 attention

36 punishment

exercise 2

Define these terms.

1 Reinforcer: _____

_____

2 Reinforcement: _____

_____

3 Punisher: _____

_____

4 Punishment: _____

5 Extinction: _____

_____

6 Time out: _____

_____

7 Response cost: _____

_____

8 Negative reinforcer: _____

_____

Answers for exercise 2

Term	Essential Points
1. Reinforcer (Reinforcing stimulus)	a) following stimulus b) strengthens or increases the future occurrence of the response class
2. Reinforcement	a) the procedure of using a reinforcer
3. Punisher (Punishing stimulus)	a) a following stimulus b) weakens or decreases the future occurrence of the response class
4. Punishment	a) the procedure of using a punisher
5. Extinction	a) no longer presenting reinforcers after response class to be weakened, but perhaps presenting them for other responses b) weakens the response class
6. Time out	a) loss of access to all reinforcers for a period of time as a consequence of making some responses b) weakens the response

| 7. Response cost | a) taking away specified units of reinforcers after a response is made |
| | b) weakens the response |

| 8. Negative reinforcer | a) terminating a stimulus following a response |
| | b) strengthens the response |

discussion questions

1   State the procedures used in dealing with Peter's obnoxious behavior.

2   In the case of Peter, what kind of consequent stimulus was involved in placing him in his room? Explain your answer.

3   In the case of Peter, what kind of consequent stimulus was involved in his mother's giving attention to him for appropriate behavior?

4   Specify three general procedures for dealing with classroom behavior problems.

5   Give one of the three main procedures for the use of consequences and illustrate it with an example.

6   Give another principle for the use of consequences and illustrate it with an example.

7   Give another principle for the use of consequences and illustrate it with an example.

8   Define and give an example of *negative reinforcement*.

9   Define and give an example of *response cost*.

10   Define and give an example of *time out*.

11   Define and give an example of *extinction*.

12   What is the critical difference between time out and extinction?

13   Specify the difference between reinforcer (or reinforcing stimulus) and reinforcement.

14   Specify the difference between punisher (or punishing stimulus) and punishment.

15   How could the principle of reinforcement be used in international affairs?

16   Identify two uses of reinforcement in the business world.

17   Identify a use of response cost by the local police department.

18   Give an example of the punishment principle from your everyday experience.

19   Give an example of negative reinforcement from your everyday experience.

unit 4

The Criticism Trap

objectives

After completing this unit you should be able to—

1 Tell what the criticism trap is and how it gets going.
2 Cite experiments supporting the analysis of the criticism trap.
3 Specify ways to escape the criticism trap and cite supporting data.
4 Make a chart to collect behavior data and graph the results.
5 Define and give examples of the "being helpful" trap.

lesson

**The More the Teacher Says "Sit Down,"
the More They Stand Up**

It was 9:20 A.M. The team-taught first grade had forty-eight children in it. Two rooms were available for the class, with a movable divider between them. The children's desks were grouped into six tables of eight children each. They had been assigned work to do at their seats, while the two young teachers taught reading in small groups. Two observers entered the room, sat down, and for the next twenty minutes they recorded the number of children out of their seats during each ten-second period. The observers also recorded how often the teachers told the children to sit down, or to get back to their seats. During the first six days of observation about three children were out of their seats every ten seconds. The teachers would say "sit down" about 7 times in a twenty-minute period (see figure 4.1).

Then some very strange events began to occur. The teachers were asked to tell the children to sit down more often. During the next twelve days, the teachers said "sit down" 27.5 times each twenty minutes. *The children stood up more*—on an average of 4.5 times in ten seconds.

The sequence was tried again. For the next eight days, the teachers went back to saying "sit down" only 7 times in twenty minutes. Out-of-seat behavior declined to an average of 3 times every ten seconds. Again the teachers were asked to tell the children to sit down more often (28 times in twenty minutes). Again the children stood up more—4 times every ten seconds.

Finally the teachers were asked to quit telling the children to sit down, but rather to praise sitting and working. They did this, and fewer than two children stood every ten seconds, the least standing observed.

What can be going on? How do we explain such happenings? There is one further perplexing piece of information. The children actually *did sit down when asked by the teacher to do so;* the result wasn't just due to a few children standing a lot.

Consider the following:

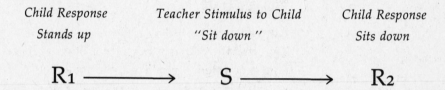

Child Response	Teacher Stimulus to Child	Child Response
Stands up	"Sit down"	Sits down
R$_1$ ⟶	S ⟶	R$_2$

The teacher's saying "sit down" *followed* standing up. When the teacher said "sit down" more often, the children stood up more often; when the teacher said "sit down" less often, the children stood up less often. S (saying "sit down") must have been a reinforcing stimulus for R$_1$ (standing up). Saying "sit down" was a stimulus following a response which strengthened that response. It was a reinforcer for R$_1$.

But S had another effect concerning R$_2$ (sitting). The children did sit down when told to, so S must *also* have been a signal (a discriminative stimulus) for R$_2$.

A Beautiful Trap! Imagine, the teacher thought that telling the children to sit down worked, because they *did sit down*. But that was only the immediate effect. The effect on standing might have been missed altogether by the teacher if careful observations had not been made. Her words were in fact having exactly the opposite effect on standing from what she desired.

A Caution. Do not conclude that an effect like this will always be found. If the teacher had praised sitting and working a lot (behavior incompatible with standing), saying "sit down" would not likely have had a reinforcing effect. But in the absence of praise and other reinforcers for working and sitting, the behavior most reinforced by the teacher's attention was standing.[1]

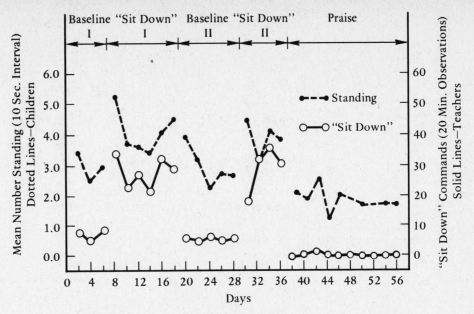

Figure 4.1 Standing up as a function of "sit down" commands and praise (Data points are averages of each two days.)

Two More Examples of the Criticism Trap

In one study we took a good class and made it into a bad one for a few weeks by having the teacher no longer praise the children. When the teacher no longer praised the children, off-task behavior increased from 8.7 percent to 25.5 percent. The teacher criticized off-task behavior and did not praise on-task behavior. When the teacher was asked to increase her criticism from 5 times in 20 minutes to 16 times in 20 minutes, the children showed even more off-task behavior. Off-task behavior increased to an average of 31.2 percent, and on some days was over 50 percent. *Attention to the off-task behavior increased its occurrence when no praise was given for working.* Introduction of praise back into the classroom restored good working behavior.[2]

Imagine the situation of the teacher who primarily disciplines by scolding rather than praising. A child misbehaves, the teacher catches him and scolds him, and he stops for the time being. *Scolding and criticizing seem to work. The teacher is reinforced for scolding and is likely to do it again.* The undesirable behavior will increase, and then it will be necessary to scold more. It is a vicious circle. Only by seeing clearly what is going on can the teacher avoid this trap and behave in ways that will produce the desired long-range effects.

In the introduction to unit 3, we discussed a four-year-old boy, Peter, who was very demanding and difficult to control. His mother did not know what to do to improve the situation. The clear use of reinforcement for good behavior and punishment for objectionable behavior produced a dramatic change in Peter (and his mother). It isn't known exactly how the situation between Peter and his mother got going, but it is quite clear that Peter got most of his attention from his mother by misbehaving. If Peter did behave, his mother probably used that time to do her chores and care for her other three children. It is not difficult to imagine that from infancy on, Peter got more and more attention from his mother for misbehavior rather than for desirable behavior. His mother was caught in the criticism and scolding trap.

How To Escape the Criticism Trap

To escape the criticism trap, it is necessary to establish conditions that increase praise and decrease criticism. This can be accomplished by

1 using prompts or reminders to praise more
2 getting practice in how to praise
3 making it possible to be reinforced for praising more (Usually the improvement in class behavior is a good reinforcer for teachers.)

How to Prompt the Use of Praise

Make the misbehavior of one child the signal to find and praise another child who is behaving well. For example, if Johnny is out of his seat when he should be

...UM AND IT'LL CUT YOUR MASCARA BILL IN HALF.

sitting working on an assignment, the teacher might say, "I see Jimmy is in his seat and doing a good job working on his arithmetic." This may prompt Johnny to return to his seat and begin to work, at which time the teacher might say, "Johnny, Carol, and Mike are being good workers." Making the *misbehavior* the signal to praise someone else does two things: first, it immediately takes the teacher's attention away from the misbehavior; and second, it gives the misbehaving child a gentle prompt as to what he should be doing. If the teacher is praising Jimmy, she can't be criticizing Johnny. Thus, if the teacher follows this rule, she will praise more and criticize less.

Give out tokens to prompt your praising.   Imagine a situation in which the teacher has to give out an average of fifteen tokens every day to thirty children. The tokens are little plastic chips that can be kept on a key ring. They can be exchanged later for time in an activity corner (or some other reinforcer). Now also imagine that the teacher is instructed to tell the children what they did well or improved on to earn the tokens. The stage is set for the teacher to be praising at least 450 times in about four hours. The tokens help to prompt praising more often. The effect of this procedure on teacher behavior is dramatic. This procedure also works for parents who find it difficult to stop criticizing their children. In order to use this procedure, the teacher needs only a supply of things she can pass out and some payoff for which they can be exchanged. She could also use edibles like raisins or jelly beans instead of tokens to prompt herself to praise.

Put up signs to remind yourself to praise.   One teacher placed a number of signs on the wall behind the small group of children she was teaching. She could see the signs but the children could not. The signs said:

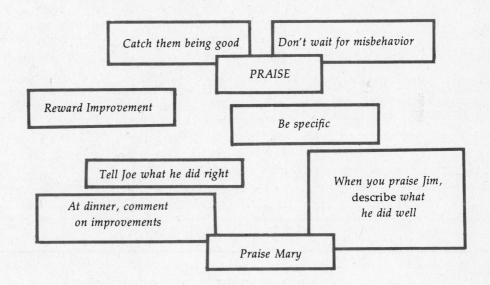

Figure 4.2 Signs

These signs were designed to help the teacher work more effectively in teaching a small group. In any classroom, it is possible for the teacher to find places where she can put signs that prompt behavior she wants to increase.

Getting Practice in How to Praise

Some adults have not learned how to say nice things to children. The words just are not there. If this is the case, it may be necessary to practice a variety of ways of positively handling common classroom situations. Unit 10, Using Social and Activity Reinforcers, provides materials that can be used for this practice. The key is to specify a classroom situation in which you want to use praise to strengthen desired behavior, and then to practice doing it in a variety of ways. For example:

Classroom Situation (S)	*Teacher Response (R)*
The children have just returned from recess, and several are still out of their seats or talking rather than starting on the next assignment.	Praise the children who are in their seats and working.
In class discussion, the children are required to raise their hands if they wish to answer, but some do not.	Ignore the children who blurt out. Say, "Billy's got his hand up. What answer would you give, Billy?"
The children are going to the bathroom. Some are walking quietly down the hall, but others are running and laughing.	Praise the children who are walking quietly and ignore those who are running. (Note that it may be necessary to back up the praise by some more powerful reinforcer.)
The class is standing in line to go into the lunchroom. Some of the children push in at the head of the line rather than wait their turn.	Praise the children who wait in line, and back up the praise by picking them to go into the lunchroom first. Do not censure the children who break into line.
The class is doing written assignments. You notice that one of the children is obviously copying.	Ignore the child who is copying. Praise a child who is doing his own work. After the child who has been copying begins to do his own work, you should praise him for working hard.

Getting Reinforcement for Praising More

The two procedures to be discussed involve keeping a record of the teacher's behavior. In the first, the teacher records his own behavior. In the second, an

Name _____ Observation Period <u>9:30 to 10:00</u>

Comments: <u>Activity consists of seatwork and reading group.</u>

<u>Recording only praise to children working at their seats, not praise to</u>

<u>reading group.</u>

Date	Number of Praise Comments	Starting Time	Stopping Time	Total Minutes Observed	Rate per Minute
2/17	6	9:30	10:00	30	.20
2/18	3	9:35	10:05	30	.10
2/19	5	9:34	10:04	30	.17
2/20	4	9:30	10:00	30	.13
2/21	3	9:32	10:02	30	.10

Note: To get rate per minute, divide number of praise comments by total minutes observed.

Figure 4.3 Recording sheet

observer is used. For most adults, seeing evidence that a desired change is occurring is a good reinforcer. But it is also very likely that keeping a record or chart of progress serves as a cue to persist in the new task. That is, today's count of praise comments may be a reinforcer for praising more today, and looking at today's chart tomorrow may remind you to try even harder tomorrow.

Change Program 1: Count Praise Behavior. Praise comments are any statements of affection, approval, or praise directed to a child or a group. These include such single words as "Good," "Correct," "Excellent," "Nice," "Great," and "Wonderful," and such sentences as "That's a good job," "Remarkably well done," "That's an improvement," "I'm so proud of you," and "That's interesting." A more complete listing of praise comments and other potential social reinforcers is covered in unit 10.

Step 1: Decide on a recorder. You might use a wrist-band golf score counter, a hand counter used by housewives in figuring grocery bills, or just a tally sheet.

Step 2: Determine an observation period. Select one or two fixed periods during the day when you are going to count every praise comment you make. These might be twenty- to thirty-minute periods. Record starting and stopping time for the observation period.

Step 3: Obtain a baseline. Before trying to change the rate of praise, just record how often you currently praise in the observation situation. You should also have a recording sheet like the one given in figure 4.3.

Step 4: Graph the results daily. Divide the number of praise comments by the number of minutes of observation to obtain a rate-per-minute measure. If the observation periods selected differ markedly in the opportunity for praising children, you might make a separate chart for each time period during the day for which observations are regularly made. If the difference is slight, the rates for the different periods may be averaged. Your data can be plotted on a chart like this:

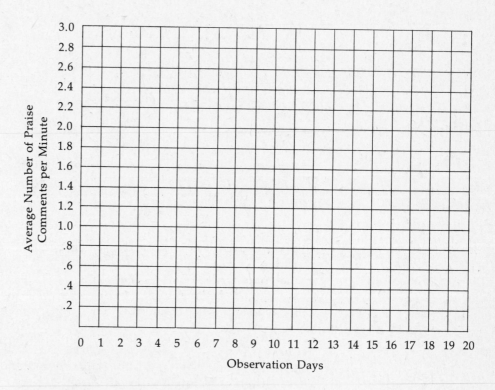

Figure 4.4 Rate of praise comments

Step 5: Attempt to increase the rate of praise: Use any of the suggestions given above to prompt praising while continuing to record the frequency of praise comments during the specified time periods. Continue to plot the results daily and keep the chart where it can be seen every day.

Change Program 2: Have an Observer Record Praising and Criticizing Behavior. When an observer is available, the steps to be taken are as follows:

Step 1: Determine a recording method. The observer could use a clipboard and attach a stopwatch to the top with tape. Daily recording sheets could be dittoed or mimeographed as in figure 4.5. Each of the 120 boxes on the recording sheet represents a ten-second time interval. The recording sheet is used as follows:

a) The observer first memorizes the codes (symbols) for teacher behavior given in table 4.1.

b) Practice with the observer in order to learn the procedure. If two observers are rating the same teacher at the same time, they should discuss with each other any differences in their ratings. There should be disagreement in no more than one out of five ten-second intervals by the end of the training period (80 percent accuracy).

c) At the beginning of the observation period, the observer watches the teacher and places a code symbol in the first box for each codable type of behavior occurring during the first ten seconds. The observer then moves to a new box every ten seconds until five boxes, or fifty seconds, have been covered. During the last ten seconds in each minute the observer can rest or make notes. More than one occurrence of a codable behavior can be recorded in each box.

TABLE 4.1 TEACHER RATING CATEGORIES

Symbols	Classes	Class Definitions
P	Praise Comments	This category includes paying attention to appropriate behavior with comments indicating approval or commendation for achievement, such as "That's good," "You're studying well," "Fine job," and "I like you."
C	Critical Comments	This category includes verbally calling attention to undesirable behavior. This may be of high intensity (yelling, scolding, or screaming) or of low intensity ("Go to the office," "You know what you are supposed to be doing," and so on). Calling the child to the desk to talk things over and threats of consequences are also included.
___	No codable response by teacher	

Teacher _____ Observer _____

Time Start _____ Date _____

Time Stop _____

	1	2	3	4	5
1					
2					
3					
4					
5					
6					
7					
8					
9					
10					
11					
12					
13					
14					
15					
16					
17					
18					
19					
20					
21					
22					
23					
24					

Frequency   Rate Per
                        Minute

1. P _____ _____

2. C _____ _____

Observation Minutes
$5/6 \times 24 = 20$
Rate per minute equals
   frequency divided by 20

Code Summary
1. P Praise Comments
2. C Critical Comment
3. — No Codable
         Response for
         10 Seconds

Comments: _____

_____

_____

Figure 4.5 Observer recording sheet

Step 2: Determine an observation period. (See program 1.)

Step 3: Obtain a baseline. (See program 1.)

Step 4: Graph the results daily. It is possible to make two graphs: rate of praise comments and rate of critical comments. (Note that in determining rates, observations are made for only fifty seconds out of each minute. This means that the total observation time should be reduced by one-sixth before dividing response frequency by observation minutes.)

Step 5: Introduce the change procedure. The steps to be taken here are the same as in program 1, except that it is helpful for the observers to give the teacher specific suggestions every day on how she might have handled situations in a more positive way. In any case, daily feedback on the results of the observations should be given to help in planning further changes.

summary

The criticism trap involves being reinforced on a short-term basis for making critical comments. Making such comments, in turn, has the long-term effect of strengthening the very problem behavior the teacher is trying to reduce. To escape the criticism trap, it is necessary to increase praise and decrease criticism. This can be accomplished by providing signals or reminders to praise more, by receiving practice in how to praise, and by setting up conditions that reinforce praising. In most cases, some kind of recording procedure is helpful in learning to escape the criticism trap.

broadening your perspective

In the criticism trap, the teacher (or parent, or spouse) reinforces the very behavior she is trying to get rid of. There is a related trap we might call the "being helpful" trap, in which the teacher reinforces repeated mistakes by giving more attention to errors than to good work.

The Case of the Poor Speller

Michael was eleven years old. He was of average intelligence, but had been placed in a residential treatment center because of his behavior problems. During his English class, his teacher noted that whenever Michael was called on to spell a word that had been previously studied, he would pause, make a distorted face, and mumble letters not related to the word. The teacher would then ask him to sound out the word and after considerable time and attention, the correct spelling would come out. The teacher began to suspect that her attention might be maintaining the poor spelling.

The teacher decided to test this idea. After Michael had turned in a spelling test with muddled combinations of barely legible letters, the teacher sent him to the blackboard. She told him that she was going to give him a test. "I will read a word and you will write it correctly on the board." The teacher gave a word. Michael mispelled it more than ten times while the teacher sat at her desk ignoring him (busy reading papers). Michael would misspell a word and look to the teacher, but she would not respond. He would erase it and "try" again. Sometimes he would say, "I can't remember it." After ten minutes, Michael spelled the first word correctly. His teacher said, "Good, now we can go on." A second word was followed by a similar scene. As they painfully worked through ten words, the time Michael took to get to a correct spelling decreased. At the end the teacher wrote an A on his spelling chart and asked him to help her color some Easter baskets. In a month's time with consistent reinforcement for good spelling, instead of bad, Michael's bizzare spelling disappeared. Michael had been given real help.[3]

The Digit Reverser

Bob was an eight-year-old enrolled in a Basic Skills class. He was considered one of the better students by his teacher. But nearly every time he added numbers producing a two-digit sum, he would reverse the numerals. For example, he would write 31 as the sum of 5 and 8. Because of this *behavior*, Bob received several neurological and eye examinations. He was also given lots of extra help by several teachers. The problem remained.

A check of Bob's skills showed he could discriminate 31 from 13, 24 from 42, and so on. In fact, he would point out reversals on his paper if the teacher missed them. On several occasions he was seen erasing a correct answer and replacing it with a reversal. An experiment was undertaken to see what was going on.

Sets of twenty problems yielding two-digit sums were made up for each day. They involved the same kind of work, but with different examples. Over four weeks' time, each possible sum was used seven times. Problems with sums having identical digist (11, 22) and with sums of 10 were not used.

During the study, Bob raised his hand when he had completed the twenty problems and his teacher would then check the answers. For seven days (baseline), the teacher marked C if an answer was right and X if it was wrong. For wrong answers, the teacher would say, "This one is incorrect. You see, you reversed the numbers in the answer." Bob was then taken through each problem he missed and "helped" to get the right answer with the aid of counters and number lines. For these first seven days, Bob made *18 to 20 errors each day*.

For the next seven days, Bob's teacher simply marked all answers C. No comments were made nor help given with wrong answers. For right answers, the teacher might give Bob a pat on the back, a smile, and say, "This one is *very* good." For the first three days under this condition, Bob's errors remained near 20. Then for the next four days they *dropped to 5, 1, 4, and 0.*

There could be little question that the teacher had been caught in the "being helpful" trap.[4]

Using Praise to Increase Praise

Ace Cossairt and colleagues decided that if praise is good for helping the kids learn, why not see if it helps the teachers too. Three teachers were studied in their third and fourth grade classrooms. They devised a special math lesson to provide a controlled setting in which to observe changes in teacher behavior. The teacher was to teach the children to pay attention when he was giving instructions. The students were given folders with math problems in them. The teacher would give instructions for a row of problems at a time, such as: "Add the first problem, subtract the second problem, leave out the third problem, and add the fourth problem." When the task was completed, the children closed their folders and waited for the next instruction. Observers recorded two behaviors, Teacher Praise for Attending and Students Attending to Teacher, using an interval recording procedure.

After recording a baseline condition, two of the teachers were introduced to the following procedures one at a time:

1 *Instructions.* The teachers were given written and oral instructions that teacher attention and praise could be effective in changing student behavior. In the daily written instructions was the message, "Teacher praise for attending to instructions sometimes increases this behavior."

2 *Feedback.* After each observation, the teacher was told the number of intervals the children attended to instructions and the number of intervals the teacher gave praise for attending.

3 *Feedback plus praise.* Social praise was added to the feedback. For example, Ace might say, "You had the whole class attending to you" or "John really responds to your attention," or "You sure know how to hold their attention with your praise."

The results were very instructive. *Instructions* produced a small change for one teacher, but not the other. *Feedback* produced a moderate increase in praise for both teacher A and B. *Praise* from the trainer produced a dramatic increase in both teachers' use of praise. For teacher C, who received all three procedures at once, a sharp increase in praise occurred. In all three cases, students' attention to teacher increased from around 20 percent to nearly 100 percent. Post checks made two or three weeks later showed some decrease in the amount of teacher praise being used and a small drop in student attention, but most of the gains were being maintained.[5]

self-test

If you get nine or ten right, skip the Programed Practice and go on to the next exercise. If you make more than one error, do the Programed Practice, go back to the text to correct mistakes, and then do the next exercise.

1 When the children stand up, the teacher says, "Sit down." If standing up increases in frequency, then saying "sit down" must be acting as a _____.

2 Since the response of sitting down follows the signal closely, the long-range increase in standing up would probably go unnoticed, and the teacher would think that saying "sit down" _____.

3 She is _____ for scolding because it seems to work.

4 The criticism trap develops only when criticism is the main way in which a child gets _____ from adults.

5 Three procedures can help one get out of the criticism trap: first, use signals or _____ to praise more; second, practice how to praise; and third, find a way to get _____ for praising more.

1 reinforcer

2 worked

3 reinforced

4 attention

5 reminders, prompts; reinforcers

6 In the lesson, two ways were discussed for the teacher to get reinforced for criticizing less and praising more. Both involved keeping some kind of _____ of the teacher's behavior.

7 Keeping records can help _____ the desired behavior by showing improvement.

6 record

8 Keeping records may also serve as a _____ to keep trying to do better.

7 reinforce

9 Related to the criticism trap is the "being helpful" trap. In this trap, the teachers reinforce repeated mistakes by giving more _____ to errors than to good work.

8 prompt

NUMBER RIGHT _____

9 attention

exercise 1 programed practice

Write one word in each blank.

1 Research indicates that when teachers use criticism they sometimes get exactly the _____ effect to the one they desire.

2 In one study, when teachers increased the frequency with which they told the children to "sit down," the children _____ _____ more.

1 opposite

3 Saying "sit down" followed the child's response of standing up. If standing up increased in frequency, then saying "sit down" must have been acting as a _____ .

2 stood up

3 reinforcer

4 signal, cue

5 worked

6 observation

7 criticism

8 reinforced

9 reinforced,
  strengthened

10 attention

11 praise; criticize

12 reminders,
   prompts;
   reinforcers

13 praise

14 prompt

15 signs

4 Saying "sit down" was also a _____ for the child's response that followed it (sitting down).

5 Since the response of sitting down followed the signal quite closely and the increase in standing up might not have been noted, the teacher might have thought that saying "sit down" _____.

6 Only careful _____ and recording of the events can reveal the trap.

7 The teacher who tries to control her children mainly by scolding rather than praising is likely to get caught in the _____ trap.

8 She is _____ for scolding because it seems to work.

9 The very behavior she does not want will be _____.

10 The criticism trap develops only when criticism is the main way in which a child gets _____ from adults.

11 To escape the criticism trap the teacher must establish conditions that permit her to _____ more and _____ less.

12 Three procedures can help one get out of the criticism trap: first, use signals or _____ to praise more; second, practice how to praise; and third, find a way to get _____ for praising more.

13 One way to prompt praising behavior is to make the misbehavior of one child the cue to _____ another who is behaving well.

14 Another thing a teacher can do to _____ praising behavior is to pass out tokens to the children and set a definite number to be awarded in a day.

15 Teachers can also post _____ to remind themselves to praise.

16 Carrying a hand counter or a tally sheet to record praise statements could also be used to _____ praising behavior.

17 Some teachers may need to _____ praising children in order to learn new responses.

18 In the lesson, two ways were discussed for the teacher to get reinforced for criticizing less and praising more. Both involved keeping some kind of _____ of the teacher's behavior.

19 Keeping records can help _____ the desired behavior by showing improvement.

20 Keeping records may also serve as a _____ to keep trying to do better.

21 In change program 1 the teacher keeps a record of his or her own _____ behavior and trys to increase it.

22 Change program 2 involves the use of an _____ to keep a record of the teacher's praising and criticizing behavior.

23 Both programs require some way of _____ the behavior to be increased.

24 Finally, in order to see the changes as they occur over time, it is important to make a _____ of the behavior being recorded.

25 Related to the criticism trap is the "being helpful" trap. In this trap, the teacher _____ repeated mistakes by giving more _____ to errors than to good work.

16 prompt

17 practice

18 record

19 reinforce

20 prompt

21 praise

22 observer

23 recording

24 graph

25 reinforces; attention

26 In one example, Michael's bizarre spelling behavior disappeared when the teacher _____ attention from bizarre spelling and _____ good spelling.

27 In another example, Bob was found to keep making the same digit reversals when the teacher constantly corrected his mistakes. When attention was switched to _____ responses, Bob learned to do it the right way.

28 Cossairt showed that _____ teachers for increasing their praise behavior produced the desired effect.

26 withdrew;
   reinforced

27 correct

28 praising

exercise 2

This exercise deals with change program 1, which was discussed earlier in the unit. Your task is to complete the rate-per-minute scores for days 2/24 through 3/7 in figure 4.6, and to plot all the rate-per-minute scores on the graph on page 74 (fig. 4.4).

Name _____ Observation Period 9:30 to 10:00 _____

Comments: _____Activity consists of seatwork and reading group._____

Recording only praise to children working at their seats, not praise to

reading group.

	Date	Number of Praise Comments	Total Minutes Observed	Rate per Minute
Initial Praise	2/17	6	30	.20
	2/18	3	30	.10
	2/19	5	30	.17
	2/20	4	30	.13
	2/21	3	30	.10
Changed Praise	2/24	23	30	
	2/25	30	30	
	2/26	34	30	
	2/27	31	30	
	2/28	40	30	
	3/3	19	30	
	3/4	50	30	
	3/5	32	30	
	3/6	40	30	
	3/7	44	30	

Figure 4.6 Recording sheet

The correct rate-per-minute scores are:

Date	Rate per Minute
2/24	.77
2/25	1.00
2/26	1.13
2/27	1.03
2/28	1.33
3/3	.63
3/4	1.67
3/5	1.07
3/6	1.33
3/7	1.47

The correct graph should look like this one:

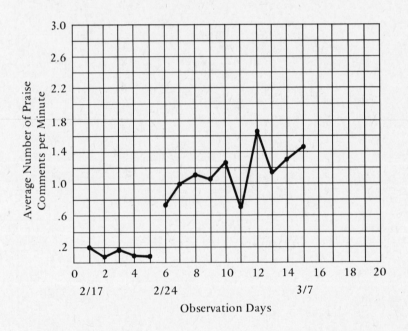

exercise 3

This exercise gives you practice in scoring observer ratings, a skill needed in change program 2. Complete the Observer Recording Sheet (figure 4.7) by making the appropriate entries for the "Frequency" and "Rate per Minute" columns. To determine the rate per minute, divide the frequency by 5/6 times 24 minutes, or 20.

Teacher _Becker_   Observer _Thomas_

Time Start _8:27_   Date _August 1, 1969_

Time Stop _8:51_

	1	2	3	4	5
1	P	—	—	—	—
2	—	—	—	—	—
3	P	—	—	P	—
4	P	—	—	—	—
5	—	C	—	C	C
6	—	—	—	—	—
7	—	P	—	P	—
8	—	—	—	—	—
9	—	P	—	—	—
10	C	C	—	—	—
11	—	—	P	—	—
12	—	—	—	P	—
13	C	C	C	C	—
14	—	P	—	—	—
15	P	—	—	—	—
16	—	—	—	—	—
17	P	P	—	—	—
18	—	—	P	P	P
19	—	—	—	—	—
20	—	—	C	—	P
21	CP	—	P	P	—
22	—	—	P	—	P
23	—	—	—	—	—
24	—	—	P	P	—

Frequency Rate Per
Minute

1. P _____ _____

2. C _____ _____

Observation Minutes
5/6 × 24 = 20
Rate per minute equals
frequency divided by 20

Code Summary
1. P Praise Comments
2. C Critical Comment
3. — No Codable
Response for
10 Seconds

Comments: _____

Figure 4.7 Completed observer recording sheet

The correct frequencies and rates are:

	Frequency	Rate per Minute
1. P	24	1.20
2. C	11	.55

discussion questions

1 Specify exactly what the trap is in the criticism trap.

2 Describe a study that illustrates the criticism trap.

3 What are the two main principles to use in getting out of the criticism trap?

4 Describe a program to help someone get out of the criticism trap.

5 Describe experimental studies of successful procedures for getting parents and teachers to increase praise behavior.

6 What is the "being helpful" trap?

7 How is the "being helpful" trap like the criticism trap?

8 Look over project 2 and be prepared to raise any questions you have about it.

project 2

Name _____

Date Due _____

Section _____

A Self-Management Experiment Increasing Your Praising Behavior

This is a two-week project. For the first week you will be recording the frequency of your praising or criticizing behavior. For the next week, you will be using one of the techniques described in unit 4 to increase your praising behavior.

Part A. Baseline

Following the project instructions are the forms you will need. They include a summary sheet to record the rate of your praising or criticizing behavior for ten days and a graph to place the data on. If you use an observer, the observer will need ten Observer Recording Sheets.

1 *Define the behavior to be observed.*
2 *Choose a measuring procedure* from those discussed in unit 4.
3 *Determine a time of day* when the behavior you want to change is frequent. This time should be used regularly as your observation period.
4 *Record the behavior daily* for ten days. *Graph* the results each day.

If you do not have a class available to work with, pick some other recurring situation in which you are too critical and work to change your behavior. Adapt the recording method as needed.

Part B. Increasing Praise and Reducing Critical Comments

After recording your behavior for five days to obtain a baseline, complete the program as follows:

1 Return to unit 4 and select one of the change proecdures described there.
2 Write out your change plan, and discuss it with your group leader before proceeding.

Name _____

Date Due _____

Change Plan

Outline the procedure to be used to increase praise and decrease criticism.

_____

_____

_____

_____

_____

_____

_____

_____

_____

_____

_____

_____

Rate of Praise Comments and Critical Comments

Praise Comments: Solid line
Critical Comments: Dotted line

Observer Recording Sheet

Teacher _____ Observer _____

Time Start _____ Date _____

Time Stop _____

	1	2	3	4	5
1					
2					
3					
4					
5					
6					
7					
8					
9					
10					
11					
12					
13					
14					
15					
16					
17					
18					
19					
20					
21					
22					
23					
24					

	Frequency	Rate Per Minute
1. P	_____	_____
2. C	_____	_____

Observation Minutes
$5/6 \times 24 = 20$
Rate per minute equals
  frequency divided by 20

Code Summary
1. P Praise Comments
2. C Critical Comment
3. — No Codable
      Response for
      10 Seconds

Comments: _____

_____

SUMMARY SHEET

Name _____

Date Due _____

Name _____ Observation Period _____

Comments: _____

_____

_____

Date	Number of Praise Comments	Starting Time	Stopping Time	Total Minutes Observed	Rate per Minute

unit 5

Varieties of Reinforcers and Punishers

objectives

When you complete this unit you should be able to—

1 Tell the difference between learned and unlearned reinforcers and punishers.

2 Discriminate social reinforcers from token reinforcers and activity reinforcers.

3 State the Premack principle.

4 Define *contingency* with reference to the reinforcement or punishment of behavior.

5 Explain how adult attention might come to be a reinforcing event for a child.

6 State in general how neutral stimuli or activities can become reinforcing events for children.

7 Suggest a procedure for determining whether a particular activity (making a puzzle) might be used to increase the frequency with which a child does arithmetic problems.

8 State why the Premack principle has special significance for the teacher.

lesson

In unit 3 we saw that reinforcers can be used to strengthen behavior and punishers to weaken it. This unit is aimed at helping you identify reinforcers and punishers, and at teaching a rule about how to create new reinforcers and punishers.

Reinforcing and punishing stimuli can be divided into two major categories on the basis of knowledge of their history. The first category has been named, at various times and places, primary, unconditioned, or unlearned. The second category has been called secondary, conditioned, or learned. The terms can be used interchangeably. We prefer to use the terms *unlearned reinforcers* (and *punishers*) and *learned reinforcers* (and *punishers*) because these terms most directly describe the procedure used to determine whether a reinforcer or punisher falls into one or the other category. That is, the distinction is based on whether or not a prior learning history is necessary for the stimulus event to be a reinforcer or punisher.

Unlearned Reinforcers and Punishers

Unlearned reinforcers most typically include such stimulus events as food, water, warmth, and activity. Events such as these will usually strengthen the behavior they follow without having to be paired first with some other reinforcer.

Unlearned punishers include such stimulus events as loud noises, pain, excessive heat or cold, and the like. Unpleasant events such as these will usually weaken the behavior they follow without having to be associated with some other punisher first.

Learned Reinforcers

Stimulus events that have no effect on behavior (neutral stimuli) can become reinforcers or punishers if they are closely followed by reinforcers or punishers.

Praise from teachers, like "Good job" and "That's pretty good," becomes a reinforcer for most children if it is closely followed by other good things (food, warmth, affection, special privileges, fun activities). Stimulus events that become reinforcers because of a history of being followed by other reinforcers are called *learned reinforcers*.

> PRINCIPLE: *To make some neutral event (such as praise, a grade, a checkmark on a chart, or money) a reinforcer, closely follow the occurrence of such an event with an effective reinforcer.*

Examples of the principle. To teach the value of money we might give a young boy two cents to buy bubble gum at the store and have him exchange the coins for the gum. Money is closely followed in time with chewing bubble gum. Later we might be able to use money as a reward at home for doing a good job.

To teach children to respond to praise, a new teacher might tell Jimmy, who just completed his seatwork, "Jimmy, you did such a good job finishing your exercise that you can choose a puzzle from the shelf to play with for the next ten minutes."

Susie's teacher decided to use stars on a card at Susie's desk to help motivate her to work more. Susie was told that she would get one star for each worksheet she completed. Each star earned could be traded for playtime in the activity corner where there was a doll house she liked to play with. The first day, Susie needed only two stars to earn five minutes of play; after that each star could be exchanged for one minute of play. The stars were closely followed by a reward. Susie learned to like to earn stars.

To the turned-off adolescent who has repeatedly failed in school because he was never taught to read well, grades may mean nothing. However, if the situation is structured so that he can learn, and if good grades can be exchanged for driving lessons or use of the family car, it is possible for him to come to value grades. When good grades are followed by a reinforcing consequence, they become reinforcers in their own right. Through the same process, he could also come to like reading.

Technical Note

The student of psychology will recognize that this principle is a restatement of the principle of respondent conditioning. In the model of respondent behavior, an eliciting stimulus evokes a respondent:

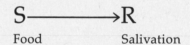

$$S \longrightarrow R$$

Food   Salivation

Stimuli that elicit respondents fall into two categories, just as reinforcers and punishers do. They may be *unlearned* eliciting stimuli or *learned.* Unlearned eliciting stimuli are called unconditioned stimuli (US), and learned eliciting stimuli are called conditioned stimuli (CS). To establish a neutral stimulus as a conditioned eliciting stimulus, it is necessary to first present the neutral stimulus and then to follow it with the unconditioned stimulus. For example, the sight of food (initially a neutral stimulus for the infant), if repeatedly followed by the taste of food (unconditioned stimulus), will come to elicit salivation by itself. In a similar way, as discussed in unit 15, stimuli associated with painful events come to elicit reactions we call fear.

Note that the consequences for operant behavior (reinforcers and punishers) often are eliciting stimuli for respondents. In fact, some theories of why reinforcers or punishers have effects on operants focus on this point. But the important point for the teacher or parent is that the procedure of pairing a neutral stimulus with a known reinforcer (or punisher) can establish new reinforcers (or punishers).

Learned Punishers

Words like "No," "Don't," "Stop that" become punishers if they are closely followed by a slap on the wrist, a spanking, or a loss of privileges. For Peter, mother's warning ("Stop that") quickly became an effective punisher; it was followed by being placed in his room and became a signal that punishment would occur if the warning was not followed.

Types of Learned Reinforcers

Social Reinforcers

Social reinforcers involve the teacher's behavior—tone of voice, words of praise, giving attention, smiling, touching, and being near. Most teaching is based on the use of social reinforcers as the immediate consequence for good behavior. For example, the teacher says, "That's right," when Billy answers correctly. He may *pat Aaron on the back* for working well or tell Tony to *bring his work to be checked* when he is finished. In each of these examples, the underlined words are aspects of teacher behavior that can function as social reinforcers.

For most children, social reinforcers are established as important early in life because parents repeatedly give attention and physical contact along with reinforcers such as food, warmth, and relief from painful events.

Token Reinforcers

Token reinforcers are another important kind of learned reinforcer. They consist of such things as points, gold stars, trading stamps, or poker chips, that have been made reinforcing by being paired with other reinforcers.

Money is a very important token reinforcer in our society. But money by itself is useless. It has value to us only because it is a basis for obtaining other reinforcers.

Poker chips quickly acquire value for the gambler. Trading stamps become valuable to the housewife who finds they can be traded for things she wants.

We can make a variety of objects token reinforcers and use them to motivate children to do things. Tickets, bottle caps, and bubble gum cards have at various times been used. They can be collected, saved, and usually exchanged for other reinforcers. It is very useful for a teacher to know how to use token reinforcers and social reinforcers in teaching.

Activity Reinforcers

Premack Principle

David Premack is a psychologist who did a number of basic studies demonstrating that more preferred activities can be used to reinforce less preferred activities.[1] The Premack principle states that any higher-frequency behavior that is *contingent* upon a lower-frequency behavior is likely to increase the rate of the lower-frequency behavior. Here, contingent means that if the less-preferred behavior occurs, the student is then permitted to perform some more-preferred behavior. The preferred activity is used to reinforce behavior the teacher wants to strengthen.

The following examples use the Premack principle:

"You may go home when you finish your assignment."

"When the whole class is quiet and seated, we can go out to recess, a row at a time."

"Jimmy, you raised your hand, so I'm going to call on you to answer."

"Alice is all finished. She can help me hand out these corrected papers."

"Those who score 100 percent on this spelling test may go out to recess five minutes early today."

"Archibald's row is quiet and ready. They may go to lunch first."

"Jeff has been working hard. He can clean the erasers for me today."

"When everybody is seated at the table and quiet, father will say grace and then we can eat."

The next two examples are NOT examples of the Premack Principle.

"You can go play if you will do your homework later."

IT'S THE FIRST STEP IN A SURVEY OF
HIGH FREQUENCY BEHAVIOR.

"We'll have an extra five minutes of recess if you will work harder when we get back to class."

In these two examples, the order of behavior is backwards. The more-preferred activity comes before rather than after the less-preferred activity. Reinforcers do not work when given before the behavior.

A Teacher Learns to Use the Premack Principle

Mrs. Stone had been battling with Justin. She had deprived him of recess because he had not completed his exercises, and Justin just pouted for the rest of the day. He could see no point to finishing his exercises, since he could not go to recess anyway. Mrs. Stone happened to mention this difficulty to the school social worker in the lounge. The social worker recognized the problem as an ineffective use of punishment and suggested a slight modification of procedure. "Tomorrow you tell Justin at the beginning of the work period that when he finishes his assignment he can go to recess. If he finishes before recess, he can go out early. If he finishes after recess starts, he can go out for as much recess as there is left." The early recess possibility was cleared with the principal and Mrs. Stone tried it. Justin was finished seven minutes before recess and extremely pleased with himself. Mrs. Stone was amazed at the difference made by using recess to reward working rather than using loss of recess to punish not working.

Why Activity Reinforcers Are Important

If preferred activities can function as reinforcers, then by observing what children do frequently, the teacher can determine what might be used as a reinforcer for a particular child. This is an extremely valuable idea for teachers learning how to motivate children in positive ways. Lloyd Homme once observed that four preschool children he wanted to teach to read spent most of their classroom time "running and screaming." So he made a rule. "Sit and listen for two minutes, and I'll let you run and scream." Gradually, he required more sitting, listening, and working for less running and screaming. In a short time, the children were hardworking and well-behaved.

With careful observation, the teacher can find a host of activities readily available to be used as reinforcers.

Are Activity Reinforcers Learned or Unlearned?

The discerning student has noticed that we did not classify activity reinforcers under the heading of learned reinforcers. This was quite intentional. If all operant behavior is learned, then activity reinforcers are learned. This is probably the case. But there is a gray area. For example, sucking by the young infant occurs without a history of prior learning. However, before many days of life, sucking can be shown to be under the control of consequences (an operant). From a practical point of view, it really doesn't make much difference. Preferred activities can be easily identified and used by the teacher as reinforcing events.

A General Procedure for Using Reinforcers

The key to the use of reinforcers is to make the reinforcer *contingent* on a desired performance. If, and only if, the desired performance occurs, the reinforcer is given. Reinforcers are not given for undesired behavior.

After the child has learned to work for several reinforcers, it is possible to teach him to work for new unfamiliar reinforcers by treating them as if it were as much fun as the old ones he knows about. "If you finish this reading on time, I'm going to let you do your arithmetic sheet. How about that?" This approach is similar to the one Tom Sawyer used to convince his friends that whitewashing a fence was a supremely reinforcing activity.

summary

1 Reinforcing and punishing stimuli can be first divided into *unlearned* and *learned* varieties. Other names for these two classes are: *primary* and *secondary; unconditioned* and *conditioned.*

2 Neutral stimulus events can become reinforcers if their occurrence is followed closely by known reinforcers. We teach children to respond to praise by pairing it with food, warmth, and other reinforcers.

3 Events can be made punishers by pairing them with punishers. "No" followed closely by a hand slap can quickly teach the two-year-old to stop reaching for the lamp when mother says "No."

4 Three groups of reinforcers important to the teacher are social reinforcers, token reinforcers, and activity reinforcers.
   a) *Social reinforcers* involve the teacher's behavior—words of praise, attention, smiles, nearness.
   b) *Token reinforcers* are things such as money, poker chips, points, and gold stars that can be exchanged for other reinforcers.
   c) *Activity reinforcers* are activities children like to participate in when given a chance. These might include running, games, art activities, singing, eating, recesses, going home.

5 The Premack principle states that any behavior a child will readily engage in can be used to reinforce behavior he will not readily engage in. You simply require that the less-preferred activity be performed before the more-preferred activity is allowed. The more-preferred behavior is contingent on the less-preferred behavior.

6 The general procedure for using reinforcers is to make the reinforcer contingent on the occurrence of the desired response. If the correct behavior occurs, the reinforcer is given; if the correct behavior does not occur, the reinforcer is not given.

broadening your perspective

Smiles and Touch

Does it really pay to smile and show affection to your student through a pat on the back, a hug, or a gentle touch? Most research on the effect of teacher attention on child behavior has focused on social reinforcement of the praise variety. A study by Alan Kazdin and Joan Klock shows that if you hold verbal praise at constant level while increasing the number of smiles and touches, these social reinforcers have important effects on their own.

Their study was carried out in a class of thirteen moderately retarded children aged seven to twelve. During baseline observations, verbal praise was given, but smiles and touch were infrequent. In the experimental condition, smiles contingent on good working behavior increased to 10 percent of the 15-second observation intervals, and contingent touches occurred in as many as 30 percent of the intervals. The overall effect on attentive behaviors of the children was to increase this behavior from an average of 50 percent to nearly 80 percent. To clearly show that smiles and touch were functioning as reinforcers, they followed the first experimental condition with a return to baseline conditions where there were few smiles and touches. Attentive behavior dropped back to the 50 percent level. A return to the experimental condition quickly reestablished a high level of attentive behavior.

Note: The experimental design in this study is called an ABAB design. The A stands for a baseline condition and the B for the experimental condition. Each condition was studied twice to demonstrate the effects of teacher behavior on child behavior.[2]

A Lesson in Tactics

Polly was a three-year-old who lacked both motor and social skills. In preschool, she participated very little in the program. She did not show cooperative play and rarely talked to or touched other children. The staff decided to use social reinforcement (teacher attention, smiles, and touch) to increase Polly's use of the play equipment. The idea was that if Polly were more involved with the play equipment, she would naturally have more encounters with other children and thus improve her social skills.

At first the teachers had to *prime* her to use the equipment. For eight days (after a baseline condition), they would place her on a different piece of equipment (trike, jungle gym, swing, and others) and stay near her, showing approval as long as Polly used the equipment. After eight days the priming was stopped, but social reinforcement continued. Polly's use of the play equipment rose from near zero to over 50 percent of the observation intervals. In later phases of the experiment, use of play equipment exceeded 70 percent of the time intervals. As side effects of this tactic, Polly's social interactions with other children increased in the form of touching, talking, and cooperative play. Her somewhat bizarre baby talk, hand flapping, and hopping behaviors also decreased considerably. She was behaving more like a happy three-year-old.[3]

The Joys of Free Time in a Junior High Class

The seventh grade class contained thirty-two students, eight of whom showed high levels of disruptive behavior (70 percent off-task). The study was carried out in a pre-lunch math period and a post-lunch geography period. The first approach to increasing productive behavior was to structure the class activities more clearly. As the students entered the class the teacher handed out the day's lesson so that each student knew what he or she was supposed to do. Rules for conduct were also included in the handout. This procedure by itself had little effect on study behavior.

Next, a group reinforcement procedure was introduced, first during math only, and later during geography. The teacher made a set of 18 cards on a rotary file, so the cards could be flipped one at a time. The students were told that they could now earn privileges by helping to make a better classroom. By following the class rules, they could earn 18 minutes of free time each day. During the free time they could talk with friends, play games, work on other assignments, read magazines and comics, play records, use the tape recorder, write on the blackboard, color, or have any other activity that would not disturb others. However, anytime during the work period that a student violated a rule, a card was flipped and the group lost a minute of free time.

The effect of this use of the Premack principle was to increase the appropriate behavior of the eight target students to over 80 percent in both math and geography.[4]

Contingent Swimming

During a summer camp session, the Premack principle was used with eight boys who wouldn't brush their teeth regularly. During baseline, there was little tooth brushing in the morning, evening, or after lunch. To demonstrate the value of using contingencies, the counsellors introduced a requirement that the boys would have to brush their teeth before they would be given permission to go swimming. The brushing of teeth immediately increased to 100 percent most days. There were many other opportunities to use this kind of reinforcement at the camp. Trips to town, movies, and nature hikes, for example, were made contingent on cleaning up the cabin, making beds, or participating in group construction projects with good results. It sure beats nagging![5]

Praise Even Works in the High School

Much of the early work in behavioral analysis was done with elementary school children. Secondary school teachers, on first exposure, are prone to say, "It'll never work with my kids." Well, it can!

Loring McAllister and several others worked with a high school English teacher with twenty-five low-track students. Their ages ranged from sixteen to nineteen. A control group, taught by the same teacher, consisted of a similar class where experimental changes were not made.

The target behaviors were inappropriate talking and turning around in the seat. These behaviors occurred frequently during baseline observations and disrupted instruction.

In the experimental condition, being quiet was worked on first. The teacher was to give praise to the entire class, such as, "Thank you for being quiet," or "I'm delighted to see you so quiet today." During the first two minutes of class, praise was given after each thirty seconds in which there was no inappropriate talking. During lecture, discussion, or recitation, praise was given at the end of fifteen minutes on the average. When seat work was assigned, praise came at the end of the period, if it had been earned. A summary statement was made at the end of each class period, such as, "Thank you all for being so quiet today," or, "There has been entirely too much talking today. I hope you can do better tomorrow."

The teacher also used criticism when the students got too noisy, statements like, "John, be quiet," or "Jane, stop talking." However, threats or other punishments were not to be used.

After effective changes had occurred for quiet behavior, the teacher focused on turning-around behavior.

The results showed a remarkable drop in inappropriate talking from about 25 percent of the observation intervals to under 5 percent. The control classroom with the same teacher showed no change. When praise was given for not turning around, it decreased from 15 percent to 4 percent. Again the control group showed no change.[6]

Praise can work with hard-to-teach high school kids!

Note. The procedure used in this study, in which first one behavior is changed and then another, is technically called a multiple-baseline design. The independent variable responsible for change in the students is more definitely seen as the teacher's behavior, when at *different* points in time, two or more behaviors change as the experimental procedure is applied to them. A multiple-baseline design is often helpful when it is not desirable to return to the baseline condition to demonstrate experimental control over a given effect.

self-test

If you get nine or ten answers right, skip the section on Programed Practice and go on to the next exercise. If you make more than one error, do the Programed Practice, refer to the text to correct mistakes, then go on.

1 learning,
training

2 punishers,
punishing
stimuli

3 followed

4 behavior

5 things,
tangibles,
objects

6 before

7 observing,
watching

8 (c)

9 contingent

10 high, higher;
low, lower

1 Unlearned reinforcers and punishers do not require previous _____ in order to function as reinforcers.

2 Loud noises, pain, and excessive heat or cold are unlearned _____ for most people.

3 Events can become reinforcers if they are closely _____ by effective reinforcers.

4 Social reinforcers involve the _____ of people (praise, smiles, attention, nearness).

5 Token reinforcers consist of _____ such as points, gold stars, money, and poker chips.

6 The Premack principle requires that a less-preferred activity be performed _____ a more-preferred activity can occur.

7 We can tell what is likely to be reinforcing for a given child by _____ what he likes to do when given some freedom.

8 Put an X on the one that is NOT a social reinforcer: (a) "good" (spoken), (b) a smile, (c) a gold star, (d) a pat on the back.

9 The _____ use of reinforcers means that if the child performs in the desired way, he gets the reinforcer; if not, he does not get it.

10 The Premack principle states that any _____-frequency behavior can be used to strengthen any _____-frequency behavior.

NUMBER RIGHT _____

exercise 1 programed practice

1   Reinforcers can be used to strengthen behavior; punishers can be used to _____ behavior.

2   Unlearned reinforcers and punishers do not require previous _____ in order to function as reinforcers.

3   Food, water, warmth, and activity are _____ reinforcers for most people.

4   Unlearned reinforcers are also called _____ reinforcers or _____ reinforcers.

5   Loud noises, pain, and excessive heat or cold are unlearned _____ for most people.

6   Learned reinforcers are also called _____ reinforcers or _____ reinforcers.

7   Events can become reinforcers if they are closely _____ by effective reinforcers.

8   Money can be made a reinforcer if it can be exchanged for other _____.

9   Words of praise can be made reinforcers by closely following them with other _____ such as food.

10   By consistently following "Stop that" with placing Peter in his room if he failed to stop, Peter's mother made the phrase a learned _____ for Peter.

---

1 weaken

2 learning, training

3 unlearned, unconditioned

4 unconditioned; primary

5 punishers, punishing stimuli

6 conditioned; secondary

7 followed

8 reinforcers

9 reinforcers

10 punisher

11 Social reinforcers involve the _____ of people (praise, smiles, attention, nearness).

12. "Thank you," "Good job," and "Great" are examples of _____ reinforcers.

13 Token reinforcers consist of _____ such as points, gold stars, money, and poker chips.

14 For many housewives trading stamps have become _____ reinforcers.

15 Trading stamps are token reinforcers rather than social reinforcers because they are _____ that can be _____ for other reinforcers.

16 The following (is) (is not) an example of use of the Premack principle: "Be dressed by 7:30 and I will drive you to school."

17 The following (is) (is not) an example of use of the Premack principle: "You can go to recess if you will finish your work when you get back."

18 The Premack principle requires that a less-preferred activity be performed _____ a more-preferred activity can occur.

19 We can tell what is likely to be reinforcing for a given child by _____ what he likes to do when given some freedom.

20 Preferred activities can be used to strengthen _____-preferred activities.

21 Reinforcers must be made contingent on responses to be strengthened. This means that if the correct behavior occurs, the _____ is given; if the correct behavior does not occur, the reinforcer is _____ given.

11 behavior

12 social

13 things,
tangibles,
objects

14 token

15 things, tangibles
objects;
exchanged

16 is

17 is not

18 before

19 observing,
watching

20 less

21 reinforcer,
reward; not

22 If Reginald laughs when Mickey makes funny faces, and Mickey starts making funny faces more often, Reginald's laughing is a _____ reinforcer.

23 Laughing is a social reinforcer because it involves the _____ of a person and serves to strengthen making funny faces.

24 Which one is NOT a social reinforcer: (a) "good" (spoken), (b) a smile, (c) a gold star, (d) a pat on the back.

25 Which is NOT a token reinforcer: (a) trading stamps, (b) money, (c) points, (d) praise.

26 A learned reinforcer based on the teacher's behavior is called a _____ reinforcer.

27 Token reinforcers can be collected and exchanged for other _____.

28 Examples of _____ _____ are words of praise, smiling, being near, and a pat on the back.

29 The Premack principle is based on the idea that generally any behavior a child will readily engage in can be used to reinforce any _____ of lesser strength.

30 The Premack principle is very important to the teacher because she needs only to _____ what her child frequently does to find out what is a _____ activity for the child.

31 Establishing a contingency would be like setting up a rule that if, and only if, the child performs a desired behavior, he will get a particular _____.

22 social

23 behavior

24 (c)

25 (d)

26 social

27 reinforcers, rewards

28 social reinforcers

29 behavior, response

30 observe, watch; reinforcing, preferred

31 reinforcer, reward, payoff

32 The _____ use of reinforcers means that if the child performs in the desired way, he gets the reinforcer; if not, he does not get it.

33 In the classroom, the teacher's behavior (social reinforcers), tangibles (token reinforcers), and the child's own preferred activities can all be used to _____ desired behavior.

34 The Premack principle states that any _____-frequency behavior can be used to strengthen any _____-frequency behavior.

32 contingent

33 strenthen, increase reinforce

34 high, higher; low, lower

exercise 2

Define these terms.

1 Learned or conditioned reinforcer: _____

_____

2 Learned or conditioned punisher: _____

_____

3 Social reinforcer: _____

_____

4 Token reinforcer: _____

_____

5 Unlearned or unconditioned reinforcer: _____

_____

6 Unlearned or unconditioned punisher: _____

_____

7 Premack principle: _____

_____

8 Contingency: _____

_____

Answers to exercise 2

Terms	Essential Points
1. Learned or conditioned reinforcer	a) is a formerly neutral stimulus that has been repeatedly paired with a reinforcer b) is presented following a response c) causes the response to occur more frequently in the future
2. Learned or conditioned punisher	a) is a formerly neutral stimulus that has been repeatedly paired with a punisher b) is presented following a response c) causes the response to occur less frequently in the future
3. Social reinforcer	a) is a formerly neutral stimulus that is based on the behavior of a person b) is presented following a response c) causes the response to occur more frequently in the future
4. Token reinforcer	a) is a formerly neutral stimulus that is tangible b) is presented following a response c) causes the response to occur more frequently in the future
5. Unlearned or unconditioned reinforcer	a) is a stimulus that has not been previously paired with a reinforcer b) is presented following a response c) increases the frequency of the response (strengthens the response)

6. Unlearned or unconditioned punisher

    a) is a stimulus that has not been previously paired with a punisher

    b) is presented following a response

    c) decreases the frequency of the response (weakens the response)

7. Premack principle

    a) states that if a higher-frequency behavior (more-preferred activity) is made contingent upon a lower-frequency behavior (less-preferred activity)

    b) it is likely to strengthen or increase the lower-frequency behavior

8. Contingency

    a) is a procedure

    b) governs the delivery of consequent stimuli

    c) states: if, and only if, response A occurs will reinforcer (or punisher) X be given

exercise 3

Identifying Classes of Potential Reinforcers. Suppose you are a child; each of the following events occurs following your behavior and functions as a reinforcer for you. Indicate what kind of reinforcer each event would be. Write *S* before each example of a social reinforcer, *T* before a token reinforcer, *U* before an unconditioned reinforcer, and *A* before each reinforcing activity or privilege.

_____ 1. Someone says, "You're pretty smart."

_____ 2. You get to play teacher.

_____ 3. Check marks are placed on a card (exchange for a toy later).

_____ 4. You are given food.

_____ 5. You're chosen for running errands.

_____ 6. Someone winks at you.

_____ 7. You are given M and M's.

_____ 8. The grocer gives you trading stamps.

_____ 9. Everyone gets extra recess.

_____10. Someone says, "You make me happy."

_____11. You are given raisins.

_____12. You win poker chips.

_____13. You get some popcorn.

_____14. "Good work" is written on your paper.

_____15. You choose the game at recess.

_____16. You are given money.

_____17. The group cheers you.

_____18. You are appointed to pass out papers.

_____19. Someone smiles at you.

_____20. You get to lead the salute.

_____21. You are given candy.

_____22. You are given a part in a play or skit.

_____23. Everyone goes on a field trip.

_____24. The audience claps for you.

_____25. You get hugged.

_____26. You are given lemon drops.

_____27. You get to play with a model airplane.

_____28. You get to play baseball.

_____29. Someone pats you.

_____30. He touches you.

_____31. She looks at you.

_____32. You get to work a puzzle.

_____33. You get some peanuts.

_____34. You get to play with a balloon.

_____35. You are given animal crackers.

_____36. Someone kisses you.

_____37. You get an extra minute to present at show and tell.

_____38. You are chosen for group leader.

Answers to exercise 3

1	S	11	U	21	U	31	S
2	A	12	T	22	A	32	A
3	T	13	U	23	A	33	U
4	U	14	S	24	S	34	A
5	A	15	A	25	S	35	U
6	S	16	T	26	U	36	S
7	U	17	S	27	A	37	A
8	T	18	A	28	A (or S or both)	38	A (or S or both)
9	A	19	S	29	S or U		
10	S	20	A	30	S or U		

discussion questions

1 State the Premack principle and give an example of its use.

2 Define and give an example of an _unlearned reinforcer_.

3 Define and give an example of a _conditioned reinforcer_.

4 Define and give an example of a _conditioned punisher_.

5 Define and give an example of an _unlearned punisher_.

6 Define _social reinforcer_ and give an example.

7 Define _token reinforcer_ and give an example.

8 How are social reinforcers and token reinforcers the same?

9 How are social reinforcers and token reinforcers different?

10 Define _contingency_.

11 Give an example of contingent reinforcement.

12 Give an example to show how a child might learn to respond to an adult's attention as a reinforcing event.

13 Specify five classroom activities that might function as reinforcers for appropriate behavior if the activity were made available contingent on desired behavior.

14 Suggest a procedure for determining whether a particular activity (finger painting) might be used to increase the frequency with which Johnny does arithmetic without actually trying it as a reinforcer.

15 State what special significance the Premack principle has for the teacher.

16 The studies presented in Broadening Your Perspective describe the use of both group and individual contingencies. What is the difference in these procedures?

17 What is noncontingent reinforcement? Give an example.

18 Be prepared to discuss with your group leader how the same stimulus (e.g., food) can have a reinforcing function for operant behavior and an eliciting function for respondent behavior.

19 Be prepared to give new examples of the relationships cited in question 18.

unit 6

Differential Reinforcement: Use of Discriminative Stimuli in Classroom Management

objectives

When you complete this unit you should be able to—

1 Define differential reinforcement and explain how it is used to establish discriminative stimuli.
2 Give examples of discriminative stimuli commonly used in the classroom.
3 Define and give examples of prompts.
4 Give two rules for using prompts.
5 Describe a behavior chain.
6 State the two functions of discriminative stimuli in a chain.
7 Give one procedure for establishing a behavior chain.
8 Explain a procedure for teaching children to follow the classroom rules.
9 Explain one benefit from following a daily routine.
10 Describe a procedure to teach children to follow instructions.

lesson

In unit 2, we noted that the basic model of operant behavior is an $S \rightarrow R \rightarrow S$ model. A preceding stimulus, called a discriminative stimulus or S^D, sets the occasion in which an operant response is likely to be followed by a reinforcing stimulus or the avoidance of punishment. Basically, discriminative stimuli tell you *when to do what*. The degree to which we depend on them in our everyday behavior is not always obvious. But think about the simple process of getting from one place to another in your own house.

Suppose you were blindfolded. What would you do without visual cues (S^D's) to guide your movements? You would probably bump into things or reach out to feel your way. We are very dependent on a series of visual stimuli to let us know when to stop or when to reach out and open the door—in short, when to do what.

We learn about movement in space by experiencing consequences: punishment in the form of bumps and falls or reinforcement from getting where we want to go. We are *differentially reinforced* for the way we read cues that tell us how to move safely. There are two aspects to differential reinforcement. Let S^R stand for a reinforcing consequence. Let S^P stand for a punishing consequence. Let EXT stand for no consequence or an extinction condition. Now consider this example; we have two discriminative stimuli (S^D_1 and S^D_2) and two responses (R_1 and R_2).

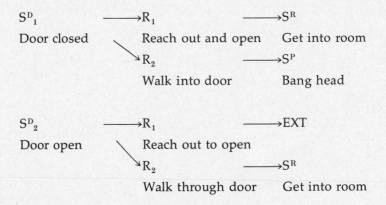

The two aspects of differential reinforcement are:

Appropriate responses are reinforced. In the presence of S^D_1, R_1 is reinforced.

Inappropriate responses are not reinforced. In the presence of S^D_2, R_1 is not reinforced. R_2 is not reinforced in the presence of S^D_1.

We learn which response to make in the presence of which stimulus. In the classroom, the teacher encourages this process by reinforcing acceptable or right responses. If the teacher says, "Take out your spelling books," and Mary does so, the teacher might say, "I'm glad you're ready to work, Mary." If Mary heads for the door, however, the teacher would have to say, "Get back in your seat." Teaching children to abide by rules, follow instructions, and know what to do next all involve teaching them to respond to discriminative stimuli.

Differential reinforcement is also essential to concept teaching. The only difference is that, in the case of concept teaching, reinforcement is given for making the same response to a *set* of stimuli that have common properties, although each instance differs in some ways. For example, cars, trucks, and airplanes are all responded to as *vehicles* and share the properties of being manufactured things that can take people places. Instances of Ford, Chevys, and Plymouths are all responded to as *cars.* This aspect of stimulus control will be developed extensively later (volume 2). Our goal here is to learn about the role of discriminative stimuli in classroom management. But first we need to develop two additional concepts involving discriminative stimuli—prompts and behavior chains.

Prompts

Once a child begins to respond to discriminative stimuli such as verbal instructions, signals, or words on the blackboard, these can be used to help get responses going in the presence of new discriminative stimuli. In teaching reading, we make use of the fact that children can imitate our sounds to get them to make specified sounds in the presence of letters or words. We can prompt getting ready to work with a reminder, "It's time for class now." Rules can also serve as prompts. Prompts are established $S^D \rightarrow R$ relationships that can be used to facilitate learning new $S^D \rightarrow R$ relationships.

There are two important principles in the use of prompts. First, *be sure the new S^D occurs before the prompting S^D.* When teaching a student to read the sound *mmm*, point to the letter *m* first before prompting with, "This sound says *mmm*. Say *mmm*." If the new S^D comes first, the student learns to respond to that rather than to rely on your prompt, which comes later. If the prompt comes first, then the student will rely on you to keep prompting him.

The second principle is to *fade your prompts as soon as possible.* In *fading*, you gradually withdraw the extra help so that the children respond to the S^D you are teaching. In the classroom, it is most efficient if they learn appropriate study behaviors during work periods without constant reminders. Initially, you might put the rules on the board and repeat them as necessary to remind the children of expected behaviors. When the behaviors occur, reinforce them with praise, attention, going to lunch early, or whatever. As they become established, point out the rules and reminders less often, but give reinforcement to maintain them. Fading can be accomplished by delaying the presentation of the prompt, using it less and less, eliminating parts of it, or weakening its intensity. (Volume 2 of this text gives a greater consideration to the use of prompts.)

Behavior Chains

Most activities in school consist of sequences, or chains, of behavior. Going to recess can be broken down into the component behaviors of getting up from the desk, going to the coat rack, putting on a coat, lining up at the door, walking down the hall, and going out to the playground. Writing a theme usually involves reading in a topic area, making an outline, writing sentence after sentence, and editing the product. In a chain, simple behaviors under the control of discriminative stimuli are joined into a sequence of behavior. The whole sequence is reinforced at its completion. Formally, the $S \rightarrow R \rightarrow S$ model of operant behavior can be extended into a model that looks like this:

$$S^D_3 \longrightarrow R_3 \longrightarrow S^D_2 \longrightarrow R_2 \longrightarrow S^D_1 \longrightarrow R_1 \longrightarrow S^R$$

| "Group three, get ready for reading." | Bob takes out his book. | The book in hand is a cue to get up and go to reading corner. | Bob goes to reading corner. | The chairs in the reading corner cue sitting. | Bob sits. | "I can see Bob's ready for reading." |

There are two important questions we can ask about a behavior chain: What reinforces R_3 and R_2? And how does one go about establishing a chain?

The Reinforcers in a Chain

In unit 4 we noted that learned reinforcers (or conditioned reinforcers) can be established by following a neutral stimulus with a reinforcing stimulus. S^D_1 precedes S^R and so, with repeated pairing, it is likely to become a conditioned reinforcer. Similarly, S^D_2 would also become a conditioned reinforcer if repeatedly paired with S^D_1. Thus we see that each S^D in a behavior chain tends to acquire a conditioned reinforcing function for the response that precedes it, and a discriminative function for response that follows it.

Establishing Behavior Chains

The most common method of establishing a behavior chain in the classroom is to first prompt each step in the chain and then fade the prompts. For example, the chain for going to the reading group could have initially consisted of three separate instructions. The teacher would first ask group three to "Get out your reading books. Good, everyone has his book," followed by, "Now walk quietly to the reading corner." And finally, he might say, "Let's all sit in our chairs. You got ready for reading very quickly. I like that." After several repetitions, it would be unnecessary to say more than, "Group three get ready for reading," because they now know what to do.

Strategies for Classroom Management

Effective classroom management requires planning. The teacher needs to think out the behavior management plan ahead of time. What are the rules?

What are the consequences for following them? The teacher must organize and structure the day's activities to support the management plan and teaching goals. The physical environment should be structured to support teaching activities. Following are some reports from teachers who have been trained to use behavioral analysis principles. While reading these selections, attempt to pinpoint various applications of the principles we have been discussing.

Getting a Class Started

by Constance Carlson, Hays School, Urbana

This year of teaching is my second experience with the contingent use of teacher attention in the modification of child behavior. Last year I took a course in behavior modification and successfully learned to extinguish the tantrums of one child and to work with a point system for two other children. Since I was convinced of the merits of the approach, I was eager to use it this year.

On the first day of school these rules were written and displayed permanently in the front of the room:

Raise your hand when you wish to talk.
Walk in the room and halls.

Keep your hands and feet to yourself.

Be polite.

When you finish your work you may find something to do from the back of the room.

The children were reminded of the rules by—

1   Having the children read them each morning
2   Making praise comments contingent on following the specific rules and making references to the rule in the praise comment: "Johnny, I like the wa_ you walk in our room"; "I called on Johnny because he raised his hand."
3   Only attending to behavior within the limits of the rules

Possibly because the children were new to each other as well as uncertain of my ways, they were easy to control at the beginning of the school year. Since many of the children were strangers to each other, they relied heavily on teacher approval and only slightly on peer interactions.

In the classroom situation few rules are broken when the children are doing lessons together or doing seat work, since the working behavior is usually incompatible with talking loudly or running around the room. Most rule breaking occurs after assigned work has been completed. My method of punishing a child for breaking a rule was to withdraw a reinforcer.

In their free time the children were allowed to choose activities such as molding clay, water color painting, reading, using sewing cards, playing games, or using flash cards. If a child could not work quietly without disturbing the reading group or his own neighbors, he had to put away whatever he was doing. When the child had returned to his seat and had begun to work quietly, he was praised by name for the appropriate behavior.

Often I could stop a problem behavior by praising another child who was following the rule. If praising a neighbor or withdrawing a free activity failed, pointing to a chair that was next to the wall and away from all group activity usually worked. The offender sat in the chair until he was ready to follow the rules again. Usually a two- or three-minute time out was sufficient. To make a time-out period more effective, I tried not to change my facial expression or to raise my voice. As little attention as possible was given to the offender. Often his peers were not even aware that any punishment had been given.

I do not deny that problems have occurred during the year. However, because of having taken the behavior modification course, I was better able to handle the situations that did occur. After the first few months of school, the children formed peer groups, which functioned both in and out of school. It became more difficult to isolate undesirable behavior from the reinforcing effects of peer attention. At the beginning of the year it had been possible to control peer effects by telling the children that if their neighbor forgot a rule, they could help him by ignoring whatever he was doing wrong.

This worked beautifully for a period of time; but as the peers became more tightly knit, it became harder to isolate deviant behavior. As this happened, more time out was necessary.

In retrospect, I began this school year by (a) specifying the desired behavior—that is, making my rules clear and positive; (b) ignoring deviant behavior until it was impossible to do so; and (c) praising behavior that I wanted to strengthen. The attitude in the classroom was warm and accepting. If a child broke a rule, he knew that the consequences were a result of his own action, not a judgment inflicted upon him by a harsh disciplinarian. Using this positive approach made me feel very comfortable with the children. Because very few punishers were needed, my own anxious or emotional feelings were at a minimum and the atmosphere in the room was pleasant and happy for me. The children were friendly to each other and positive in their reactions toward school. In fact, several parents told me that their children hesitated to report sore throats at home because the children did not want to miss school.

I would summarize by stating that my classroom control was maintained throughout the year by the "specify, praise, ignore" method. Time out within the room was used occasionally and worked effectively because the children regarded the room activities as positive and pleasant.[1]

Setting a Calm Model

by Mary Thomas, Hays School, Urbana

As a result of training in behavior modification principles, I attempted to change my classroom environment completely. I previously scurried about, chattered constantly, and often found myself yelling at the children. It came to me while studying the nature of imitation that I was teaching the children, through modeling, the exact frenzied behavior I could not control. I began to walk about the room more slowly; I talked more softly, distinctly, and slowly. I carefully explained what I wanted and waited for questions. I allowed the children more time to talk in the early morning. I stopped chattering about my every thought. I made a point of calling on the children by name for answers. When I wanted a class response I cued the children by saying "Ready" or "Class." I began deleting all useless words and unnecessary parts of lessons. I reduced the environment to the barest essentials.

The results are astounding. My class now works quietly for long periods of time and is able to clean up much more quickly than before. The children are more relaxed and speak more quietly. They can change from one task to another easily. In general, a calm atmosphere prevails. This has reduced my fatigue and tension. This is extremely important because as my tension rises, so does the noise level in the room. Now I feel the children are not as anxious about their efforts and feel freer to bring their questions to me. When I do explode occasionally, I get instant attention.

There have been, of course, many other changes in my teaching techniques, some of which I am probably not even aware of. But through the use of behavior modification I have been able to achieve a calm environment and systematic behavior control.[2]

Specify, Praise, and Ignore

The procedures followed by these teachers can be summarized as follows:

1   Specify, in a positive way, the rules that are the basis for your reinforcement. These serve as discriminative stimuli for appropriate behavior, and they are made important by providing reinforcement for following them. Rules may be different for different kinds of work, study, or play periods. As the children learn to follow the rules, repeat them less frequently (fading), but continue to praise good classroom behavior.

2   Catch the children being good. Reinforce desirable behavior. Focus on reinforcing tasks important for social and cognitive skills. Relate the children's performance to the rules. Be specific: "You watched the board all the time I was presenting the example. That's paying attention." "That's a good answer. You listened very closely to my question." "Jimmy is really working hard. He'll get the answer. You'll see." Between work periods, relax the rules. Do not be afraid to have fun with your children when the work period is over.

3   Ignore disruptive behavior unless someone is getting hurt. Prompt the correct behavior from the children who are misbehaving by praising those who are working well. When you see a persistent problem behavior, look for the reinforcer. It may be your own behavior.

A Kindergarten for Individualized Instruction

This example shows the interrelation of program, class structure, and management of the children. This kindergarten teacher was attempting to prepare her students to work on their own for periods long enough to permit her to teach reading and math, at first in small groups, and then on an individualized basis. She divided her children into four groups and assigned them color names (reds, greens, blues, and purples). The classroom was divided into four study areas, each with a table for six children. There was a music area with a rug where all the children could sit together, and an area by a blackboard where a group could come to work with the teacher.

Adjacent to each work area were materials and supplies for a particular kind of fun activity. One table had the clay-modeling materials and some individual games. Another had a record player with headsets for eight children and picture books. One was a painting table with art supplies. The fourth table had coloring books, cut-and-paste supplies, and puzzles.

The teacher began the year by assigning the same simple task (coloring) to all the children, while she supervised. When the routines of getting set up, working, and cleaning up were established, she assigned two tasks at once. "This morning, children, after you complete your worksheets (coloring and cut-and-paste), you may start a second activity on your own, using the materials on the shelves near your group's table." She walked around the room telling the whole class what the options were for each group. "Each day of the week you will get a chance to move to a different activity area. Everyone will have a chance to do everything each week."

Name tags, color-coded by group, were on appropriate tables when the children came in. When the groups shifted areas each day, the children only had to look for their colors and their names to know where to sit. Frantic questions such as, "Where do I go?" were eliminated from the beginning by good planning.

The next step was to introduce a work activity relating to reading or arithmetic, before the fun activity. Since the children could now go through two activities on their own with little supervision, the teacher could begin to teach small groups in reading and math in the period from 9:15 to 10:45. The children were motivated to complete their work assignments by the availability of fun activities, as well as by the teacher's praise. The teacher also set up an interesting way of encouraging the children to clean up or finish their second tasks without a lot of pressure or confusion. At 10:45, she would put on a record at the music area. The first child with his tasks completed, cleaned up, and put away could come and sit in the group leader's chair. The other children came when ready and sat on the floor to play imitation games directed by the group leader. The children had five minutes to clean up before the formal music period started. The whole operation was so smooth that it ran itself. These children were working in an environment that was teaching them good work habits in an enjoyable way. The teacher's job seemed to an observer to require little effort. She put her effort into planning and structuring her classroom rather than into correcting mistakes after they happened.

The next step was to individualize the activities in the work period. Folders were prepared containing the materials and instructions for each child. There was a place to pick them up and turn them in when completed. When the children wanted the teacher's help, they stood up a little red tent that was kept in their folders, rather than waving their arms in the air for several minutes.

Organizing the Day

The procedures used in this kindergarten provide examples of some general rules for planning a day.

1   Not all children finish a task in the same amount of time. Allow for this by including a *cushion activity* (which is also a reinforcer) between tasks that all children are required to complete. In giving a general assignment, also assign a secondary activity that is permitted upon completion of the assignment.

2   Planning should provide *systematic prompts or reminders* for what each child should do next. Much confusion and wasted time can be eliminated by clear signals about what to do next. Such things as color-coded name tags, signs, lists on the blackboard, verbal reminders, individual folders, check-out stations, and turn-in boxes assist in the process.

3   Planning should provide for day-to-day *consistency in routine*. This reduces the need for reminders of all sorts. The completion of one task then becomes the cue for the start of the next. Sequences of tasks are chained together. If the teacher haphazardly moves from one activity to the next on impulse, it becomes very difficult for the children to learn good work habits.

4   Motivation is maintained when *completion of one activity is automatically rewarded* by the start of a new activity: "When you finish your workbook exercises, you may get one of the games from the activity corner." "When you finish your worksheets and turn them in for checking, then you can paint."

5   Planning should provide for a periodic *change of pace*. Quiet work might be followed by talking or singing. Serious material might be followed by a game. Sitting might be followed by running or a more vigorous activity. Often, just a minute or two of a vigorous activity is all that is needed to ready a group for more serious work again.

Teaching Children to Follow Instructions

Effective instructions are usually given quietly and matter-of-factly, but are specific about the behavior desired: "When we are all sitting in our seats, with desks cleared and arms on desk, I will call on one row at a time to line up. Jimmy's row was ready first, so they may line up first."

In giving instructions designed to teach children to follow instructions, go out of your way to be arbitrary in specifying the details of what the children should do. If there are black and yellow squares on the floor, ask everyone to sit on a yellow square between designated chalk lines. This provides more specific cues for the desired behavior. The children think it is fun to follow more exacting rules. It becomes a game. At other times specify the order in which things must happen, even though it doesn't matter:

First, you put away your reading workbook. Then, you put away your reader. Then, you put away your crayons. Finally, you may take out your arithmetic book and turn to page six. Have you got it? Jimmy, what do you do first? Good. Molly, what do you do next? Let's see everyone do it once right away. Now go ahead.

For those of you concerned with the management of classes at the junior high and high school level, additional procedures and examples will be given in Unit 12.

summary

Operant behavior can be brought under the control of preceding stimuli through the use of differential reinforcement. In the presence of the appropriate stimuli, appropriate responses are reinforced. Inappropriate responses are not reinforced. Discriminative stimuli are the cues that let students know when to do what—when to work, when to play, what to do when working, what to do when a task is finished.

Prompts are discriminative stimuli a child can already respond to (such as instruction words) that can be used to get appropriate responses in a new learning situation. The new stimulus should be given before the prompt. Prompts are gradually withdrawn when they are no longer needed, and the new $S^D \to R \to S^R$ relationships are established. This gradual withdrawal is called fading.

Behavior chains consist of sequences of behavior interconnected by discriminative stimuli. The chains are held together because each S^D also becomes a conditioned reinforcer. To establish a behavior chain, each step is initially prompted. The prompts are gradually faded as the completion of one part of the chain provides the cues for the next part.

There are many ways to use discriminative stimuli in classroom management. Rules can be used to let the children know what is expected classroom behavior. But rules need to be made effective by reinforcement: following rules is praised; violating rules is ignored. Equipment and furniture arrangement in the classroom can also provide discriminative stimuli for appropriate behavior. Different activity areas or seating arrangements can serve as cues for the teaching or play activities to go on in them. The daily program should allow for different rates of task completion. For example, assigning a cushion activity along with an instructional task lets the children know what to do when the instructional task is completed. At the same time, a cushion activity may be used to reinforce behavior on the instructional task. Name tags, signs, lists on the blackboard, individual folders, check-out stations, and turn-in boxes can serve to prompt expected behaviors without a lot of teacher's nagging and children's questions. By maintaining some consistency in the daily routine, it is possible to make the completion of one task the cue for the next. Chains of behavior are established and reduce the need for teacher prompting.

In teaching children to follow instructions, it is important to be very specific in stating what to do under what conditions. Specific instructions teach the children exactly what stimuli to respond to in what sequence.

Keep in mind that learning to respond to discriminative stimuli is what makes us responsive to our tasks, sensitive to others, and socialized.

broadening your perspective

An Approach to Litter Control

In 1970 the average American disposed of a ton of solid waste. This figure is expected to double by 1980. The accumulation of nondegradable waste presents a serious ecological problem.

Scott Geller, John Farris, and David Post decided to see if prompts could influence consumers to buy beverages in returnable bottles, rather than throw-away containers. We will omit some of the details of their design, but the essence of it was the use of four different experimental conditions during

BUY
RETURNABLE
SOFT DRINK
BOTTLES

SAVE MONEY
CONSIDERING DEPOSITS RETURNABLE
BOTTLES ARE 10¢ CHEAPER PER CARTON

SAVE TAXES
YOUR TAX DOLLARS WILL NOT BE SPENT
CLEANING UP HIGHWAYS

FIGHT POLLUTION
RETURNABLES ARE RECYCLED
NONRETURNABLES ARE PERMANENT POLLUTANTS

SHOW CONCERN
HELP US FIGHT POLLUTION   THANK YOU

NOTICE
WE WILL RECORD YOUR PURCHASE
ON THE CHART
THIS EFFORT TO FIGHT POLLUTION WILL BE
REPORTED IN LOCAL NEWSPAPERS AND AT
THE AMERICAN PSYCHOLOGICAL ASSOCIATION

Figure 6.1 Handbill for experiment in prompting

different two-hour periods of the day at a neighborhood store. On different days, the conditions in effect at each period were systematically varied.

The four conditions were these:

1 *Baseline.* No change, buying behavior was recorded.
2 *Prompts.* A handbill was passed out as the customer entered the store (see figure 6.1). The *Notice* part of the handbill was omitted during this condition.
3 *Prompt plus chart.* In addition to the handbill (with the notice circled in red), a chart was posted recording the number of customers who bought more than 50 percent of their drinks in returnable bottles, and the number who bought in throw-aways. As the customer left the cashier, the chart was advanced one number in the appropriate column.
4 *Prompt plus chart plus group pressure.* This condition was like 3 except that four observers stood around the chart when the customer entered and left the store.

The results showed that the prompting condition increased the number of customers buying returnables from 60 to 80 percent. Conditions 3 and 4 showed some slight increases in effects over Condition 2, but the effects were not significant. It was concluded that prompting could be an effective aid in pollution control.[3]

Tests as Discriminative Stimuli for Studying

High school and college teachers alike try to promote daily study behavior so that the students will keep up with the lectures and not be faced with last-minute cramming. Research literature supports the value of evenly spaced study periods for retaining information.

Investigators at Southern Illinois University studied the effects of daily, weekly, and three-week tests on study behavior. Volunteer students participated in a special section in which they would get most of their instruction through readings and programed material. The dependent variable was the number of minutes spent each day in the "reading center." The independent variable was testing on a daily, weekly, or three-week basis.

All students received a course outline describing the requirements, and especially emphasizing that course grades would be based on the accumulation of quiz points. The students were free to use the study area from 3 P.M. to 6 P.M., Monday through Thursday. Study behavior was recorded by observers. Tests were given Tuesday through Friday in the daily test condition and on Friday in the other conditions.

With daily testing, the students studied regularly, about sixty minutes a day. With weekly testing, studying was irregular early in the week and increased as Friday approached. With three-week testing, daily study behavior was very low (average of twenty minutes) right after a test, and gradually increased to a peak (nearly two hours) just before the test.

In planning an instructional program, the wise teacher will consider ways in which a quiz schedule can be used to promote regular studying.[4]

The Experimental Study of Classroom Structure

In a day-care center Larry Doke and Todd Risley analyzed how the structure of activities affects participation in planned activities. Figure 6.2 shows the layout of the day-care center for fourteen disadvantaged children. Observers recorded the children's participation in planned activities throughout the school day. The primary experimental conditions examined the effects of an options schedule and a no-options schedule (figure 6.3). Within the no-options schedule, a group-dismissal procedure was alternated with an individual-dismissal procedure. In the group-dismissal condition, all the children had to complete specified *exit requirements* before moving to the next activity. In the individual-dismissal procedure, each child could meet the exit requirements and move on to another activity.

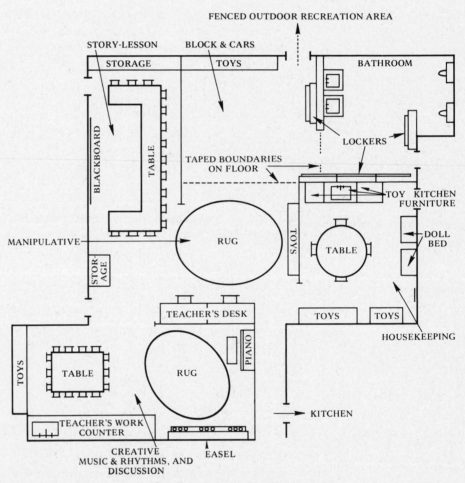

Figure 6.2 Arrangement of indoor preschool activity areas

OPTIONS ACTIVITY SCHEDULE

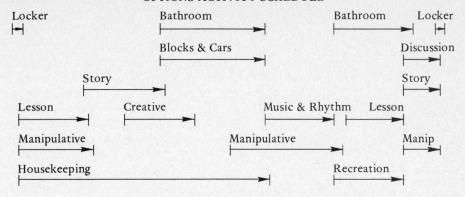

NO-OPTIONS ACTIVITY SCHEDULE

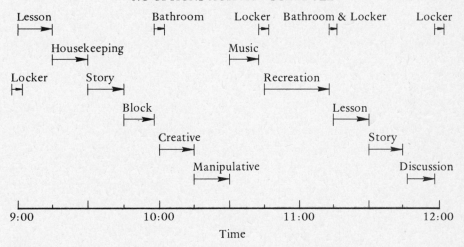

Figure 6.3 Schematic of Options and No-Options activity schedules

The results showed a high level of participation under both schedules when individual dismissal was used. However, group dismissal led to a drop in participation because the children had to wait for others to finish. Within an activity, participation also declined when there were not enough materials available for each child.

These results are not unlike effects commonly observed in classrooms at all levels, when some children finish assignments before others and have not been given an optional cushion activity to keep them involved.[5]

Self-Prompting in the Learning of Arithmetic

Tom Lovitt and Karen Curtiss demonstrated that the teacher doesn't have to do all of the prompting. The children can be taught to prompt themselves. The study was carried out with an eleven-year-old boy in a special class. Bill had trouble with arithmetic. The teacher noticed that he more often got the right answer when he said the problem to himself first. It was decided to investigate this phenomenon under controlled conditions.

Three separate experiments were carried out. The first used problems of the class $\square - 2 = 6$. "Some number minus two equals six." The number in the box had to be 10 or less. In the second experiment, the number in the box could range up to 100. The third experiment used problems of the class $4 - 3 = 9 - \square$, with numbers under 10. Bill was given twenty problems a day in experiments 1 and 2, and ten problems a day in experiment 3.

Each experiment had three conditions, no verbal self-prompting, verbal self-prompting, and no verbal self-prompting. In the no verbal condition, Bill was given the work sheet and asked to complete each item. During the verbal self-prompting condition, Bill was told to read the problem aloud before doing it. In the third condition, he was told he no longer needed to read the problem aloud.

The results of each experiment showed the percent of problems correct per minute sharply rose with self-prompting. Furthermore, when self-prompting was terminated, the rate went even higher, since it took less time to do each problem when the verbal step was removed. Self-prompting had helped Bill to learn to be more accurate, and this special help could be faded out with additional benefit.[6]

Behavior Change Is Not Magic

A teacher might expect a child to improve through therapy with a social worker or psychologist; and the teacher won't have to do anything about it. A study by Robert Wahler shows otherwise. Children can behave differently in various situations as a function of differential reinforcement in those situations.

Two boys, aged five and eight, were referred to a clinic for behavior problems serious enough to warrant psychological help. Interviews with the parents established that the boys also had problems at home. Steve showed a lot of oppositional behavior: he would not do what adults asked him to do. Louis showed a lot of disruptive behavior: he was out of his seat, interfering with other children, and playing with objects he shouldn't. These behaviors, along with their counterparts—cooperative behavior for Steve and study behavior for Louis—were recorded by observers at home and school.

After baseline measures, a change in the parents' handling of Steve and Louis was instituted at home. Social reinforcement was given for cooperative behaviors for Steve and study behaviors for Louis. Steve also received a time-out punishment for noncompliance. Their behaviors improved at home, but not at school. When change procedures were introduced at school too, the boys' behavior dramatically improved there.

The behavior that occurs in particular situations (in the presence of particular discriminative stimuli) depends on what is reinforced in that situation.[7]

self-test

1 A symbol for a discriminative stimulus is _____ .

2 In bringing behavior under the control of discriminative stimuli _____ reinforcement is used.

3 When using prompts it is important to _____ the prompt as soon as possible.

4 Fading is accomplished by _____ withdrawing the prompt.

5 In a chain, several _____ and R's occur before the reinforcer.

6 An S^D in a chain functions as a _____ _____ for the response that comes before it and a discriminative stimulus for the response that follows it.

7 In good classroom management the teacher should specify in a positive way the _____ that are the basis for reinforcement.

8 As the children learn to follow the rules, repeat them less _____ , but continue to _____ good classroom behavior.

9 Planning should provide for systematic _____ as to what each child should be doing or is to do next.

NUMBER RIGHT _____

1 S^D

2 differential

3 fade

4 gradually

5 S^D's

6 conditioned reinforcer

7 rules

8 frequently, often praise

9 reminders, cues, prompts

exercise 1 programed practice

1 A discriminative stimulus sets the occasion when an operant response is likely to be _____ .

1 reinforced

2 before

3 S^D

4 S^R; S^P

5 differential

6 response;
   stimulus

7 response

8 prompt

9 prompt

10 fade

11 gradually

12 delayed;
   reduced

2 In using prompts, the new S^D is presented _____ the prompt.

3 A symbol for a discriminative stimulus is _____.

4 Reinforcing stimuli can be referred to by the symbol _____. Punishing stimuli can be referred to by the symbol _____.

5 In bringing behavior under the control of discriminative stimuli _____ reinforcement is used.

6 In using differential reinforcement, reinforcement is given when the appropriate _____ is made to the appropriate _____ and not otherwise.

7 Learning involves both what _____ to make and what stimulus to make it to.

8 Discriminative stimuli that a child can already respond to can be used to _____ responses in new learning situations.

9 Rules and reminders can be used to _____ appropriate classroom behavior.

10 In using prompts it is important to _____ the prompt as soon as possible.

11 Fading is accomplished by _____ withdrawing the prompt.

12 In fading, the prompt is used less and less, its introduction is _____ to give the children a chance to respond without it, part of it may be eliminated, or the physical intensity of the prompt may be _____.

13 simple;
    sequence

14 S^D's

15 conditioned
    reinforcer

16 prompt;
    prompts

17 praise

18 modeling,
    imitation;
    prompted

19 rules

20 reinforcement

21 frequently,
    often; praise

22 specific,
    descriptive

---

13 In a behavior chain, a series of _____ behaviors under the control of discriminative stimuli are combined into a longer _____ of behavior.

14 In a chain several _____ and R's occur before the reinforcer.

15 An S^D functions as a _____ _____ for the response that comes before it and as a discriminative stimulus for the response that follows it.

16 The most common method for establishing a behavior chain in the classroom is to first _____ each step and then fade the _____.

17 Mrs. Carlson made classroom rules effective by the specify, _____, and ignore method.

18 Mary Thomas realized that she was teaching through _____ the frenzied behavior she could not control in her children. Her behavior _____ the children's behavior.

19 In good classroom management the teacher should specify in a positive way the _____ that are the basis for reinforcement.

20 Rules are made important by providing _____ for following them.

21 As the children learn to follow the rules, the teacher should repeat them less _____, but continue to _____ good classroom behavior.

22 Be _____ about the behavior that exemplifies paying attention or working hard.

23 Relax the rules between _____ periods. Do not be afraid to have fun with your children when the work period is over.

24 When you see a persistent problem behavior, look for the _____.

25 The _____ organization of your classroom can influence behavior.

26 Structure different areas of your room to _____ various types of activities.

27 Don't get stuck behind a _____. Keep yourself where the action is.

28 The discussion about setting up a kindergarten for individualized instruction gives some ideas about the relation between program, _____ _____, and management of children.

29 That kindergarten teacher divided her children into groups and assigned each group a _____name. The color codes were used to _____ where the children were to sit each day.

30 After all the children had learned to handle a simple task, the teacher assigned _____ tasks at once.

31 When the children _____ the first assigned task, they could start a second activity on their own.

32 When the children could go through the two activities on their own with little _____ by the teacher, the teacher could begin to teach groups in reading and math.

33 Having a fun activity follow a study activity is an application of the _____ principle.

23 work

24 reinforcer

25 physical, structural

26 support, encourage, permit

27 desk

28 classroom structure, physical structure

29 color; prompt

30 two

31 completed, finished

32 prompting

33 Premack

34 This principle states that any high-_____ behavior can be used to strengthen any lower-frequency behavior by making the higher-frequency behavior _____ _____ the lower-frequency behavior.

34 frequency; contingent on, follow

35 This teacher prompted clean-up time by playing a _____ in the music area.

35 record, phonograph, song

36 The teacher's job seemed to an observer to require little _____. She had put her effort into _____ and structuring her classroom.

37 The children used a little _____, which was kept in their folders, to signal the teacher for help. The tents were _____ stimuli for the teacher to come and give help.

36 effort; planning

38 Because not all children finish a task in the same amount of time, planning should include a _____ activity (which is also a reinforcer) between study periods.

37 tent; discriminative

39 Planning should provide for systematic _____ as to what each child should be doing or is to do next.

38 cushion

40 Planning should provide for day-to-day _____ in routine. When this is done, the completion of one task becomes the _____ for the start of the next.

39 reminders, cues, prompts

40 consistency; cue, reminder, prompt

41 Good motivation is maintained when completion of one activity can be _____ rewarded by the start of a new activity.

42 To teach children to follow instructions, be arbitrary in specifying the _____ of what the children should do.

41 automatically, immediately

42 details

43 This provides more specific _____ for the desired behavior. Also,

the children think it is fun to follow more exacting rules. It becomes a

_____.

43 prompts, cues;
   game

discussion questions

1 Define differential reinforcement and state how this procedure is used to establish discriminative stimuli.

2 Give examples of discriminative stimuli commonly used in the classroom.

3 Define and give examples of prompts.

4 Give two rules for using prompts.

5 Describe what is involved in a behavior chain.

6 State the two functions of discriminative stimuli in a chain.

7 Give one procedure for establishing a behavior chain.

8 Explain a procedure for teaching children to follow the classroom rules.

9 How did Mary Thomas's behavior change after she realized the kind of model she was presenting to her class?

10 Summarize the same procedures involved in the "specify, praise, and ignore" approach.

11 Give an example of how one might arrange a classroom to support specific types of teaching activities.

12 Describe the steps taken by a kindergarten teacher to make it possible for her to individualize instruction and identify the discriminative stimuli which she established.

13 Explain one value in following a daily routine.

14 Describe a procedure to use in teaching children to follow instructions.

15 Explain why rules or instructions tend not to be effective by themselves.

16 Name five prompts you might encounter in a typical day outside of the classroom.

17 What is the effect of fixed-interval testing on study behavior?

18 Give an example of self-prompting other than the one given by Lovitt and Curtiss.

19 Consider the method used by Doke and Risley to study the effect of classroom structure and suggest another study that could be carried out with this method.

20 When is praise a prompt?

21 Are people's personalities fixed regardless of setting?

unit 7

Differential Reinforcement: Shaping

objectives

When you complete this unit you should be able to—
1 Describe the steps to take in order to develop behavior that is not currently in a child's behavior repertoire.
2 Define the terms *shaping, differential reinforcement,* and *shifting criterion for reinforcement* and give examples to illustrate each.
3 List the kinds of behavior most likely to require shaping in the classroom.
4 State the conditions under which shaping should not be used by the teacher.
5 Define physical prompting.

lesson

A Woman Learns to Shed her Clothing

Ted Ayllon reports a study of a woman who had been hospitalized for nine years as psychotic. She was overweight and constantly stole food; she hoarded towels in her room; and she wore excessive amounts of clothing. She might wear six or seven dresses at one time, with several pairs of stockings or several sweaters. This behavior led others to treat her as unusual, to say the least.

Ayllon eliminated the food stealing by having a nurse remove the woman from the dining room without eating, if she did steal. She stole only six times in the next sixty weeks, and her weight dropped from 250 to 180 pounds. He eliminated the towel hoarding by bringing the patient more and more tow-

135

els, as many as six hundred a week (Ayllon had to hoard the hospital's supply). She soon got tired of folding and stacking towels and begged for no more. She started removing them from her room on her own. She just had too much of a good thing: she was satiated.

The procedure used to eliminate wearing too much clothing is of special interest in this unit. The patient's body weight was determined regularly, and she was required to step on a scale before entering the dining room. Initially she could enter only if she weighed under her body weight plus twenty-three pounds. This number was chosen since she usually wore twenty-five pounds of extra clothing. If the patient's weight exceeded the requirement, the nurse would say, "Sorry, you weigh too much. You'll have to weigh less." If the patient did not meet the requirement, she would miss that meal. At times the patient would remove clothing right then to meet the requirement and get to eat. Sometimes she removed more than was needed to meet the requirement. If this occurred, the weight required was lowered for the next meal. Over an eleven-week period, the weight requirement was gradually lowered to a normal three pounds of clothing. When the patient started dressing normally, she also began to participate in social events at the hospital. The patient's parents took her home for a visit for the first time in nine years.[1]

Shaping Procedures

When the response you want is not in the student's repertoire or when you have no way to prompt the response, it is necessary to use shaping procedures. In shaping, reinforcement and extinction are skillfully used together to build new behavior. There are two essential aspects of shaping:

1. *Differential reinforcement.* In the context of shaping, differential reinforcement means that the responses that meet a certain criterion are reinforced, while those that do not meet the criterion are extinguished (not reinforced).

2. *Shifting criterion for reinforcement.* The response criterion to be reinforced is gradually changed in the direction of the behavior you want the learner to end up with (target behavior).

In the case just presented, the patient was reinforced with food if her weight was below a given amount. She was *not* reinforced with food if her weight was above a given amount. *Differential reinforcement* was used. In addition, the requirement or criterion for reinforcement was slowly changed to lead the patient to wear less and less clothing. There was a *shifting criterion* for reinforcement, approaching a target behavior of wearing a normal amount of clothing.

In previous units, several examples were given where *shaping* was used as a part of a program, or where it was suspected that problem behavior was shaped up by the way in which parents or teachers responded to it. Very likely Peter's mother shaped his objectionable behavior by giving Peter more and more attention for misbehavior and less and less attention for appropriate behavior. A teacher can shape a bad class by giving attention to misbehavior and not to desired behavior. Time on-task and persistence are usually taught through shaping. Catching the children getting better is another technique of shaping. Responses showing improvement are reinforced; others are not. Differential reinforcement and a shifting criterion for reinforcement are used.

How to Shape

In shaping, the teacher goes through the following steps:

Steps to Take	Example
1 Define the target behavior.	**1** I want Jimmy to do 20 addition problems in twenty minutes without coming to me.
2 Decide what behavior to build from.	**2** Jimmy will now do 1 problem in two minutes with me there to help him.
3 Establish a reinforcer.	**3** He will earn points on a card. For every 25 points he earns, he gets to choose one game at recess.
4 Outline the program of steps to get to the target behavior.	**4** Choose a set of problems that Jimmy can do.
	4.1 Jimmy is given a paper with 1 problem on it. I help him do it.
	4.2 Jimmy is given a paper with 1 problem on it. "Now you do this one by yourself and I'll come check it."
	4.3 A paper with 2 problems is given. "Do these and raise your hand when you have finished. I'll come and check them."
	4.4 A paper with 5 problems is given. "Do these and raise your hand."
	4.5 A paper with 10 problems is given. "Let me know when you have finished."
	4.6 A paper with 15 problems is given. "Let me know when you have finished."

Steps to Take (continued)	Example (continued)
	4.7 A paper with 20 problems is given. The time Jimmy takes to complete them is recorded.
	4.8 A paper with 20 problems is given. "If you finish in less then X minutes you will get a 5-point bonus." X is one minute less than the time measured in step 4.7.
	4.9 Continue step 4.8 until papers are regularly completed in less than twenty minutes, slowly lowering the time requirement. (This program is carried out over several days.)
5 Start training with your first criterion for reinforcement.	5 Jimmy is given step 4.1 and immediately reinforced.
6 Decide when to shift to a new criterion for reinforcement. (Stay with each new requirement no longer than is necessary to meet the criterion.)	6 Move right on to step 4.2 because step 4.1 was done easily.
7 If the criterion is not met, return briefly to an earlier step or add a new step in between and try again.	7 When Jimmy went from 5 to 10 problems, he failed to finish them without help. He returned to 5 problems and then went to 8 problems.
8 Repeat steps 6 and 7 until the target behavior is achieved.	8 Jimmy learned to work 20 problems in under twenty minutes.

In shaping, the teacher has to know where he is going, what steps to take to get there, and when to go ahead or back, according to the performance of the child. The dilemma faced in shaping is that if the teacher stays too long at one step, time is lost and behavior is strengthened at an undesired level. If the teacher moves on too quickly, he may lose the child when the criterion for reinforcement is not met.

Some Responses That Usually Require Shaping

Working longer, working faster, paying attention, and staying in one's seat are examples of behavior for which shaping is commonly used.

Speech problems often require careful shaping to get the proper sounds going. To teach a child to say "ssss" rather than "thhhh" when he encounters *s*, the speech teacher might have the child practice saying "ssss" with his teeth closed. The child is reinforced each time he makes the sound with his teeth closed, and not reinforced if his teeth are open. Once the child is making regular "ssss" sounds in isolation, the teacher begins to reinforce "ssss" in words, and then in conversational speech.

A teacher might shape a quiet child to talk more or to talk louder. The program might start with questions or situations that you know the child will respond to and gradually move to general classroom discussion.

Most programs used to teach manuscript or cursive writing involve some shaping. The child usually starts by writing larger letters and then learns to write smaller ones. The criteria are slowly increased. In a program developed by B. F. Skinner, a special pen and chemically treated paper are used to give the child immediate differential reinforcement. If the child makes a correct line, it comes out gray. If the line is incorrect, it comes out yellow. The width of the band that will produce a gray line (correct) is made narrower later in the program; thus the criterion for reinforcement is changed by narrowing the area that is considered a correct response. Figure 7.1 shows sample exercises from various stages in building cursive writing. Note how prompts are faded and the response requirements are increased.[2]

Gym skills and many athletic skills are developed best through a shaping process. One first-grader in a rural school that places emphasis on basketball spent most of his gym periods trying to shoot baskets. *He made two all year.* You have never seen such an unhappy child. The whole experience was punishing, to say the least, and quite pointless. Simply by switching from a ten-foot-high basket and a regular basketball to a seven-foot-high basket and a volleyball, some real training could have taken place. Also, the child would have become enthusiastic about the sport instead of sick of it.

Throwing a ball, catching a ball, batting, jumping, and running for speed or distance are all skills that can be taught either in ways that ensure success and enthusiasm, or in ways that produce punishment and disillusionment. The key to such training is shaping. Differentially reinforce success according to an increasingly harder requirement, but never go to a harder requirement until there is success at an easier one.

An Astromonk Is Taught to Respond Quickly

The essentials of the shaping process can readily be seen in an example from work in training animals (where it is quite clear that one could not accomplish the task simply by using instructions).

The target behavior is to get a space monkey, Herman, to press a response button within 1 second after a warning tone sounds. Herman currently makes no responses in less than 2 seconds, and is averaging 4 seconds in responding to the tone. What do you do? You can't tell him to "Hurry up, Herman," or "Do it faster." You might act it out for him, but there is no

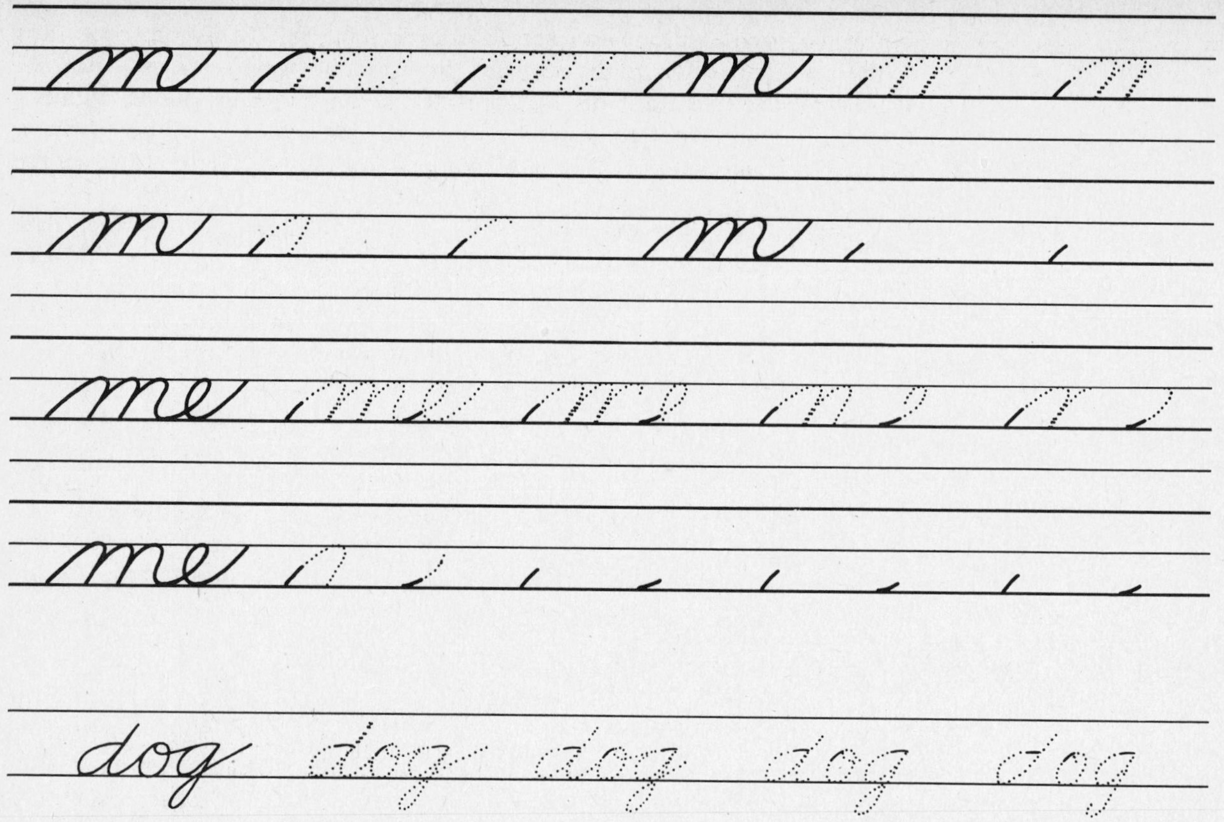

m m m m m m

m m m m m m

me me me me me

me me me me me me me me

dog dog dog dog dog

dog dog dog dog dog

My dog wags his tail.

My dog wags his tail.

My dog wags his tail.

My dog wags his tail.

Figure 7.1 Prompts for building cursive writing

guarantee he would pay attention to the speed of your response. If you just wait for him to make a response in less than 1.5 seconds, it might never happen. In fact, you could extinguish Herman's responding altogether, since no response would be reinforced.

Shaping can change the situation. The following procedure was used:

1 Half of Herman's responses occurred in less than 4 seconds. So the first criterion for reinforcement was set at 4 seconds. This criterion provided reinforcement about half of the time and was more than enough to keep him going. Banana pellets were used as reinforcers.

2 Before long most of Herman's responses were occurring in less than 4 seconds, and even a few in less than 1 second. So the requirement for reinforcement was moved from 4 seconds or less to 3 seconds or less.

3 When the new requirement was met on most trials, the criterion was shifted to 2 seconds, then to 1.5 seconds, and finally to 1 second. The target behavior was achieved. Herman now responded regularly in a way in which he had not responded at all earlier. A dawdling spacemonk was changed into a speedy spacemonk.

When Shaping Is Needed

Shaping is a terribly inefficient process compared with prompting. If the teacher had to shape every new response, the children would end up pretty dumb. Therefore, the first rule is this: *Shaping is used when there are no prompts that can be used to get the target behavior going.*

It is not possible to tell a child, "Sit and work hard for an hour and I'll give you a special treat," and get him to do it, if in the past the child has never worked at any one thing for more than two minutes.

If Ayllon had insisted that the woman wearing twenty-five pounds of clothing remove all the excess before she could eat, she might have eventually done so; but he probably would have had to battle with her and deprive her of food for some time. The hospital staff might have considered this cruel and inhumane. It is also possible that the behavior change might not have been accomplished at all. Shaping is often the gentle and reasonable way to teach new behavior with a minimum of emotional distress.

The teacher should be careful, however, not to get caught in the trap of shaping (accepting poor answers) when it is unnecessary to do so. When imitation or instructions can be used to get the target behavior going, do not accept less than the target behavior.

In most classroom applications of shaping, instructions are used along with shaping. Classroom rules can prompt desired behavior. When the teacher reinforces working longer, working faster, paying better attention, writing more clearly, writing more cleverly, sitting longer, or whatever, she should relate the behavior being reinforced to the rules for good classroom behavior.

HIS SHAPING PROGRAM BEGAN WITH SMALL JUMPS.
AT EACH TRIAL, HE HAS TO STAY UP LONGER FOR
A REINFORCEMENT.

summary

Shaping is a process that involves differential reinforcement and a shifting criterion for reinforcement. Differential reinforcement refers to reinforcing responses that meet current criteria and not reinforcing (extinguishing) other responses. A shifting criterion for reinforcement means that the responses to be reinforced are gradually changed to approach the target behavior.

The steps involved in shaping are to define your target behavior, decide what behavior you are going to build from, select a reinforcer, outline a program to achieve your target behavior, begin training on the program requirements, shift to a new requirement when the first one occurs with regularity, return to an earlier requirement if failure is encountered, and progress through your program until the target behavior is achieved.

Although shaping is inefficient, it is required to get behavior going when instructions, imitation, and other prompts cannot produce the target behavior.

broadening your perspective

Using Physical Prompting in Shaping New Behavior

The procedures used by Sebastian Striefel and Bruce Wetherby to train a severely retarded eleven-year-old boy are an illustration of shaping. Jerry had been trained previously to remain in his seat, keep his hands on his lap, make eye contact with a person calling his name, and to imitate. He showed no vocal behavior except a kind of crying sound.

Each task was broken down into a number of simpler tasks. For example, for the task "raise your hand," Jerry at first would do nothing. So the teacher would physically prompt the response by moving Jerry's hand to the appropriate position and holding it there. Reinforcement in the form of praise and ice cream followed. On subsequent trials the teacher would move the hand less and less—three-fourths of the way, half way, just get his arm started, just touch his hand. The physical prompting was faded out as the criterion for reinforcement was raised. Jerry had to do more and the teacher less. Eventually, just the instruction was enough.

Training was conducted for twenty-two instructions, such as, "drink from glass," "clap your hands," "eat with spoon," "drop ball," "blow on feather." Jerry mastered twenty of the twenty-two instructions as tested by random sequence presentation. An attempt to get generalization to new instructions using combinations of trained actions and objects was not successful.[3] This failure was probably a function of the training sequence, which failed to force separate discrimination of action and object in a given instruction. The subject could be reinforced for just attending to one part of the instruction, if that provided a unique cue. We will return to this kind of problem in volume 2, where we examine procedures for teaching concepts and operations as a general case.

The Training of Autistic Children

Ivar Lovaas and a group working with him at UCLA have carefully studied the processes of building, step by step, more normal behavior repertoires in twenty autistic children. Because they were so hard to control, most of them had been rejected from schools for the emotionally disturbed or the retarded. Their behaviors included not responding to auditory stimuli, attempting to walk through objects as if they were not there, failing to reach out to be picked up by people, being distant and not affectionate, stimulating themselves by rocking, spinning, or flapping, being either mute or echolalic, not following simple instructions, showing no social play or self-help behaviors, and being self-destructive by head banging and scratching or biting themselves.

The first step in treatment was the elimination of self-stimulatory and self-destructive behaviors. While they continued, the children would not even pay attention to the teacher. These behaviors were eliminated by use of extinction, mild punishment, and reinforcement of incompatible behaviors. During this training the teacher also taught the children to attend to him. The behavior was strongly prompted by physically holding the child's head in the right position when the child did not respond to, "Look at me."

The part of the central training program that involved language took nearly 80 percent of the time in a two-year program. If the child was mute, these five steps were followed: (1) Reinforcement was given for any vocalization. (2) Reinforcement was given only for vocalizations made within five seconds of a vocalization by the teacher. (3) Reinforcement was given only for vocalizations similar to those made by the teacher. (4) After one sound was imitated, such as "aaaah," another was introduced ("mmmmm"), and imitation reinforced. Then the two sounds were alternated randomly to force the discrimination between them. (5) Additional sounds would then be presented, reinforced, and differentiated from earlier sounds. The sounds could then be hooked together into words.

Once a child had ten words (if the child was echolalic and could already imitate, he started here), a program to teach functional speech was initiated. The children were taught names for foods; then they would have to request the foods by name to get each bite. Gradually, the children were moved through more complex language forms, such as pronouns, action words, and correct tense usage. They were required to talk about what had happened to them earlier in the day, to make plans, and so forth. At the same time work began on social skills, such as showing affection, dressing themselves, table manners, and greetings.

Of the many results of Lovaas's studies, a major finding concerns what happened to the children after training. Children who had to be returned to the custodial care of an institution lost the gains they had made. This probably occurred because there was no systematic reinforcement provided to maintain the gains. However, for those children whose parents were trained to be the primary therapists, a basis for maintaining gains was established.

The IQ scores of all the children rose considerably, from untestable (or below test range) to an average of around 50. While in no case producing a totally normal person, these studies produced results with a problem that no other treatment method has helped at all.[4]

Shaping Attending Behavior

Phillip was a bright underachieving fourth-grader. He showed a variety of disruptive behaviors in his regular class and was referred to a special class for children with behavior problems. In the special classroom run by Hill Walker and Nancy Buckley, who used a token reinforcement system, Phillip did better but still was very distractible, especially when doing arithmetic. An individual training program to shape attending behavior was set up.

Each day, Phillip came into a special session that was broken into three ten-minute periods, with three-minute breaks after the first two periods. Extraneous cues were reduced to help focus attention. Programed subtraction and addition lessons were used for the study materials. During a baseline condition, Phillip attended about 25 percent of the time. In the experimental condition, Phillip could earn points for each so-many seconds of continuous attending. A click was used to let Phillip know he had earned a point. He had to earn 160 points before he could exchange them for a model he had picked out.

The following schedule was used to shape attending for longer periods:

TABLE 7.1 GRADUATED SCALE FOR CHANGING
RESPONSE INTERVALS AND ADMINISTERING
REINFORCERS

No. of Successfully Completed Intervals	Duration of Interval	No. of Reinforcers Received
		(Events) (Points)
20	30 sec.	20 × 1
10	60 sec.	10 × 2
5	120 sec.	5 × 4
2.5	240 sec.	2.5 × 8
1.2	480 sec.	1.2 × 16
1 *	600 sec.	1 × 20

*Completed three intervals to criterion.

Phillip was trained to work for a full ten minutes with no breaks. At the end of this training he was showing practically 100 percent attending, as measured by an observer's recordings.

This change in behavior was transferred back to the experimental classroom by reinforcing Phillip with one point for each thirty minutes (on the average) that he met the criterion for good attending. He averaged about 90 percent attending in the classroom.[5]

self-test

1 Giving too much of a reinforcer to weaken its effectiveness is an application

of the procedure of _____.

2 One essential procedure in shaping is the use of _____ reinforcement. This means that responses meeting a certain criterion are reinforced, and those that do not meet the criterion are _____.

3 A second essential procedure in shaping is the use of a _____ _____ for reinforcement. Gradually, responses more like the _____ behavior are required.

4 In developing a shaping program—

a) First, define the _____ behavior.

b) Next, decide what behavior to _____ on.

5 The teacher should avoid moving so fast that failure often occurs, or too slowly, which may _____ a behavior at an undesired level.

6 Shaping is used when there are no _____ that will produce the target behavior.

7 Shaping is generally more _____ than prompting for getting responses going.

NUMBER RIGHT _____

3 shifting
   criterion;
   target, desired

4 a) target,
      desired
   b) build

5 strengthen,
   reinforce

6 prompts

7 inefficient

exercise 1 programed practice

1 In a study of a hospitalized psychotic woman, Ayllon eliminated food stealing by having a nurse remove the patient from the dining room without _____ if she did steal.

2 Taking away this patient's food if she stole is an example of punishment by _____ of reinforcers.

3 Hoarding towels was eliminated for this same patient by giving her _____ _____ _____ towels until she got tired of them.

1 eating

2 withdrawal,
   withholding

3 more and more

4 satiation

5 shaping;
   reduced,
   decreased

6 shifting
   criterion

7 two

8 differential;
   not reinforced,
   extinguished

9 shifting
   criterion;
   target, desired

10 improvement

11 a) target,
      desired
   b) build
   c) reinforcer
   d) steps

---

4 Giving too much of a reinforcer to weaken its effectiveness is an application of the procedure of _____.

5 Wearing excess clothing was eliminated by using a _____ procedure. If the patient weighed more than a given amount, she was not admitted to the dining room to eat. The weight allowance for clothing was gradually _____ until the patient was dressing normally.

6 Reduction of the weight allowance from time to time is an example of a _____ _____ for reinforcement.

7 Shaping is a process that consists of _____ essential procedures.

8 One essential procedure in shaping is the use of _____ reinforcement. This means that responses meeting a certain criterion are reinforced, while those that do not meet the criterion are _____.

9 A second essential procedure in shaping is the use of a _____ _____ for reinforcement. Gradually, responses more like the _____ behavior are required.

10 Another way of talking about shaping is to talk about reinforcing _____ or getting better.

11 In developing a shaping program—

   a) The teacher must first define her _____ behavior.

   b) Next she decides on a behavior to _____ on.

   c)·A _____ is selected to use in strengthening behavior.

   d) A program consisting of progressive _____ is then devised to get from what the child can do to the target behavior.

e) Training is begun with the first requirement for reinforcement. When the first requirement is met, the teacher shifts to a _____ requirement.

f) When the requirement for reinforcement is not met, the teacher _____ briefly to an earlier step, or adds a new step in between.

g) Training continues through the steps of the program until the _____ behavior is mastered.

12 The teacher should avoid moving so fast that failure often occurs. He should also avoid moving too slowly, in which case he may _____ a behavior he doesn't really want.

13 In a program developed by B. F. Skinner, a special pen and chemically treated paper are used to give the child _____ _____ reinforcement.

14 In this program, if the child draws the correct line, it comes out gray. If he is incorrect, it comes out _____. The width of the band that will produce a gray line is _____ later in the program.

15 Narrowing the width of the band that will produce a gray line is an example of changing the _____ _____ _____.

16 Some responses commonly requiring shaping are working longer, working _____, paying attention, and staying in one's _____.

17 Many athletic skills are best developed through a _____ procedure. Children learn new skills through many _____ trials.

---

e) new, higher

f) returns

g) target

12 strengthen, reinforce

13 immediate differential

14 yellow; narrowed, decreased

15 criterion for reinforcement

16 faster; seat

17 shaping; successful

---

18 reinforcing;
   target

19 criterion

20 prompts

21 imitation;
   shaping

22 inefficient

18 Herman, the astromonk, was trained to be speedy by first _____ responses that he made in four seconds or less. The _____ behavior for Herman was to make all responses to a tone in less than one second.

19 The _____ for reinforcement was gradually changed from four seconds to one second.

20 Shaping is used when there are no _____ that will produce the target behavior.

21 When instruction or _____ can be used to achieve target behavior, the teacher should not use _____.

22 Shaping is generally more _____ than prompting in getting responses going.

discussion questions

1 Describe how a shaping procedure was used to eliminate wearing excess clothes by a mental patient.

2 State the two essential procedures in the process called shaping.

3 Define *differential reinforcement*.

4 Define *shifting criterion for reinforcement*.

5 Give an example of differential reinforcement as it is used in the classroom.

6 Give an example of a shifting requirement for reinforcement as it is used in the classroom.

7 Specify one behavior that a teacher might try to get going through shaping.

8 Describe the steps involved in building a shaping program.

9 How do shaping principles enter into Skinner's writing program?

10 Explain why shaping is a good procedure to use in developing athletic skills.

11 Describe a procedure for training a subject to respond quickly.

12 State the rule about when to shape.

13 Give an example to show the use of physical prompting in shaping.

14 Describe the steps in the language training program used by Lovaas in therapy with autistic children.

15 Describe a procedure for shaping attending for ten minutes with a child who can attend for only ten seconds.

A Two-Week Project in Changing Behavior

Part A.   Baseline

For students who have a classroom to work in, this project is to be carried out with a child from your class. For others, the instructor will arrange for class-room visits at a fixed time each day for two weeks, or the target behavior and situation can be modified to apply to the behavior of a friend.

1 *Define the target behavior.* For those in a classroom, the target behavior is *time on-task* when the child is assigned an exercise or project to do on his own. If necessary, make up ten to twenty minutes of seat work each day for ten days for a group of children. Time on-task is defined as ten sec-onds of continuous working at the task or paying attention to the teach-er's instructions.

2 *Select a child to be observed.* For this study, select a child who is off-task much of the time.

3 *Measure the target behavior.* Record your observations on the recording sheet. Use a stopwatch or a watch with a second hand. For each 10 sec-onds of observation, record whether the child is on-task (—) the whole 10 seconds, or off-task (X) for any part of the 10 seconds. Do not count as off-task looking around for less than 2 seconds unless the head turns more than 90 degrees.

— in a box stands for on-task for a complete 10-second interval
X in a box stands for off-task for any part of a 10-second interval

For each day's observation, *time on-task* is expressed as a percentage of the total number of observation intervals.

$$\frac{\text{On-Task Intervals}}{\text{Total Intervals Observed}} = \text{Percent On-Task}$$

You are to collect data for one week and discuss it with your group leader before proceeding.

Part B. Experimental Change Program

1 *Choose a suitable reinforcer for on-task behavior.*

2 *Devise a method for delivery of the reinforcer at the right time.* Consider your criterion for giving a reinforcer and how it might change with time. The reinforcer should be given quickly without interfering with on-task be-havior.

3 *Measure the target behavior.* Record your observations on the recording sheet using the method given above.

4 *On the back of the report form, briefly describe your reinforcement procedures.* On the front of the report form, record the new on-task percentages and graph the results daily.

Recording Sheet

Name _____

Observer _____ Teacher _____

Subject _____ Date _____

Time _____ School _____

Observed Behavior: _____

Minute	Observation Intervals (Ten Seconds Each)						Comments
	1	2	3	4	5	6	
1							
2							
3							
4							
5							
6							
7							
8							
9							
10							
11							
12							
13							
14							
15							
16							
17							
18							
19							
20							

Project Report Form

Child's Name _____ Observation Time _____

Target Behavior _____ Setting of Observation _____

_____

Daily Data

	Baseline			*Experimental*	
	Date	Percent On-Task Behavior		Date	Percent On-Task Behavior
1.	_____	_____	6.	_____	_____
2.	_____	_____	7.	_____	_____
3.	_____	_____	8.	_____	_____
4.	_____	_____	9.	_____	_____
5.	_____	_____	10.	_____	_____

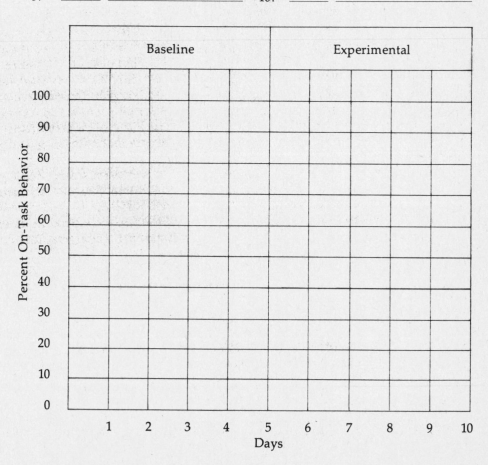

unit 8

When to Reinforce

objectives

When you complete this unit you should be able to—

1 Define these terms: continuous reinforcement
                         intermittent reinforcement
                         fixed-ratio schedule
                         fixed-interval schedule
                         variable-ratio schedule
                         variable-interval schedule
                         resistance to extinction
2 Describe the characteristics of various schedules of reinforcement and what happens when they are terminated.
3 State the implications of scheduling for teaching persistent behaviors.
4 Explain why immediate reinforcement is important and state ways of achieving it or overcoming delays.
5 Explain why reinforcing improvement is important.

lesson

It is important for the teacher to learn when to reinforce and when not to. The timing of reinforcement can determine its effectiveness and is related to the durability of the behavior being reinforced.

Reinforce Immediately

Teacher Trains Billy to Dawdle

Billy worked beautifully in a reading group where he could get immediate attention from his teacher. But the minute Billy was required to do programed reading exercises on his own, he seemed to lose all interest in reading. He opened his book to the right page and started the first item, but then he turned away from his work and looked out the window or turned to watch Susie, next to him. His teacher eventually noticed this and came to him. She assumed he needed extra help, so she worked with him on each item on the page, having Billy read out loud. She provided immediate attention and reinforcement for working. When she left, she told Billy to finish his assignment. Ten minutes later when she checked back, he had made no further progress. She again went over the work item by item with him. He always got the right answers. The next day his teacher told him, "I know you can do these exercises, now get with it." Billy turned to his work briefly and did a few items, but soon went back to dawdling. His teacher noticed this and scolded him again. "Billy, do I have to stand over you every minute?" Again, Billy worked as long as his teacher was watching him.

Billy's teacher was making several mistakes:

1 She withdrew all reinforcement for working as soon as she discovered he could do the work. Reinforcement was not immediate enough to keep Billy working.

2 When Billy was put on his own, his teacher gave attention only to not working—to his dawdling. Billy received no praise for the few items he had completed. Dawdling rather than working seemed to be reinforced.

To correct this situation, his teacher needed to structure the situation to provide more immediate reinforcement for working. For example, after seeing that he could do the work, she might have instructed Billy to raise his hand after he completed each of the next five items so that she could check them. Then she might require Billy to do two or three items before checking, then maybe a page of six items. The key to success is to structure the situation to get immediate reinforcement going for working, not for dawdling.

Carefully Watch What Is Reinforced

We teach others how to behave by what we reinforce. Reinforcers strengthen the behavior they follow. If reinforcement does not immediately follow the response we want to strengthen, it is possible that some other response might be reinforced. By the time Billy's teacher gave him attention, he was no longer working. Not working was being reinforced by her nagging attention. Any delay in reinforcement (time between the response and the reward) increases the chances that wrong behavior will be taught.

How to Provide Immediate Reinforcement

When told to use immediate reinforcement, many teachers say, "That's impossible! You've got to be kidding. How can I give immediate reinforcement to twenty-five (or forty) children at the same time?" As a matter of fact, you can't in a typical classroom. There are three ways to deal with this dilemma. Two of them involve ways of providing immediate reinforcement. First, you can go to teaching machines or programed books to provide immediate reinforcement for responses. Second, use small-group instruction (as in the Engelmann programs) where the teacher works with five to eight children at a time and is able to respond to each child as needed. For either approach to be efficient, it is necessary to have well-programed course materials. The third procedure makes use of the fact that, with most verbal children, it is possible to overcome a delay period by using words. When reinforcement is given, the teacher *specifies* exactly what the child did that was right. She tells the child why a reinforcer is being given. If answers are written down on an assignment paper that the teacher has corrected, the child can be instructed to go back over his right responses and to correct his wrong responses. Delays can be bridged by a careful use of words, but more immediate reinforcement is better.

Conditioned Reinforcers Are Usually Preferred

The principle of immediacy applies to any reinforcer, conditioned or unconditioned. Most of the time the teacher uses immediate conditioned reinforcers in teaching, and occasionally backs these up with unconditioned reinforcers. Conditioned reinforcers such as "You're right," "That's good," "I like that" are preferred in the classroom because they are easy to give immediately and do not interfere with the teaching. If a child were given candy, the food in the mouth would make it difficult for him to answer questions. If the reinforcer were a play activity, this too would interfere with the ongoing teaching. It is important to choose reinforcers that do not compete or interfere with teaching. Eventually, the learning tasks themselves should contain the reinforcers.

Reinforce Improvement

One problem with grading according to a standard level of performance is that those who know the most to begin with usually get the most reinforcement. Under such conditions, the students who know less to begin with are reinforced less for trying. The teacher defeats his own objectives with this kind of grading. Those who need to learn the most are reinforced the least and therefore are likely to learn less.

The teacher needs to be sensitive to signs of improvement and make reinforcement contingent on getting better. Catch the children getting better and praise them for this behavior. All the children in the classroom have an equal opportunity to earn rewards when the teacher defines his task in this way. Remember also that what is just a small step for one child may be a big step for another. In teaching a child to work on his own, application of this rule requires that we first praise the child for completing short tasks, and gradually expand the task to be completed before reinforcement.

Schedules of Reinforcement

Very often we are interested in teaching children behavior that will continue when there is no one around to reinforce it. This can be done if we understand the effects of various schedules of reinforcement on behavior and how to establish these schedules.

Continuous Reinforcement

When every response is reinforced, a continuous schedule is in effect. Continuous schedules have the advantage of getting new learning to occur quickly. However, if reinforcement stops, extinction is likely to take place rapidly.

Intermittent Reinforcement

When only some responses are reinforced, the schedule is said to be intermittent. Intermittent schedules are defined on the basis of whether the schedule focuses on the number of responses (ratio schedules) or on the passage of time (interval schedules), and on whether the schedule is predictable (fixed) or unpredictable (variable). This two-way classification leads to four types of intermittent schedules. Table 8.1 summarizes the properties of each.

Fixed-Ratio Schedules. In a fixed-ratio schedule, reinforcers are given for every X responses. An FR-5 schedule means that after every five responses, a reinforcer is given. Such schedules are common in industry and go under the name *piecework:* a set number of completed tasks is worth so much money. The teacher might use a fixed-ratio schedule with seatwork assignments. Each ten exercises completed correctly in the programed reader is worth one point. Each five arithmetic problems completed correctly is worth a minute of recess. Fixed-ratio schedules produce high rates of responding while they are in effect. After terminating a fixed-ratio schedule, extinction follows less quickly than with continuous reinforcement, but more quickly than with variable reinforcement.

Fixed-Interval Schedules. On this schedule, reinforcers are given for the first response to occur after X minutes (or seconds or hours) have passed. But there are problems. If reinforcement occurs only at regular intervals, the student will learn to discriminate when it pays off to work and when it does not. Right after reinforcement, the student learns to take it easy until the next

TABLE 8.1 Four Kinds of Intermittent Reinforcement Schedules[1]

Name Schedule	Definition of Schedule	Effects on Behavior	
		Schedule in Effect	Schedule Terminated (Extinction)
Fixed Ratio (FR)	Reinforcer is given after each X responses.	High response rate	Irregular burst of responding. More responses than in continuous reinforcement, less than in variable ratio.
Fixed Interval (FI)	Reinforcer is given for first response to occur after each X minutes.	Stops working after reinforcement. Works hard just prior to time for next reinforcement.	Slow gradual decrease in responding.
Variable Ratio (VR)	Reinforcer is given after X responses on the average.	Very high response rates. The higher the ratio the higher the rate.	Very resistant to extinction. Maximum number of responses before extinction.
Variable Interval (VI)	Reinforcer is given for first response after each X minutes, on the average.	Steady rate of responding.	Very resistant to extinction. Maximum time to extinction.

time. In unit 6 we discussed a study by Mawhinney et al. that compared the effects of daily, weekly, and three-week testing intervals. For the longest interval between tests, studying was lowest right after a test and gradually increased as time for the next test approached.

On a fixed-interval schedule, the teacher tells the class, "Today, I am going to check you every ten minutes to see if everyone is working. If when I check, everyone is working, you will earn one minute of recess." With this approach, the children get busy just before each ten-minute check by the teacher.

On the other hand, it is possible to give reinforcers on a fixed-interval basis for convenience, but to set the criterion for reinforcement so that it works like a continuous schedule. The teacher simply states the rules and says, "For each ten minutes that no one violates the rules, the whole class will earn two minutes of recess. If a violation occurs, the ten-minute period starts over." The reinforcer is given for good behavior *over the whole period*, not just for the time immediately before the reinforcer is due.

Variable-Ratio Schedules. Variable-ratio schedules give reinforcement for every X responses *on the average*. For example, a VR-5 schedule might reinforce after one response, then after four, then after seven, then two, then nine, and so forth. The range varies from one to ten, but would average five. Variable-ratio schedules lead to high steady response rates while they are in effect, and they are very resistant to extinction; that is, the behavior continues a long time after reinforcement is stopped. Most games of chance operate on variable-ratio schedules. The gambler who persists at a slot machine hour-after-hour even though he is losing shows the powerful control exerted by variable-ratio schedules. Winning a little every once in a while can keep a lot of behavior going. When persistence is the goal, variable-ratio schedules may help to achieve it.

Variable-Interval Schedules. These schedules give reinforcement for the first response after X minutes *on the average*. For example, a VI-5 schedule might reinforce a response after one minute or after seven minutes. The range of times might be from one to ten minutes and average five. Variable-interval schedules (like variable-ratio schedules) produce high rates of responding when the schedule is in effect and high resistance to extinction. They are very useful for reinforcing continuous-stream behaviors such as attention to the task, time on-task, and so forth.

I'M GOING TO SWEAR OFF AS SOON AS I FIGURE OUT THE SCHEDULE

Using Schedules in the Classroom

To get new learning going quickly, start with continuous reinforcement. As the behavior becomes established, *gradually* shift from a continuous schedule to some form of intermittent schedule. If you suddenly shift from reinforcing every response to reinforcing every hundredth response, the student may quit long before he gets to a hundred. A gradual shift is necessary to prevent extinction from occurring. A good sequence to remember is: to get it going, reinforce every time; to keep it going, reinforce now and then.

Teaching On-Task Behavior—the Wrong Way

The class has been assigned a task the teacher knows they can do. She walks around the room to check their work and answer questions. Jeff just sits and looks in the air until the teacher comes near; then he turns to his work and seems busy. The teacher praises him for working. When she passes, he returns to his daydreaming. The same pattern is repeated frequently. Jeff is being trained to work only when the teacher is near. Jeff is reinforced each time he works (continuous reinforcement), but he does not work continuously. Jeff does what is reinforced: working when the teacher is near. A clear signal is provided (the teacher's approach) as to *when* working is likely to be reinforced. Jeff is receiving predictable continuous reinforcement.

Teaching On-Task Behavior in a Way That Works

A colored card with fifty squares on it is placed on Jeff's desk. When the card is filled, Jeff gets to choose the game for the next recess. The teacher has a kitchen timer (which makes a soft *ding* when it goes off) on her desk. She also has a little card with the following numbers on it: 30″, 2′, 1′, 20″, 4′, 1″, and so forth. Jeff is instructed that the teacher will check to see if he is working each time the bell dings. If Jeff is working, the teacher will nod and Jeff can put a mark on his card (teacher also keeps score at her desk when she resets the timer). The timer is set according to the numbers given above. Unpredictable intermittent reinforcement is given. Jeff can't predict when reinforcement is coming. To keep from losing points he has to keep working. Slowly the time intervals are increased. Then the bell is eliminated, with the teacher checking now and then on her own. After Jeff has learned to complete his tasks, the points are dropped and the teacher only gives praise and occasional privileges for good work.

Predictable reinforcement will lead to working (or paying attention) only when reinforcement is likely to occur. Variable reinforcement will lead to steady working or persistent behavior.

Be Careful Not to Reinforce the Wrong Behavior

If a behavior is reinforced only now and then, it follows from what we know about intermittent reinforcement that such behavior is likely to be persistent.

If Jerome's tantrums are usually punished but sometimes get his parents or teacher to give in, the tantrums may become quite persistent. Teachers or parents can accidentally train children into bad habits by occasionally giving in. To change an undesirable behavior, the teacher must be very consistent in not rewarding that behavior.

summary

1 Immediate reinforcement is most effective. However, delays can be overcome by telling the students exactly what they did that you liked.
2 Reinforce improvement.
3 To get behavior going, reinforce each time. To keep it going, reinforce on a variable-intermittent schedule.
4 Avoid predictable reinforcement when persistence is desired.
5 Avoid occasionally reinforcing undesired behavior. Be consistent.

broadening your perspective

The Grading Lottery

In 1958, Ogden Lindsey discussed the problem of the high school English teacher who works on composition. To learn to write compositions, the student needs to get in there and do it; but the more compositions an English teacher assigns, the more the teacher is punished by losing evenings and weekends grading papers. Lindsey suggested that as many as fifteen compositions could be assigned in a semester; but for any one assignment, the teacher would grade only four to six papers. An intermittent grading schedule is used. The papers would be selected randomly, with some juggling to be sure each student had at least three papers graded in the semester. Since the student could not know if a given paper would affect his grade, he was safe only if he tried to do a good job with all of them. The students would get the practice they needed and reasonable teacher feedback; and the teacher would not be excessively punished.[2]

At Southern Illinois University, a group of students working with Bill Hopkins studied the effects of an intermittent grading procedure on the acquisition of printing skills by six kindergarten children.[3] Prior to the start of the experiment, the children had completed the first thirty-five pages of *Handwriting with Write and See* by Skinner and Krakower.[4] For the experiment, the children were given daily worksheets with guidelines and model letters. Thirteen upper case letters were used, along with the upper case Z. Each worksheet had a model for one letter with places to copy it twenty-seven times. At the bottom it also had a model of Z and a place to make nine copies. A teacher demonstrated correct writing at the board each day before the worksheet was started.

The experimental conditions were as follows. First, in baseline, the children completed their worksheet and went out to play for a period of fifteen minutes from when the first child finished. No papers were graded. Next, papers were graded and feedback given on the daily target letter, but not Z. The grading was intermittent: 50 percent of the children's papers were graded each day, and the children could not tell if they would be graded or not until they turned in their papers. If a child was not graded that day, he could go immediately out to play. When grading occurred, he waited for the teacher to correct his paper and give feedback. In the next condition, the children were intermittently graded, but a contingency was placed on their performance. They had to exceed a specified percent correct each day, or they would have to take another worksheet and do it over to meet criterion before they could go out to play. This clearly meant losing play periods if the work was too sloppy. Criteria were set individually for each child and adjusted as needed to *shape* doing better. For some children 30 percent correct was acceptable; for others 70 percent was the minimum performance.

The results showed about a 30 percent accuracy during baseline. This did not change when intermittent grading was introduced. Only when the intermittent grading was used with a contingency did accuracy go up. Accuracy rose to nearly 80 percent in fact.

After these results had been demonstrated, the same procedures were now applied to Z only, and no longer to the other letters. Up to now there had been no improvement on Z. Again, intermittent grading alone did not change Z performance. Grading plus the contingency did lead to a remarkable improvement. Thus, the main findings were replicated using this multiple baseline design.

The Work Rates of Congressmen

Figures 8.1 and 8.2 demonstrate that the work rate of congressmen follows the expected pattern for a fixed-interval reinforcement schedule. Before considering these figures it is necessary to discuss how they are drawn. The horizontal axis is a familiar one, reflecting the passage of time, in this case two years. The vertical axis is new to us. Instead of reflecting *number of responses*, or *percentage of observation intervals*, it reflects the *cumulative number of responses*.

These figures show that Congress passes few bills early in a new legislative session, but as the time for adjournment in October approaches, more bills are passed. The slope of the cumulative curve gets steeper. The charac-

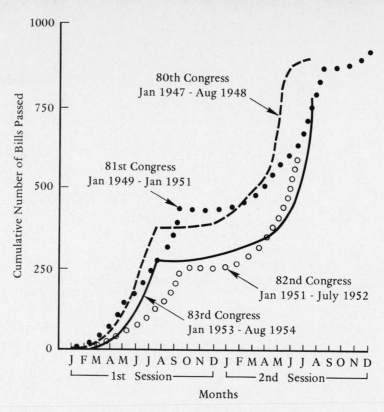

Figure 8.1 Cumulative number of bills passed during the legislative sessions of Congress from January 1947 to August 1954

teristic shape of a cumulative curve produced by a fixed-interval schedule is called a *scallop*. The data also reveal that in the second session, prior to going to the voters for reelection, many more bills were passed than in the first session of each Congress.[5]

The behavior of congressmen in passing legislation is very similar to that found for college students on a three-week fixed-interval schedule for testing.

Getting Onto an Intermittent Schedule

Frank Kirby and Frank Shields describe one procedure for getting a distractible thirteen-year-old boy to work more persistently at his arithmetic. After baseline observations where Tom did twenty problems a day on a worksheet without social reinforcement, a reinforcement condition was begun. Tom was instructed to bring his paper to his teacher for checking at specified times. The teacher would then check it and praise Tom for the work completed. For the first two days, praise and the correct answers were given after

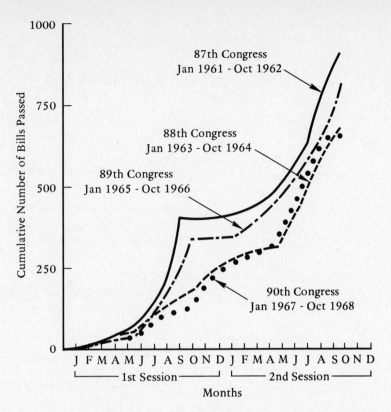

Figure 8.2 Cumulative number of bills passed during the legislative sessions of Congress from January 1961 to October 1968

each two problems. For the next two days, praise was given after every four problems. For the next two days, praise was given after every eight problems, and finally, after sixteen problems. Rate of problem completion tripled under this reinforcement schedule to a rate of 1.5 problems per minute. A reversal condition in which no checking and praising were done reduced Tom's performance to twice the baseline level. A second reinforcement condition similar to the first reestablished responding at three times the baseline rate.[6]

Using a DRL Schedule with High School Girls

In a DRL schedule, *differential reinforcement* is given for *low* rates of a response class. Samuel Dietz and Alan Repp used a DRL schedule with fifteen high school senior girls enrolled in an office procedures class. The dependent variable was the number of times a class member changed the subject from the academic topic to some other, usually social, topic. During baseline the class went off the subject 6.6 times per fifty-minute period. A progressively reducing DRL schedule was introduced. To earn a free-time class on Friday, the number of subject changes had to be less than 6 on Monday through Thursdays. The next week the criterion was moved to 3 or fewer, then to 2, and then to 0. The girls met the criterion in every case.[7]

Delayed Reinforcement

Karen was a 12-year-old girl who was described by her teachers as very "self-conscious" and having a "poor self-image." She was not pretty, was poorly dressed and groomed, and had poor posture. She was careless in her math work. An observer identified four behaviors that it might be helpful for Karen to change: (1) her writing was too small and hard to read; (2) she touched her face with her hands a lot; (3) posture while working was slouched; (4) her voice was too quiet when she recited.

A video-tape recorder was used to record Karen's behavior for twenty minutes each day during math. After school each day the tape was shown to Karen, and she was given poker chips for improved behaviors. The chips could be exchanged for items like bracelets, pens, and dresses. One behavior at a time was focused on for change (multiple-baseline design). The delayed procedures were very effective in producing the desired changes in Karen.[8]

self-test

1 To be most effective, do not permit a _____ between response and reinforcement.

2 In the early stages of learning a task, reinforce _____ correct response.

3 As behavior gets going, _____ shift from reinforcing every response to variable intermittent reinforcement.

4 The principle of immediacy applies to _____ _____, conditioned or unconditioned.

5 The teacher should be sensitive to _____ and reinforce it.

1 delay, lapse

2 every

3 gradually

4 all reinforcers

5 improvement, getting better

6 In a _____-_____ schedule, reinforcers are given for every X responses on the average.

7 Extinction occurs most rapidly after termination of _____ reinforcement.

8 Resistance to extinction refers to how long or how often one will keep making a response after reinforcement has been _____.

9 In order to make responses resistant to extinction, the teacher must use _____ intermittent reinforcement.

10 To change an undesirable behavior, teachers must be very _____ in not reinforcing that behavior.

NUMBER RIGHT _____

6 variable-ratio

7 continuous

8 stopped, terminated

9 variable

10 consistent

exercise 1 programed practice

1 In teaching a new task, it is best to reinforce or punish _____ rather than allow a delay.

2 In the early stages of learning a task, reinforce _____ correct response.

3 After the behavior becomes more proficient you should require _____ correct responses before you reinforce.

4 You should gradually shift from reinforcing every correct response to a _____-_____ schedule reinforcement of correct responses.

1 immediately

2 every

3 more, several

4 variable-intermittent

5 predictable, continuous

6 likely, probable, near

7 reinforced

8 stimulus

9 response, behavior

10 immediate

11 teaching

12 small group

13 words; tells, specifies

14 immediate

15 all reinforcers

5 Avoid the use of _____ reinforcement for attention, working in the face of failure, and task completion.

6 Predictable reinforcement may teach the child to attend or to work only when there is a signal present that reinforcement is _____.

7 Billy's teacher also adopted a procedure that _____ dawdling rather than working on task.

8 When using the S-R-S model of teaching, we are trying to get the right response to occur in the presence of specified _____ conditions.

9 A reinforcing stimulus strengthens whatever _____ it follows under the stimulus conditions that are in effect at the time the response is made.

10 It is usually difficult for a teacher to give _____ reinforcement to an entire classroom of children. There are three ways out of the dilemma.

11 First, one could use _____ machines or books which provide immediate consequences for responding.

12 Second, one could use _____ _____ instruction where the teacher can give appropriate reinforcement to each child when he responds.

13 The third procedure uses _____ to bridge the delay. When the reinforcement is given, the teacher _____ exactly what it was that the child did that was right.

14 Delays in reinforcement can be bridged with words, but more _____ reinforcement is preferred.

15 The principle of immediacy applies to _____ _____, conditioned or unconditioned.

16 quickly, easily,
immediately;
interfere

17 most

18 improvement

19 fixed-interval

20 variable-ratio

21 variable-interval

22 fixed-ratio

23 every;
intermittently

24 continuous

25 intermittently

26 intermittently
reinforced

27 continuous reinforcement,
immediate reinforcement

16 In the classroom, conditioned reinforcers are preferred over unconditioned reinforcers, because they can be given _____ and because they do not _____ with teaching as activity or tangible reinforcers can.

17 Grading according to a standard level of performance results in the children who need reinforcement the _____ getting the least.

18 Teachers need to be sensitive to signs of _____ and reinforce them.

19 In a _____-_____ schedule, reinforcers are given for the first response to occur after X minutes have passed.

20 In a _____-_____ schedule, reinforcers are given for every X responses on the average.

21 In a _____-_____ schedule, reinforcers are given for the first response after X minutes on the average.

22 In a _____-_____ schedule, reinforcers are given for each X responses.

23 To get new behavior going, reinforce _____ response. To keep behavior going, reinforce _____.

24 Extinction occurs most rapidly after _____ reinforcement.

25 If a correct response is reinforced sometimes and not other times, then it is said to be _____ reinforced.

26 Responses that are _____-_____ are more resistant to extinction.

27 In order to teach new responses rapidly the teacher should use _____ _____.

28 Resistance to extinction refers to how long or how often one will keep making a response after reinforcement has been _____.

29 There are two kinds of predictable reinforcement: one based on a fixed period of _____, and the other based on a fixed number of _____.

30 The gambler cannot tell if he will win or not. Reinforcement is _____ as well as intermittent.

31 Jeff could tell when working would pay off and when it would not because the likelihood of reinforcement was _____ by the teacher's approach.

32 This situation with Jeff was corrected by putting him on a _____ _____ reinforcement.

33 _____ intermittent reinforcement is likely to lead to steady working or persistent behavior.

34 We can accidentally train children into _____ _____ by occasionally giving in when a child misbehaves.

35 To change an undesirable behavior, teachers must be very _____ in not reinforcing that behavior.

28 stopped, terminated

29 time; responses

30 unpredictable, variable

31 signaled, cued

32 variable intermittent

33 Variable

34 bad habits, undesirable behavior

35 consistent

exercise 2

Define these terms.

1 Continuous reinforcement: _____

_____

2 Fixed-ratio schedule: _____

_____

3 Fixed-interval schedule: _____

_____

4 Variable-ratio schedule: _____

_____

5 Variable-interval schedule: _____

_____

Answers

1 Each response is reinforced.
2 – 5 See table 8.1.

discussion questions

1 Why is immediate reinforcement important?
2 Give three ways a teacher can surmount the difficulties faced in trying to give immediate reinforcement to a whole class.
3 Why should the teacher focus on reinforcing improvement?
4 Define these terms and give an example of each:
continuous reinforcement
intermittent reinforcement
fixed-ratio schedule
variable-ratio schedule
variable-interval schedule
resistance to extinction
5 For each of the classes of schedules mentioned in question 4, describe the effects of the schedule on behavior while it is in effect, and when the schedule is terminated (extinction).
6 Explain the steps you would take to teach persistent behavior.
7 Why should predictable reinforcement be avoided for continuous-stream behaviors like on-task?
8 Explain why conditioned reinforcers are often preferred over unconditioned reinforcers in teaching.
9 Why is it important to be consistent in not reinforcing an undesired behavior?

unit 9

Review 1

This review unit is designed to remind you of some of the material covered earlier in the course. This unit is *not* designed to teach you new material, except for the overview of stimulus and response functions. If any terms or concepts are mentioned that you do not understand, you should go back to the original material and study it carefully. In addition, you should go back through the exercises you did for each unit and make sure that you know the correct answer for each item.

Stimulus and Response Functions

One way to get a handle on the basic concepts or principles underlying behavior is through the concepts of *response functions* and *stimulus functions*. In the first half of this text we have described and discussed two response functions and four stimulus functions.

Response Functions

Respondent Function	*Operant Function*
Response occurs in reaction to an eliciting stimulus	Response operates on the environment and produces effects

---

Stimulus Functions

Eliciting Function	*Reinforcing Function*
Unconditioned Eliciting Stimulus (US)	Unconditioned Reinforcing Stimulus (S^R)
Conditioned Eliciting Stimulus (CS)	Conditioned Reinforcing Stimulus (S^r)

Punishing Function

Unconditioned Punishing Stimulus (S^P)

Conditioned Punishing Stimulus (S^p)

Discriminative Function

Discriminative Stimulus (S^D)

The basic outline of behavior theory is relatively simple, even though it can be used to build or understand the most complex human activities. For each of the above stimulus and response functions, be sure you can give appropriate definitions and examples.

review

Unit 1. Human Concerns and a Science of Behavior

The opening unit discussed some common misunderstandings and questions students have about a scientific approach to the study of learning processes. Some have asserted that there is a basic conflict between humanistic values and scientific method. We see no inherent conflict between values and methods, although we grant that not all scientists have shown adequate concern for their "subjects." We believe that better knowledge of human behavior can be used to more effectively meet personal needs.

When the behavioral scientist talks about cause, he is talking about the environmental events (independent variables) that can be used to produce a change in behavior (dependent variables). Scientific laws are statements of relationships between independent and dependent variables, between causes and effects. Human behavior follows lawful processes just as the rest of the physical world does. When the scientist uses the word *control*, it is simply another name for a cause. In popular usage, control often means coercion, and usually, we don't like it. Knowledge of how behavior works (its lawfulness) should help us be more effective in our efforts to help others.

Determinism means that behavior is lawful or predictable. The term *indeterminism* refers to converse condition, namely, randomness or unpredictability. The attempt to cite Heisenberg's *Principle of Indeterminancy* to support an antideterministic position is found to be lacking, since it is based on a misinterpretation. Heisenberg was talking about a measurement problem, not the absence of causality.

Free will refers to the behavior of making choices without being coerced. Philosophically, the term also implies that the choices are not caused. Thus, free will is considered the opposite of determinism. But the opposite of determinism is chance, and the opposite of freedom-of-choice is coercion. The problem of freedom-of-choice arises in consideration of social systems. Some allow for more freedom-of-choice than others.

In a deterministic world responsibility exists in terms of the sets of agreements people make with each other. Laws of state assign or permit the assumption of various legal responsibilities. Personal responsibility is an *assumed* responsibility based on an implicit contract with others.

Accusations that behavior theory is too simplistic to handle the complexities of human cognition usually refer to an ancient form of behaviorism and are derived from a lack of knowledge of modern behavior theory.

The bribery issue confuses the misuse of reinforcers (given following misbehavior) with the use of all reinforcers. Only under certain conditions can rewards be considered bribes and are therefore to be avoided.

Several fictional causes for behavior were discussed. Looking within the "personality," as the medical model of behavior does, misses entirely the environmental events responsible for what we do. Circular explanations contain no independent variable, and so while sounding like causal statements, in reality they say nothing. That we do things for a purpose has to be logically incorrect because causality runs only forward, like time.

Placing the blame (cause) for teaching failures on the children is no longer acceptable. The teacher is responsible. Present knowledge of behavior can be used to help you learn to be an effective teacher. It can also help you manage your own life and contribute to a better world.

Unit 2. First Steps in the Analysis of Behavior

There are two functionally different classes of behavior—operant and respondent. Respondent behavior involves the reflexive action of the smooth muscles and glands. Operant behavior involves the striated muscles system or what we normally call "voluntary" behavior. Respondents are controlled by preceding stimuli which are called eliciting stimuli. Operants are controlled by following stimuli which are called reinforcing stimuli and punishing stimuli.

In the model of respondent behavior, $S \rightarrow R$, a preceding stimulus elicits a response. Operant responses can be brought under the control of preceding stimuli by the use of differential reinforcement. If an operant response is reinforced in the presence of some stimulus and not others, it will tend to occur more often when that stimulus is presented. A preceding stimulus that influences the occurrence of an operant is called a discriminative stimulus. In the model of operant behavior, a preceding stimulus sets the occasion when an operant response is more likely to get reinforced (or lead to the avoidance of punishment). In the operant model $S \rightarrow R \rightarrow S$, the consequences of behavior are very important. The teacher is mostly concerned with operant behavior.

In learning to use behavior principles to help others reach their objectives, the first step is to learn how to define behavioral events (operant behaviors) and stimulus events in objective terms. The key is to keep the definitions or descriptive examples restricted to what you can see—observables. What is he doing? What is she saying? The focus of a behavioral event is on the performance itself. Trait labels such as intelligent, aggressive, or retarded are to be avoided, as are words referring to internal events, such as feelings, motives, knowledge, and thoughts.

A good test of the adequacy of a behavioral definition is to have two observers use the definition to code a sequence of behavior and see if they come up with similar results. A percentage of agreement can be computed by dividing the number of agreements by agreements plus disagreements.

Stimulus events can be readily defined when they deal with physical events. Just use a descriptive physical language. When the stimulus events for one person involve the behavior of another (teacher's praise), then the same rules as used in defining behavioral events apply.

In selecting methods for recording behavioral events, first decide whether the behavior can be counted meaningfully. If it can, count the number of times the behavior occurs in a unit of time to get the behavior rate. If the behavior is continuous (or of widely varying durations), use a time-interval method. For a given time interval record whether or not the behavior occurs. Then use as your measure the per cent of time intervals in which the behavior occurs.

The final part of this lesson presented three behavior-change studies by teachers learning about behavior modification. The basic steps common to these studies were the definition of a target behavior, determination of a measurement procedure, determination of a change procedure, executing the change, and recording the progress on a graph to see if the procedure worked.

Unit 3. Consequences: Basic Principles

There are three main procedures for use of consequent stimuli to modify operant behavior:

1 *Reinforcement.* Follow responses you wish to strengthen with reinforcing events. Reinforcing events can include both the presentation (positive reinforcers) and termination (negative reinforcers) of stimuli.

2 *Extinction.* Weaken undesired responses by stopping the reinforcement that is keeping them going.

3 *Punishment.* Follow responses you wish to weaken with punishing events. Punishing events can include both the presentation of stimuli (which are generally called aversive stimuli), and the withholding of reinforcers. As will be seen, punishing by withholding reinforcers (as in *time out* and *response cost* procedures) is usually more effective.

Unit 4. The Criticism Trap

Parents and teachers fall into the criticism trap when they use only criticism to control the behavior of children. Because the children temporarily stop the undesirable behavior, the adult feels that the criticism is having the desired effect. Systematic observations, however, reveal that often the undesirable behavior increases rather than decreases. This is especially likely to happen when the child gets attention from adults only for misbehavior. To escape the criticism trap the teacher must establish conditions that permit praise more often and criticism less. The conditions required to change the teacher's behavior include devising ways to prompt more frequent praising, getting the praising responses going, and then devising reinforcers so that she can keep at the task long enough for changes in the children to become apparent.

Among the ways to cue or prompt the use of praise are: (1) making the misbehavior of one child the cue to praise another child who is behaving correctly; (2) giving out tokens to prompt praising behavior; and (3) putting up signs in the room to remind you to praise. Role playing, or practicing the behavior involved in praising, seems to be an effective way to develop the strength of the praising behavior. An effective way of getting reinforcement for increased praising behavior is for the teacher or an observer to keep a record of the teacher's behavior. A procedure is selected for recording praise behavior, specific periods are identified when the record will be kept, a baseline record of frequency of praise is taken, and the results are graphed daily.

Unit 5. Varieties of Reinforcers and Punishers

1 Reinforcing and punishing stimuli can be first divided into *unlearned* and *learned* varieties. Other names for these two classes are: *primary* and *secondary, unconditioned* and *conditioned*.

2 Neutral stimulus events can be made into reinforcers if they are closely followed by effective reinforcers. We teach children to respond to praise by pairing it with food, warmth, and other reinforcers.

3 Events can become punishers by pairing them with punishers. "No" followed closely by a hand slap can quickly teach the two-year-old to stop reaching for the lamp when mother says "No."

4   Three groups of reinforcers important to the teacher are social reinforcers, token reinforcers, and activity reinforcers.
   a) *Social reinforcers* involve the teacher's behavior—words of praise, attention, smiles, nearness.
   b) *Token reinforcers* are things such as money, poker chips, points, and gold stars that can be exchanged for other reinforcers.
   c) *Activity reinforcers* are activities children like to participate in when given a chance. These might include running, games, art activities, singing, eating, recesses, going home.

5   Premack principle says that any behavior a child will readily engage in can be used to reinforce behavior he will not readily engage in. You simply require that the less preferred activity be performed before the more preferred activity is allowed. The more preferred behavior is made contingent on the less preferred behavior.

6   The general procedure in using reinforcers is to make the reinforcer contingent on the occurrence of the desired response. If the correct behavior occurs, the reinforcer is given; if the correct behavior does not occur, the reinforcer is not given.

Unit 6. Differential Reinforcement: Use of Discriminative Stimuli in Classroom Management

Operant behavior can be brought under the control of preceding stimuli through the use of differential reinforcement. In the presence of the appropriate stimuli, the appropriate responses are reinforced. Inappropriate responses are not reinforced. Discriminative stimuli are cues to let students know when to do what—when to work, when to play, what to do when working, what to do when a task is finished.

Prompts are discriminative stimuli a child can already respond to (such as instruction words) that can be used to get the appropriate response to occur in a new learning situation. In using prompts, the new stimulus should be given before the prompt is given. Prompts gradually are withdrawn when they are no longer needed as the new $S^D \rightarrow R \rightarrow S^R$ relationships become established. This gradual withdrawal of prompts is called fading.

Behavior chains consist of sequences of behavior interconnected by discriminative stimuli. The chains are held together because each S^D also becomes a conditioned reinforcer. To establish a behavior chain, each step in the chain is initially prompted. The prompts are gradually faded as the completion of one part of the chain provides the cues for the next part.

The use of discriminative stimuli in classroom management was illustrated by a variety of examples. Rules can be used to let the children know what is expected classroom behavior. They need to be made effective by reinforcement: following rules is praised; violating rules is ignored or punished.

The way in which equipment and furniture is arranged in the classroom can also provide discriminative stimuli for appropriate behavior. Different activity areas or seating arrangements can serve as cues for the teaching or play activities to go on in them. The planning of the daily program should allow for different rates of task completion. For example, assigning a cushion activity along with an instructional task lets the child know what to do when the instructional task is completed. At the same time, a cushion activity may be used to reinforce behavior on the instructional task. The use of name tags, signs, lists on the blackboard, individual folders, check-out stations, and turn-in boxes can serve to prompt expected behaviors without a lot of teacher nagging and children's questions. By maintaining some consistency in the daily routine, it is possible to make the completion of one task the cue for the next. Chains of behavior are established and reduce the need for teacher prompting.

In teaching children to follow instructions, it is important to be very specific in stating what to do under what conditions. Specific instructions teach the children exactly what stimuli to respond to in what sequence.

Keep in mind that learning to respond to discriminative stimuli is what makes us smart, sensitive to others, and a socialized person.

Unit 7. Differential Reinforcement: Shaping

Shaping is one of the two major ways to get responses going in the presence of a specified stimulus. (Prompting is the second way.) The two essential procedures in shaping are differential reinforcement and shifting criterion for reinforcement. Differential reinforcement refers to reinforcing only responses that meet a certain criterion. A shifting criterion for reinforcement means that the response characteristics to be reinforced are gradually changed to become more like the target behavior that you want to teach. For example, if you are working with a child who doesn't sit in his seat and work, but runs around the room all the time, you might first reinforce him for being near his desk for short periods of time. As the child begins to spend more time near his desk, you would shift your criterion for reinforcement to standing at his desk or sitting in his chair. Later the requirement would shift to being seated and having work materials on the desk in front of him, then to doing some work, then to doing increasing amounts of work, and finally to working independently for increasingly longer periods of time.

In shaping, the teacher has to go through the following steps:

1 Define the target behavior.
2 Decide what behavior you are going to build on.
3 Establish a reinforcer.
4 Outline a program of small steps to get to the target behavior.
5 Start training with the first criterion for reinforcement (the first step in your program).

6 Decide when to shift to a new requirement for reinforcement.
7 If the new requirement is not met, either return briefly to an earlier requirement and reinforce or add a new step in between and try again.
8 Repeat steps 6 and 7 until the target behavior is achieved.

Some responses that usually require shaping in school are working longer, working faster, paying attention, staying in one's seat, making the sounds of letters, handwriting, and learning athletic skills.

Shaping is an inefficient process compared with prompting. Therefore, remember this rule: Shaping is used when there are no prompts that can be used to produce the target behavior. Sometimes teachers use shaping when they really should be using prompts. This could be caused by a desire to be gentle and positive or by an inability to use prompts effectively.

Unit 8. When to Reinforce

1 Immediate reinforcement is most effective. However, delays can be overcome by telling the students exactly what they did that you like.
2 Reinforce improvement.
3 To get behavior going, reinforce each time. To keep it going, reinforce on a variable-intermittent schedule.
4 Avoid predictable reinforcement when persistence is desired.
5 Avoid occasionally reinforcing undesired behavior. Be consistent.

review exercises

Unit 1

1 State how knowledge from the experimental study of behavior clearly implies that people are responsible for each other.
2 Give examples of how the findings from the use of scientific method can be used to support or enhance human values, to build a better world.
3 Define these terms:
   a) cause
   b) independent variable
   c) dependent variable
   d) scientific control
   e) determinism
   f) indeterminism
   g) free will
   h) predestination
4 State the basis for the belief that behavior is lawful.
5 State the differences between natural control and social control.
6 State the fallacy in the position that the "Heisenberg principle of indeterminacy implies that some events are not caused."
7 Explain how "freedom of choice" can exist in a determined world.

8 Explain how laws of nature differ from laws of state and how these concepts help to clarify these polarities:
   determinism— chance
   coercion   — freedom of choice
9 Explain how a person can be responsible in a determined world.
10 Define a circular explanation, give an example, and contrast circular explanations with causal explanations.
11 Answer the charge that behavior theory is too simplistic.
12 Explain the fallacy in the "bribery issue."
13 State why the teacher should take responsibility for the success of each student.

Unit 2

1 What is the difference between operant and respondent behavior?
2 Give three examples of an operant behavior.
3 Give three examples of respondent behavior.
4 Give examples of discriminative stimuli.
5 In what way are discriminative stimuli like eliciting stimuli and how are they different?
6 How do consequent stimuli differ from eliciting and discriminative stimuli?
7 Give examples of two different kinds of consequent stimuli.
8 What difficulty arises from descriptions based on trait labels and internal events, when it comes to the scientific study of behavior?
9 Give examples of objective definitions of behavior.
10 Give examples of nonobjective definitions of behavior.
11 What are the characteristics of easily countable behavior?
12 How do you measure behaviors that are not easily counted because of their continuous nature or highly varying duration?
13 Describe the essential steps common to behavior-change projects as reported in this unit.
Be prepared to discuss this issue:
14 Does the fact that internal events, such as feelings and thoughts, are not readily studied mean that they are not important?

Unit 3

1 Specify three general procedures for dealing with classroom behavior problems.
2 Give one of the three main procedures for the use of consequences and illustrate it with an example.
3 Give another principle for the use of consequences and illustrate it with an example.

4 Give another principle for the use of consequences and illustrate it with an example.

5 Define and give an example of *negative reinforcement*.

6 Define and give an example of *response cost*.

7 Define and give an example of *time out*.

8 Define and give an example of *extinction*.

9 What is the critical difference between time out and extinction?

10 Specify the difference between reinforcer (or reinforcing stimulus) and reinforcement.

11 Specify the difference between punisher (or punishing stimulus) and punishment.

12 Suggest a way the principle of reinforcement might be used in international affairs.

13 Identify two uses of reinforcement in the business world.

14 Identify a use of response cost by the local police department.

15 Give an example of the punishment principle from your everyday experience.

16 Give an example of negative reinforcement from your everyday experience.

Unit 4

1 Specify exactly what trap is involved in the criticism trap.

2 Describe a study that illustrates the criticism trap.

3 What are the two main principles to use in getting out of the criticism trap?

4 Describe a program that might be used to help someone get out of the criticism trap.

5 Describe experimental studies indicating successful procedures for getting parents and teachers to increase praise behavior.

6 What is the "being helpful" trap?

7 How is the being helpful trap like the criticism trap?

Unit 5

1 State the Premack principle and give an example of its use.

2 Define and give an example of an *unlearned reinforcer*.

3 Define and give an example of a *conditioned reinforcer*.

4 Define and give an example of a *conditioned punisher*.

5 Define and give an example of an *unlearned punisher*.

6 Define *social reinforcer* and give an example.

7 Define *token reinforcer* and give an example.

8 How are social reinforcers and token reinforcers the same?

9 How are social reinforcers and token reinforcers different?

10 Define *contingency*.

11 Give an example of contingent reinforcement.

12 Give an example to show how a child might learn to respond to an adult's attention as a reinforcing event.

13 Specify five classroom activities that might function as contingent reinforcers for appropriate behavior.

14 Suggest a procedure for determining whether a particular activity (finger painting) might be used to increase the frequency with which Johnny does arithmetic without actually trying it as a reinforcer.

15 State what special significance the Premack principle has for the teacher.

16 The studies presented in Broadening Your Perspective describe the use of both group and individual contingencies. What is the difference in these procedures?

17 What is noncontingent reinforcement? Give an example.

Unit 6

1 Define differential reinforcement and state how this procedure is used to establish discriminative stimuli.

2 Give examples of discriminative stimuli commonly used in the classroom.

3 Define and give examples of prompts.

4 Give two rules for using prompts.

5 Describe what is involved in a behavior chain.

6 State the two functions of discriminative stimuli in a chain.

7 Give one procedure for establishing a behavior chain.

8 Explain a procedure for teaching children to follow the classroom rules.

9 Summarize the procedures involved in the "specify, praise, and ignore" approach.

10 Give an example of how one might arrange a classroom to support specific types of teaching activities.

11 Explain one value in following a daily routine.

12 Describe a procedure to use in teaching children to follow instructions.

13 Explain why rules or instructions tend not to be effective by themselves.

14 Name five prompts you might encounter in a typical day outside of the classroom.

15 What is the effect of fixed-interval testing on study behavior?

16 Give an example of self-prompting (other than the one given by Lovitt and Curtiss in unit 6).

17 Consider the method used by Doke and Risley to study the effects of classroom structure and suggest another study that could be carried out with this method.

18 When is praise a prompt?

19 Are people's personalities fixed regardless of setting?

Unit 7

1　State the two essential procedures in the process called shaping.
2　Define *differential reinforcement.*
3　Define *shifting criterion for reinforcement.*
4　Give an example of differential reinforcement as it is used in the classroom.
5　Give an example of a shifting requirement for reinforcement as it is used in the classroom.
6　Specify one behavior that a teacher might try to get going through shaping.
7　Describe the steps involved in building a shaping program.
8　How do shaping principles enter into Skinner's writing program?
9　Explain why shaping is a good procedure to use in developing athletic skills.
10　Describe a procedure for training a subject to respond quickly.
11　State the rule about when to shape.
12　Give an example to show the use of physical prompting in shaping.
13　Describe a procedure for shaping attending for 10 minutes with a child who can attend for only 10 seconds.

Unit 8

1　Why is immediate reinforcement important?
2　Give three ways a teacher can surmount the difficulties faced in trying to give immediate reinforcement to a whole class.
3　Why should the teacher focus on reinforcing improvement?
4　Define these terms and give an example of each:
　continuous reinforcement
　intermittent reinforcement
　fixed-ratio schedule
　fixed-interval schedule
　variable-ratio schedule
　variable-interval schedule
　resistance to extinction
5　For each of the classes of schedules mentioned in question 4, describe the effects of the schedule on behavior when it is in effect, and when the schedule is terminated (extinction).
6　Explain the steps you would take to teach persistent behavior.
7　Why should predictable reinforcement be avoided for continuous-stream behaviors like on task?
8　Explain why conditioned reinforcers are often preferred over unconditioned reinforcers in teaching.
9　Why is it important to be consistent in not reinforcing an undesired behavior?

unit 10

Using Social and Activity Reinforcers

objectives

After completing this unit you should be able to—

1 Demonstrate the use of a variety of social and activity reinforcers.
2 Make your praise descriptive rather than evaluative.
3 Distinguish between reinforcers in scheduled activities and "cushion" activities.
4 Specify some themes likely to make story content more fun for children.
5 Tell how to put drama and suspense into your teaching style.
6 Demonstrate procedures for maintaining good attention.
7 Demonstrate a variety of procedures for making drills fun.
8 Discuss and demonstrate some teaching objectives for the first day of class.

lesson

Too often novices in the field of behavior modification take a mechanical approach to using reinforcers. They forget all they may have learned about how to be playful and how to convert work into fun. Perhaps this unit will serve as an antidote for being stuffy, rigid, or uptight, depending on your generation.

In unit 3 the study of Mrs. E. and her classroom revealed some interesting changes. Initially, Mrs. E. did not know how to say nice things to children. She primarily criticized them. Just telling her to praise more was not enough. She had to practice a lot of different ways before she could do it in class. Even then, for three weeks the classroom observers reported that she gave phony praise. However, her students showed great improvement; the praise was not phony to them, but very important. New behavior is often stilted and somewhat disorganized. Well-practiced behavior becomes natural. It took a while for Mrs. E. to be comfortable with her new behavior.

We learned two things from this experience. First, some people have to be *taught how to praise*. We cannot assume that everybody knows how. Second, initial efforts at praising might seem quite uncomfortable or unnatural for the person doing it, as well as for observers. However, if one stays with it, praising becomes natural. *The teacher must take the role of an actor playing at being a "fun teacher" until he or she becomes one.*

Using Social Reinforcers

Social reinforcers are forms of teacher behavior that act as reinforcing stimuli. They include such things as words of praise, friendly facial expressions, physical nearness, and physical contact. The first step in learning to be good at social reinforcement is to identify, study, and practice a variety of potential social reinforcers. Below is an initial list. In the exercise section, you will have a chance to add to this list, tie appropriate social reinforcers to classroom behavior and situations, and role-play using social reinforcers.

Praising Words and Phrases

Good.	That shows a great deal of work.
That's right.	You really pay attention.
Excellent.	You should show this to your parents.
That's clever.	I like that.
Exactly.	Show the class your picture.
Fine answer.	That's interesting.
Good job.	See how well Joan is working.
Good thinking.	Jimmy got right down to work after
Thank you.	recess; he's going to finish on time.
I'm pleased with that.	Let's all give John a round of applause.
Great.	That was very kind of you.

Facial Expressions

Smiling	Looking interested
Winking	Laughing
Nodding	

Nearness

Walking among students	Joining the class at recess
Sitting in their group	Eating with the children

Physical Contact

Touching	Stroking arm
Patting head, shoulder, or back	Shaking hand
Hugging	Holding hand
Holding on lap	

Make It Work—Use Behavior-Specific Praise

Dr. Haim Ginott, author of *Between Parent and Child,* has pointed out that often a child does not react to what we consider praise. Take a child who has been repeatedly told he is stupid and who has failed often. He is not likely to be overwhelmed with joy by a teacher telling him, "You are smart." The praise statement doesn't fit with his own experience. On the other hand, if this same child has been working hard for twenty minutes to complete ten long division problems and he gets them all done correctly, he might believe this: "I saw you working hard on your arithmetic for twenty minutes. I've checked every problem and every one is right. And you know, your writing is really neat and clear." This *describes* what the child did and shows appreciation by the detailed attention given to the child's work or behavior. Ginott says it's usually better to make praise *descriptive* rather than *evaluative*. *Describe—don't judge.* Praise specific behavior.

There is much to be said for this viewpoint. The less you know about a child, the more likely it is that descriptive praise will be effective and evaluative praise will miss the mark. However, it is also possible to make phrases such as "good," "great," and "that's clever" effective for children by initially accompanying such phrases with descriptive statements.

"Jimmy watched carefully throughout the whole lesson. That's paying attention well."

"Mary is sitting up straight with her hands on her desk, ready to listen. She's going to be a good listener."

"Aaron, you kept at that one for a long time and you finally got it. That's good working. When we work hard, we learn."

By repeatedly providing explicit examples of good working, good listening, good talking, good responding, and good thinking, we teach the children what we mean by such praise statements. Later, the statements "good listening," "clever answer," and "that's what I call smart" are not empty phrases. In the small group teaching procedures developed by Engelmann, it is important that praise be given quickly so as not to detract greatly from teaching time. Short phrases are preferred. "Good sitting" is much to be preferred to "I like the way you are sitting." "Good listening" is preferred to "I like the way you are watching the book and listening to me."

There are systematic ways to make short phrases effective. Simply describing what a child does or did that you appreciate is the first step to effective praising. Tying such descriptive phrases to short praise words is the next step in making teaching efficient. Finally, the teacher uses a mixture of short statements or gestures to signify approval or correctness, and more detailed descriptions of praiseworthy behavior. *Remember: Make praise descriptive. Praise the behavior; not the whole child.*

Using Activity Reinforcers

Next to praise, reinforcing activities are the most readily available motivating tool the teacher has. Yet, so often the teacher just gives away these potential reinforcers without using them to help motivate students.

Scheduled Activities

In using activity reinforcers, the first step is to build two lists of things the students like to do. The first should be a chronological list, containing possible reinforcing events that are scheduled to occur during the day. This list will prompt the use of these events to help teach. Figure 10.1 shows a list made by one teacher.

In using the events on your "scheduled activities list," have the children earn a privilege by doing good work or improving behavior. Say, "Toni finished her paper first. She can help me collect the papers." Or, "Jeff, you really improved in your arithmetic group today. You can choose the game for recess." Or, "Class, you have all completed your reading assignments five minutes early. That means we get an extra long recess today." Rather than just following a routine automatically, use the fun things coming up to promote social and academic learning.

Going to recess, lunch, or home.   Children are usually excited just before a fun activity. Going to recess, going to lunch, and going home often lead to considerable excitement and horsing around. The good manager recognizes from the start that these are times when the teacher has a lot of reinforcement power and can use it to teach desired behavior. A rowdy class should not be dismissed just because the teacher would like to get rid of all the noise. The consequences for noise and confusion could be partial loss of recess, a delay in lunch, or a delay in getting out to go home.

Playing teacher.   In small group instruction, playing teacher can be used to reinforce good work. Special reinforcers like this are especially helpful for working on repetitive tasks, such as learning arithmetic facts or sounds. "If you do a good job in working all these problems on your sheet, you can be teacher and write a problem on the board." Along the way, reminders are given, "Oh, I think John is going to be a teacher. He's really working . . . and so is Tommy. Look at him go . . . We're going to have a lot of teachers today."

Some other items on a scheduled activity reinforcer list might include:

Running errands	Supervising a group outside of class
Being excused from a test	Competing with another class
Taking care of class pets	Having the lesson outdoors
Choosing where to sit	Being called on to answer questions
Telling a joke to the class	Special holiday events and parties
Being in a skit	

Special events.   The last item on the above list deserves additional discussion. Our society provides many occasions for reinforcing social behavior, but often they are not used as contingencies. Throughout the seasons, the teacher can use holidays as a time for children to earn special reinforcing events. Halloween, Thanksgiving, Christmas, Valentine's Day, and Easter are some of the fun holidays for children. The teacher can use the activities, plays, and parties surrounding these events as consequences for improved behavior. For example, one teacher had her first graders work to get their names on a list to send to Santa Claus. As a general rule, the teacher should not exclude any child from an event that all children in the class are entitled to, regardless of special requirements. However, special things the teacher might do with her own class can be set up so that they are special consequences for good work.

Reinforcing Cushion Activities

The teacher also needs a list of reinforcing activities that can be used at any time during the day or during free periods. Where materials and supplies are involved, it is ideal to have an activity center in part of the room or in another room, if supervision is available. When certain classroom requirements have been met, time in free choice activities is allotted. Where space does not permit an activities center, the list should be restricted to activities that can be used at the student's desk. Here are some suggestions:

New and interesting books	Time in the library
Music listening station	Time with teacher
Pocket radio with earphone	Studying with a friend
Games of all sorts	Ping pong
Puppets	Basketball
Art materials	Puzzles
Models	Teaching machines
Construction materials	Tape recorder

Embedding Social and Activity Reinforcers in Tasks

Task-embedded reinforcers are built into the teaching presentation. They can involve the content (or lesson material) of the teacher's presentation or the style. For a play to be good, you need a good script (content) and good actors to deliver it (style). A good script provides periodic reinforcers to the audience, in the form of humor, surprises, or relief from a tense situation. Good acting involves a style of delivery that will catch and hold the audience's attention. While we do not pretend to have formal data on what constitutes good content and good style in teaching, a number of themes and procedures have been found effective with a wide variety of children.

Reinforcing Content

Most children enjoy themes involving food, people making silly mistakes, unusual animals, surprises, and the like. Arithmetic problems can be made fun by embedding some surprises in them. "O.K., this is a story about Bob. Bob started out with four teeth. He went to sleep and when he woke up,

Time	Period	Reinforcing Activities
9:00	Opening Exercises	Lead the salute "Show and tell"
9:15	Reading groups	Pass out seat work Play teacher Read to the group Read for another student Collect papers
10:15	Recess	Go to recess first Go to recess early Choose games at recess Be group leader
10:40	Arithmetic	Help teacher hand out papers Help another student Extra page of "special problems" Collect papers
11:20	Music	Lead the class in a song Extra time for music
11:40	Lunch	Go to lunch first
12:15	Spelling-Writing	Help teacher Team competition on spelling Get to do "toughies"
12:45	Special Events	Go to a movie, TV, assembly, field trip
1:25	Social Studies	Reports to the class Filmstrip
2:05	Gym	Go to gym first Earn extra gym time
2:40	Free time-study time	Use play material during study time
3:15	Go home	Go home first Go home early

Figure 10.1 A scheduled activity-reinforcer list

what do you think happened? He had grown five more teeth. Wow! How many teeth did he end up with?"

The following is an example of a fun reading story from the Distar ® Library Series.

The Hill Of Hair

Bill was a man. Bill did not like to have his hair cut. His hair hid his neck. His hair hid his arms. His hair even hid his legs.

Bill went on a bus. He said to the man on the bus, "Stop at a farm."

The man on the bus said, "Is this a man or a hill of hair?"

Bill went to the farm. He said to the man on the farm, "I need ten eggs."

The man on the farm said, "Is this a man or a hill of hair?"

Bill got the eggs and left the farm. He met a cop. Bill said, "How do I get to the pet shop?"

The cop said, "Is this a man or a hill of hair?"

So Bill went to the pet shop. The man in the pet shop said, "I will lock up this hill of hair." So he did.

Bill said, "Let me go. I am not a pet. I am a man."

But the man in the pet shop did not let him go. The man in the pet shop said, "I will see if this is a pet or a man."

So he cut Bill's hair. He cut and cut and cut.

He said, "Now I can see legs."

He cut and cut. Then he said, "Now I can see arms."
He cut and cut. "Now I can see ears," he said.
Then he said, "Now I see that this is not a pet. This is a man."
So Bill went home. He said, "I like this hair cut. Now I am not a hill of hair. I am a man with no hair."

Selecting or creating material with unusual, dramatic, or even silly content is a big step toward motivating learners. Too often it seems as if educators consider it wrong for children to have fun while learning in school. At least that is the inference one might make from a review of widely used curriculum materials.

Making Neutral Content Reinforcing

Any neutral stimulus event can become a conditioned reinforcer if the neutral stimulus is repeatedly followed by a reinforcer. "Learning for its own sake" can come about if learning activities are initially followed by reinforcing events. This simply means that the effective use of reinforcers in teaching will automatically embed reinforcers in the tasks being taught. Any steps the teacher can take to provide more reinforcement for school activities will have the effect of embedding conditioned reinforcers in those activities. The remainder of this unit deals specifically with how to accomplish this.

A Reinforcing Style

If the teacher responds as if the material were interesting and exciting, the children are more likely to respond that way too. If she laughs and makes comments about why an example is funny, the children will tend to react the same way. Unfortunately, a teacher may have good material but present it in a deadpan way. The effect of the good material is likely to be lost if the children are not prompted by the teacher's reaction that it's O.K. to have fun in school. The teacher needs to be a bit of a clown.

Creating drama and suspense. Getting and holding the audience's attention is the primary task of the actor and the teacher. Without this attention, what follows does not matter. The key to holding attention in any situation is to provide variable intermittent reinforcement for attending behavior. Variations in pacing, rhythm, loudness, and pauses are essential elements in attention-holding presentations. Such variations can be made in silly ways:

"I can say it. The window is *iiiiin* the wall. You say it with *meeeeee*"—hold the *e* while looking to see if everyone is waiting and watching—"now!"

Variations can be made in dramatic and suspenseful ways: "This is a tough one. I don't think you will be able to do it." This is followed by a dramatic pause as the teacher is poised ready to write an arithmetic problem or a letter or number for identification drill. After the children get it right, the teacher acts surprised. "I didn't think you could do that. You guys really are smart today."

There are two points in the presentation of a teaching task at which variable pausing is particularly important. The first point is between the time the teacher signals the children to pay attention to her ("Everybody listen—" *pause*) and the presentation of the task ("We are going to count to four"). By varying the time interval between the signal and presenting the task, careful attending is more likely to be strengthened. Attention is focused on what is coming next and this attending is likely to be reinforced by the eventual presentation of the task and the chance to respond. The second point is between the time the teacher presents a task ("We are going to count to four—" *pause*) and the time she signals the children that she wants them to respond ("Count to four"). These pauses are important to good teaching. They help maintain attention and insure strong responding by the children. The children see the teacher as playing a game in which she is trying to catch them not attending. If some children do not attend, or if they respond at the wrong time, the teacher can act as if she tricked them: "I caught you that time."

Variations in rhythm, loudness, or almost any other stimulus that the teacher can control are also likely to help in getting and holding attention. Another approach is to hint about what is coming next without revealing your cards. Good teaching does not present all the examples at once and then work through them. Examples are presented one at a time. That way, the display is constantly changed and constantly new. Every so often an especially dramatic or humorous example might be inserted. Picture materials for a lesson should be kept out of sight (face down on your lap for example) until it is time to use them. Let the children know you have something for them to see, but don't show what it is. Build surprises into your teaching sequences.

Converting drills into games. Races are good ways to get the children involved quickly in tasks that require a lot of practice or repetition to master. The teacher draws a score box on the board with a box for *Me* and a box for *You.*

Score Box

Me	IИ
You	IИI

"Every time I win, I'll put a mark up here. Every time you win, I'll put a mark down here." The teacher begins the race, starting with easy questions. "What's one plus two?—Three. I won. I'll bet I can get more points than you!" The teacher gets ahead in the early part and then lets the children win more and more as the race proceeds. The teacher should continue to act as if winning were really important to her and make such statements as "You were just lucky on that one. I'm still going to beat you!" The teacher can also pretend to be bothered as she loses more. "This game is no fun. I think we should change to a better game. Oh, well, I don't care about winning anyway." On subsequent days the teacher can actually let the children coax her into playing the game by acting reluctant.

Races can be used for many tasks in which a brief intensive drill is required, such as learning the sounds of letters, the names of numbers and letters, addition and subtraction facts, rhymes, and the names of parts of objects.

Deliberately Making Mistakes

In reviewing material that is already fairly well learned, the teacher should occasionally make intentional errors. Children just love to catch the teacher making errors on material they know. They are often quite indignant when a mistake is made and quickly attempt to correct the situation. The teacher might write the wrong answer on the board after *saying* the right answer. She might misread a word or an arithmetic problem. If the children miss the mistake, the teacher gloats, "I really fooled you that time! Do you really think nine plus two equals seven?" When the children catch the error they will tend to gloat and act proud. The use of foolers is fun, and it also teaches the children *not to depend on the teacher as an authority, but rather to evaluate the truth of statements for themselves.*

Taking a Negative Approach

In teaching logical or mathematical rules, the teacher can maintain attention and interest while providing practice by giving instances of the rule. The teacher first demonstrates the rule with a few instances. Then he presents a new instance and says, "I bet it won't work with this problem." When it does he continues to act surprised and a little displeased. The children are also challenged to find examples where the rule is not true.

By taking the negative approach, the teacher introduces an element of suspense into the presentation. The children get reinforced by seeing that the teacher was wrong (playfully), and they learn that the rule is true in all cases.

The First Day of Class

First impressions are very important in school. Positive or negative attitudes can be established very quickly and may determine how easy it is for you to handle any problem situation later. Make the first day dramatic for you and the students. Begin with a group activity that is aimed at getting the children involved in some subject to be covered that year. Forget the curriculum guide; try to show the children why learning in your class will be important to them.

Younger Children

With younger children, you need to focus on shorter-term payoffs, such as making adding into a race, or using letter sounds as the basis for a bingo game. Start with a short teaching lesson for the whole group, and use some of the methods suggested in this unit to make it a fun presentation and get the kids going with you. Then use what you have taught them as the basis for a game with the group. Follow this up with a short assignment that they can do on their own. Move around the room, praising examples of good work. You are teaching the rules for good working. Only after you have demonstrated that learning can be fun and that everyone is to work hard while having fun, do you focus on activities designed to help everyone get acquainted. Name tags might be handed out, and the children given a chance to introduce themselves if necessary. Then break them into teams for an upcoming recess game; or, if the children do not know each other, devise a game designed around the children's names.

Remember that the first day the objectives should be to show the children you like them as well as to show them you are going to teach them. Make yourself important to them so that later they will want to please you. Keep a surprise tucked up your sleeve for later in the day, such as passing out their first books, a visit by a pet, a small party, a new game, or a movie or TV presentation. Try to have something they can take home with them that encourages them to tell mother about their first day.

Older Children

We know a high school teacher who came into his social science class, set a tape recorder on the desk, and turned it on without saying one word. It played the number 1 popular song. When the song was over he said, "Now that I have your attention . . ." and immediately started into a series of short stories about some dramatic changes in people and systems. He indicated to the students that by understanding the principles underlying those dramatic changes, they could change their whole lives, gaining new knowledge to use in working on the problems of people and society. He ended the class five minutes early, allowing no class participation . . . ." I will see you tomorrow. You may prepare for that by doing your first assignment tonight. Assignment sheets may be picked up on the way out." The class was nearly speechless. They left quietly and thoughtfully. They looked forward to class the next day.

Periodically, this teacher would come up with a new surprise. Jokes were tucked into his quizzes. He found good movies that told a real message. "Music to take exams by" was introduced to the school. Fun examples that were personally relevant were built into lectures and discussion. As a joke, he attached a piece of candy to each of the first exams he handed back. The strange thing was that the teacher found himself spending more and more time developing good presentation material and surprises, because he was reinforced by a vitally appreciative reaction from his students.

summary

Using social and activity reinforcers involves a number of skills. Their full development will not occur just from reading a few pages. You will get some ideas of what to do when, but you also need practice. Some of the exercises we have suggested for group presentation might get you to practice the ideas presented in this unit. A good procedure for practicing is to: (1) specify a setting, (2) specify what you are trying to learn to do better (for example, use behavior-specific praise, make a routine task more fun, turn on a high school class), then (3) tape record a performance, (4) listen to it, and (5) record it again. Some alternative procedures are to practice before a mirror or team up with a friend and take turns playing teacher and student. The *out loud practice* is essential to learning new behaviors of this sort. Take the task seriously.

Social reinforcers include words of praise, friendly facial expressions, physical nearness, and physical contact. It is important to cultivate an appropriate repertoire of such behaviors. In using praise describe the behavior you like. Be factual, not judgmental. Many activity reinforcers are available. The teacher should think about developing two lists, one related to the daily schedule and a second composed of activities that can be used any time. It is important to learn to use activities contingently. Set it up so that activities the children enjoy are used as consequences for good work. Special activities such as going home, to lunch, or to recess can also be used to carefully teach appropriate group behavior at such times. Do not let a noisy class go to lunch, unless you want them to learn to be more noisy. Think carefully about the many ways you can use the seasonal holiday activities to help support learning in your class.

It is also important to make teaching more fun by embedding social and activity reinforcers in the instructional tasks themselves. Select content known to be funny, surprising, or dramatic and present the material in a way that will get and hold attention. The key to getting and holding attention is in the use of variations in pacing, rhythm, loudness, and pauses. Some other procedures for teaching in a fun style involve making games out of drills, deliberately making mistakes, and taking a negative approach to a universal rule. The possible ways in which teaching can be made fun as well as productive are limited only by one's imagination.

And finally, prepare well for that first day. It can make or break the school year.

broadening your perspective

Activity Reinforcers Motivate Adolescents Who Have Been Kicked Out of Regular School

Shlomo Cohen has been running a learning center for 150 students ejected from other schools in Anne Arundel County, Maryland. The program operates in four army barracks of World War II vintage at Fort Meade. Three of the barracks are work areas for major academic studies. The fourth barrack is used as the Student Activities Center, or reinforcer area.

Most of the teaching materials are programed and divided into tasks that last thirty to sixty minutes. A checkout is given at the completion of each task. Students freely opt into and out of the study areas. However, showing appropriate study behaviors and completing academic tasks (which they contract to do) are necessary to earn tickets good for time in the Activities Center. The activities program is announced the week before, and the students have to sign up for many of them since there is limited space. For example, a crafts period might be limited to ten students, a trip to the swimming pool to fifteen, a softball game to twenty, indoor games (ping pong, pool, and others) to ten. The vending machine area is open at specified times for snacks and drinks. Tokens to use in the vending machines (called "skins" for Skinnerian) are given out for showing desirable behavior in the Activities Center. There is also a contingency contracting system established with parents, providing home-based reinforcers (money, use of car, and so on) when the Activities Center program is not enough. (These latter procedures are discussed more fully in unit 12.)

Over a four-year period, the Learning Center has been remarkably successful. The Center is able to graduate about ten students a month and take in ten new ones. The positive focus, the use of programed materials and a contracting system, backed up by the reinforcers available in the Activities Center and home, are probably responsible for the program's success.

It is not difficult to imagine an alternative school of this sort operating within a high school or in cooperation with several junior and senior high schools. On the other hand, if some of the procedures used to motivate the teenagers in the Learning Center were used as a standard part of a high school program, there would probably be no need for an alternative school.[1]

Home-Based Reinforcement

Achievement Place is a home for court-referred, neglected boys. Jon Bailey, Montrose Wolf, and Elery Phillips explored the effects of a daily report card from school on study behavior and rule violations. An agreement was made with the five boys and their parents, that basic privileges could be earned each day by getting a good report at school. Basic privileges consisted of snacks, TV, and permission to go outside.

After a baseline period, the report card was introduced, and the teacher was instructed to give only "yeses" at first. This was to check the effect of the card, without a real contingency. At first there was some improvement, but not for long. Then, the teacher was instructed to give "yeses" for studying more than 90 percent of the time and rule violations less than 10 percent of the time (observer data were used to make these determinations). When clearly contingent "yeses" and "nos" were given, study behavior was above

90 percent and rule violations were under 5 percent of the observation intervals.[2]

Keep in mind that the activity reinforcers that back up your program at school may be provided by parents at home.

self-test

1 Ginott recommends that praise be _____ rather than evaluative.

2 Descriptive praise focuses on the details of behavior that the teacher wishes to _____.

3 Build one list of activity reinforcers tied to the daily _____ and another list of activities that can be used at any time.

4 The key to the use of activity reinforcers is to make them _____ on desired performance.

5 Good teaching requires a good script (_____) and good acting (_____).

6 Any neutral stimulus event can become a conditioned reinforcer if the neutral stimulus is repeatedly _____ by a reinforcer.

7 The key to maintaining attention in any situation is to provide _____ intermittent reinforcement for attending behavior.

8 A good way to build interest in the teacher's presentation is to _____ at material that is to be presented later without telling all about it.

9 How the teacher handles the first day of class is important in establishing the _____ of the students about the class.

NUMBER RIGHT _____

exercise 1 programed practice

1 practice

2 praising

3 improvement

4 actor

5 Social

6 descriptive

7 descriptive

8 evaluative

9 descriptions

10 higher, high;
   lower, low

11 reinforcers

12 not given

1 Telling Mrs. E. how to praise was not enough. She had to _____ lots of different ways of praising before she could do it in class.

2 Initial efforts at _____ may seem quite unnatural or uncomfortable.

3 Even though observers called Mrs. E.'s behavior "phony praise," the children who were praised showed _____ in their behavior.

4 The teacher must take the role of an _____ playing at being a fun teacher until the role becomes natural.

5 _____ reinforcers are conditioned reinforcers that involve behavior such as praising, giving attention, being near, smiling, and touching.

6 Ginott recommends that praise be _____ rather than evaluative.

7 "Jimmy watched carefully throughout the whole lesson" is an example of _____ praise.

8 "You're smart, Jake" is an example of _____ praise.

9 Short praise phrases can be made effective by initially accompanying such phrases with _____ of praiseworthy behavior.

10 The Premack principle states that any _____ frequency activity can be used to strengthen any _____ frequency behavior.

11 A common error in teaching occurs whenever the teacher gives away her _____.

12 Using reinforcers contingently means that the reinforcers are given after appropriate behavior and are _____ _____ after inappropriate behavior.

13 In using the events of your "scheduled activities list" set it up so that the children have _____ a privilege by good work.

14 A rowdy class should not be _____ just because the teacher would like to get rid of the noise.

15 The strong reinforcers tied to getting out of class can be used to _____ quiet and orderly behavior in the classroom.

16 Playing teacher might be used as a reinforcer, particularly when you need to sustain attention for long periods through _____ tasks.

17 To use events surrounding holidays as reinforcers, the teacher just needs to establish some _____ for earning the special privileges.

18 Reinforcing cushion activities are _____ by completion of other classroom requirements.

19 The key to the use of activity reinforcers is to make them _____ on desired performance.

20 Good teaching requires a good script (_____) and good acting (_____).

21 Most children enjoy _____ involving food, people making silly mistakes, unusual animals, surprises, and so forth.

22 Any neutral stimulus event can become a conditioned reinforcer if the neutral stimulus is repeatedly _____ by a reinforcer.

23 This means that the effective use of reinforcers in teaching will automatically _____ reinforcers in the tasks being taught.

13 earned

14 dismissed

15 teach

16 repetitive

17 requirements

18 earned

19 contingent

20 content;
   style

21 themes,
   stories

22 followed

23 embed

24 It is important for teachers to show by their behavior that it is all right for children to have _____ in school.

25 Getting and holding the _____ of the children is a primary teaching task.

26 The key to maintaining attention in any situation is to provide _____ intermittent reinforcement for attentive behavior.

27 Variations in pacing, rhythm, loudness, and _____ are the essential elements in presentations that hold attention.

28 The first point for variable pausing is between the time the teacher signals for _____ and the time she begins to present the lesson.

29 The second point for variable pausing is between the time the teacher completes her demonstration and the time she signals the children to _____ (to see if they have learned the task).

30 If some children do not attend, or if they respond at the wrong time, the teacher can act as if she _____ them: "I _____ you that time."

31 Unpredictable timing of the presentation of reinforcers has the effect of both _____ not attending and _____ careful attending.

32 A good way to build interest in the teacher's presentation is to _____ at material that is to be presented later without telling all about it.

33 Races are a good way to get the children involved quickly in tasks that require a lot of practice or _____ to master.

24 fun

25 attention

26 variable, unpredictable

27 pauses

28 attention

29 respond

30 tricked, fooled; caught

31 punishing; reinforcing

32 hint

33 repetition, drilling

34 early, first;
  end

35 reluctant

36 authority

37 does not;
  true

38 dramatic;
  involved

34 In the _____ part of a race the teacher gets ahead. Then she allows the children to catch up and get ahead by the _____ of the game.

35 On subsequent days the teacher can actually let the children coax her into playing the game by acting _____.

36 The use of foolers is fun, and it also teaches the children to evaluate the truth of statements for themselves rather than to depend on the teacher as an _____.

37 The negative approach involves teaching a rule and then trying to show an example for which the rule _____ _____ apply. The children learn to apply the rule to new examples, and they also learn that the rule is _____ in all cases.

38 The first day should be made _____ and instructional. It should be aimed at getting the kids _____ in what you have to teach.

exercise 2

Make a list of praise words and phrases that you would be comfortable using. There are no fixed answers for this exercise. Bring this list to the next group discussion.

1 _____

2 _____

3 _____

4 _____

5 _____

6 _____

7 _____

8 _____

9 _____

10 _____

11 _____

12 _____

13 _____

14 _____

15 _____

16 _____

17 _____

18 _____

19 _____

exercise 3

Make a list of reinforcing activities you might use as a classroom teacher. There are no fixed answers for this exercise. Bring this list to the next group discussion.

1 _____

2 _____

3 _____

4 _____

5 _____

6 _____

7 _____

8 _____

9 _____

10 _____

11 _____

12 _____

13 _____

14 _____

15 _____

16 _____

17 _____

18 _____

19 _____

discussion questions

1 Give examples of how social and activity reinforcers might be used in a high school classroom. Describe a situation and specify what you would do.

2 For each of the following incidents in full class instruction specify what you could say or do to handle the situation:
   a) The teacher needs papers passed out.
   b) It's time for recess. The room is noisy and the children are out of their seats.
   c) It's time for the Pledge of Allegiance.
   d) It's time to go home. The class is rowdy.
   e) The children are quietly working on an art project.
   f) The children return from recess in an orderly fashion.
   g) The bathroom group leader reports that everyone behaved well.
   h) Mary offers to help Linda finish cleaning up the paints so that Linda can go to recess on time.
   i) Bob's group works quietly on a science project while the rest of the class is seated and reading.
   j) Jimmy completes a three-minute task in arithmetic in three minutes. He has always taken twenty minutes before and needed a lot of coaxing.
   k) Cedrick's arithmetic paper is neater than it has ever been.
   l) Marty cleans up his messy desk without being asked.

m) Maria puts on her own boots at recess and doesn't plead for help as usual.

n) In a clear voice, John tells the class about his turtle. John usually talks softly, if at all.

3 For each of the following incidents in small group instruction specify what you could say or do:

a) Tom stays with a difficult arithmetic problem for seven minutes, without any success.

b) Five of six children are with you during a presentation. The sixth is not.

c) Charlie answers very quickly when called on in arithmetic.

d) Ann doesn't answer when called on for an individual task.

e) Bill answers when Ann is called on for an individual task.

f) A child asks to go to the bathroom in the middle of a lesson.

g) A child is on-task but is displaying mildly disruptive behavior such as foot tapping or chair rocking.

h) One child announces to the group and teacher that he doesn't like the tangible reinforcement (such as raisins or cookies) that the teacher is using for the group.

i) When asked to find something on the page, the children slap the presentation material, nearly knocking it out of the teacher's hand.

j) A child turns and talks to visitors during the teacher's presentation.

k) Virginia cries when she makes a mistake during her individual task.

l) The teacher calls on a child for an individual turn. The child nervously says, "I don't want a turn. I can't do it."

4 For each of the following times of the day, name three possible activity reinforcers the teacher might use:

a) Opening activities

b) Reading period

c) Seatwork or study period

5 Describe content material for children that is likely to be reinforcing or fun.

6 Describe the general procedure for embedding conditioned reinforcers in neutral material.

7 Describe a teaching style that is likely to create drama and suspense.

8 Indicate the two points in teaching a task at which it is important to use a variable pause.

9 Give an example of using the two pauses at the right places.

10 Present a teaching sequence showing the use of hinting.

11 Demonstrate the use of variable patterns of speech to make material interesting. Present the same task in a deadpan manner.

12 Demonstrate the procedure of making a drill into a race.

13 Demonstrate the procedure of making deliberate mistakes.

14 Demonstrate taking a negative approach in teaching the universality of a rule.

15 Outline the first day of class in kindergarten, in high school geometry.

unit 11

Designing and Using Token Reinforcement Systems

objectives

When you complete this unit you should be able to—

1 Describe the components of a token reinforcer system.
2 Indicate when such systems might be used and when they should not be used.
3 Explain why the use of special reinforcers is not bribery.
4 Describe the six main steps in designing a token system.
5 Design a token system for use in a special class.
6 Describe a variety of informal token systems.
7 Explain how to maintain the gains of special token reinforcer systems while eliminating the systems.

lesson

For many children, praise and grades are not enough to get them going. They have not learned to respond to praise from adults or to enjoy school tasks. School-work means failure and punishment; it has not paid off for them. They skip classes or drop out, turned off by teachers and school. When children have been exposed to such failure, strong, obvious, and immediate reinforcers for each response may be necessary, along with teaching programs that make success possible. Token reinforcement systems are one practical way to introduce stronger reinforcers in the classroom or at home.

In a token reinforcement system, points or some tangible, like poker chips, are given as the immediate reinforcer. Later, these are exchanged for reinforcing activities, edibles, or play materials. Token systems have been used successfully where other approaches have failed. The following examples show the power of special reinforcers.

An After-School Program for Potential Dropouts

Wolf, Giles, and Hall studied sixteen pupils from two elementary schools located in a low-income district of Kansas City. The children worked in a remedial teaching program during the summer and after school hours during the regular school year. Comparisons were made with a group that went to the regular school and did not take part in a remedial program.

The token reinforcement system used was somewhat like a trading stamp plan. The students had cards marked off into squares. The cards were checked by an instructor whenever a student had earned a point. Each checked square was a token. When a child first joined the program, points were given for each problem worked correctly. As the child did better, the amount and difficulty of the work required to earn points increased. The number of points given to a child for a particular bit of work was determined by the instructor alone or by bargaining with the child.

Filled pages of points could be exchanged for a variety of goods and events, such as the circus, swimming, the zoo, daily snacks, candy, soap, novelties, or long-range goals such as clothes or secondhand bicycles. A number of other contingencies were provided for in the program. In some instances, favorite subjects or popular activities could be attempted only after completion of work in less-favored areas. A bonus was given for attendance. Improvement in grades in the regular classroom led to a party after each grading period for all students who had improved. The students also received bonus points for reports of good behavior from their regular class teacher.

During each of the preceding two years the median gain by the remedial groups on an achievement test had been .6 year. The gain during the year of the remedial program for the token group was 1.5 years. Comments by the regular-school teachers suggest that the remedial program benefited the regular school classroom as well. Not only were the program children helped, but their increased participation and changed attitudes increased the achievement of other children in the classroom.[1]

An In-School Program for an Adjustment Class

Most early studies of token programs have used at least one adult to monitor every four or five children. O'Leary and Becker successfully devised a token program that could be used by one teacher with a class of seventeen. The children had been placed in a special class because they exhibited behavior problems and were behind in classwork—nine-year-olds working at a beginning first-grade level. Also, they were from disadvantaged homes.

For practical reasons, behavior was observed for only eight of the seventeen children. They averaged 76 percent off-task behavior before the token system was started. This included being out of their seats, talking out of turn, making noises with objects, talking to peers when it was not permitted, turning away from their work, and other behavior that did not involve paying attention to the teacher or working at a school task. The teacher had a most difficult time carrying out any procedure that might be considered teaching. She would usually leave the classroom worn out.

The token program was put into effect from 12:30 to 2:00 P.M. each day. On the first day, the class rules were placed on the blackboard, and the token procedures explained to the children. Small ten-cent notebooks were taped to each child's desk. The children were told that they would receive points in

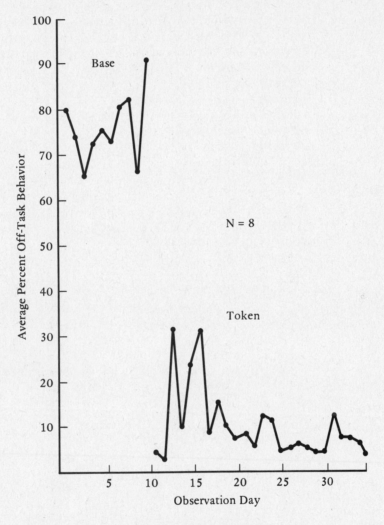

Figure 11.1 Average percent off-task behavior during base and token periods for eight children

their notebooks every fifteen minutes. For each of these periods they could get from 1 to 10 points. A mark of 10 meant that they were following the rules very well, while a mark of 1 indicated that they were not doing their tasks. After a few days, points were given for each thirty-minute period.

The points could be traded for small prizes, such as candy, comics, perfume, and kites. The variety of items increased the chances that at least one of the items would be a reinforcer for each child.

At first, the tokens were traded in at the end of the token period. Step by step, the children were required to work up to four days before trading points, and the points required for a prize were increased.

The results are summarized in figure 11.1. During baseline, the children averaged 76 percent off-task behavior. This dropped to 10 percent during the token period. It was now possible to begin to teach. The children quickly learned to respond to the teacher's praise, which was paired with the giving of points. The class became the best-behaved class in the school. The children learned to tolerate delays in trading tokens for prizes. Reports indicated that the children also behaved better in other classroom activities in which points were not given, and during music and library. The rewards for the eight-week program cost $80.76. Rewards appear to be less expensive for school districts than psychologists! Eighty dollars would pay for only three hours of a psychologist's time.[2]

"Why, That's Bribery."

As noted in the first unit, the use of rewards for learning is often interpreted as bribery. But bribery is basically different from token reinforcement: to-

LEARNING SHOULD BE FOR ITS OWN SAKE. PAY KIDS TO LEARN AND THEY'LL NEVER BE GOOD STUDENTS.

kens are *earned* rewards for good work and measurable improvement according to rules. Reinforcing consequences can be used to teach responsible behavior if the appropriate differential reinforcement procedures are followed.

Another concern of teachers is that, if toys and candy are used, the children will not discover learning for its own sake. This is just not the case. Conditioned reinforcers are established by following a neutral stimulus with a known reinforcer. If learning activities are followed by reinforcers, they will become conditioned reinforcers; then learning can take place for its own sake. To make the transition, it is only necessary to use appropriate procedures to fade out the special reinforcement system.

A Caution

Never use a stronger motivational system than you need to get the job done. If praise and grades will do the job, stay with it. If a token system is necessary, try first backing it up with free time or other activities. When you need the stronger reinforcers, use them. Then, fade them out using the procedures suggested later in this unit.

Designing a Token System

Step 1. Specify the Behaviors That Earn Tokens

When the behaviors that earn tokens are specified, the teacher knows when to give tokens, and the children know what to work for. The specification process has two stages. First, decide what general areas of behavior need stronger reinforcement; then, get down to specifics appropriate to each child.

Your general areas might include:

Study behaviors

working on-task X minutes
checking own work
using teaching machines appropriately
using references
doing homework

Social behaviors

cooperating
interacting with others
asking questions
relating experiences

Academic behaviors

reading	writing
arithmetic	spelling
language	social studies
	science

The specifics you choose will depend on what your children need to learn. Most academic tasks can be treated as countable behaviors, and some kind of ratio schedule can be used. For example, "For each ten arithmetic problems completed, checked, and corrected, you can earn 1 token." Or, "Complete the five-page story, answer the questions and do the checkout with the aide to earn 2 tokens."

Most social and study skills can be handled by requiring a fixed interval of performance according to some criterion. "For each ten minutes of working on-task without an unexcused interruption, you can earn 1 token." Another

Name _Jack_   Date _april 23_

Math
1. Flashcards: _add, xply_
2. Worksheets: _#1, 2, 3, 4, 5_
3. Mathbook: _p. 69 row 5_
               p. 308 row 10

Reading
Hegge, Kirk & Kirk Drill
               _#13_
Palo Alto: _#10 pgs 5-10_
Sullivan: _#11 pgs 35-43 p. 44 E.C._
Conquests in Reading
S.R.A.
Lippincott
Checkered Flag
Webster

Spelling
Study Words: _write them_
Test   _twice_

Language
Dr. Spello: _pgs 29, 30, 31 (top)_
Ditto: _#1_

Penmanship
Pages: _2, 3_

Extra Credit
finish all
other work
first
_p. 21 1-5_

1. Library book
_2. S.R.A._
(Green Power Builder)
3. Following Directions
_A-B_

4. Write a story
about your
favorite kind of
animal

Put five of your
words in
sentences

p. 31 (bottom)
_#2 E.C._

_p. 4 E.C._

Figure 11.2   Sample daily assignment sheet

method is to use a variable-interval checking procedure. A timer is set to go off at variable times ranging from one to twelve minutes (later, from ten to thirty). The children are checked when the timer goes off and awarded a token if they are working, being cooperative, and so on. Some social skills, like question asking, are discrete and require a ratio schedule.

In specifying behaviors that earn tokens, *be sure to specify quality as well as quantity*—so many tokens for so many right responses or corrected responses. If your concern is with study skills and academic performance, place a contingency on each. Research shows that if just paying attention is reinforced, there is no necessary academic improvement, and vice versa. Best results are obtained when both attending and academic performance earn tokens.

Gradually increase your behavioral requirements. If the children can work for only thirty seconds at a time, start there; but when this criterion is met, move to sixty seconds on-task to earn 1 token. Later the children might work for ten minutes for 3 tokens. In a similar way, initially you might give a token for each item completed correctly in a programed reader. Later, a token might be given for correct completion of a page, or five pages.

At the beginning, define your requirements so that lots of reinforcers can be given immediately. Later, the requirements for reinforcement might cover a day or a week.

Be sure to reinforce improvement! Set your requirements so that each child has a chance to "win" if he follows the rules.

It is often convenient to write out your daily assignments for each child. Let the children keep these sheets in work folders to remind them what they are to do and to allow them to monitor their own progress. Figure 11.2 shows a sample assignment sheet from one experimental classroom.[3] The students knew how many points could be earned for completion of each assignment from their daily point-summary chart (see figure 11.3).

Step 2. Develop a Menu of Backup Reinforcers

It is convenient to consider three classes of backup reinforcers: activities, foods, and play materials. Any of the activity reinforcers considered in unit 10 can be assigned point values and placed on the menu. It is possible also to equip a special activities area or room, and charge tokens (or points) for so much time there. In addition to activities, a menu might include store items:

Foods

Gum	Lemon drops
Candied cereal	Marshmallows
Peanuts	Apples
Ice cream	Raisins
Candy bars	Jelly beans
Chocolate kisses	Lollipops
Cookies	Soft drinks
Candied popcorn	

Name of Child _____ **Date** _____

Weeks 6–7: (20 pts. maximum) Give 3 times daily—9:20–10:30 **red** marks;
  10:30–12:10 **blue** marks; 12:10–1:40 **green** marks.
Week 8: (15 pts. maximum)—Give once daily.

Positive

1. Completed Assignment   ____(+2)   Math
    (wk. 6–7 +1 if 100%)   ____(+1)   Reading
                                 ____(+1)   Language
                                 ____(+1)   Writing
                                 ____(+1)   Other   _____Subtotal

2. Attend to task   ____(+1)   9:20– 9:55
                                 ____(+1)   10:30–11:00
                                 ____(+1)   11:00–11:35
                                 ____(+1)   11:35–12:10
                                 ____(+1)   1:00– 1:40
                                                         _____Subtotal

3. Entered classroom   ____(+1)   8:20
    appropriately   ____(+1)   After P.E.
                                 ____(+1)   12:30   _____Subtotal

4. Exhibited socially   ____(+1)
    appropriate behavior   ____(+1)
    (Can apply to specific   ____(+1)
    programs and other)   ____(+1)
                                 ____(+1)
                                                         _____Subtotal

                                                 _____**Total Points Earned**

Negative

1. Not attending   ____(−1)   9:20– 9:55
                                 ____(−1)   9:55–10:30
                                 ____(−1)   10:30–11:00
                                 ____(−1)   11:00–11:35
                                 ____(−1)   1:00– 1:45
                                                         _____Subtotal

2. Other inappropriate   ____(−)
    behaviors (specify)   ____(−)   _____Subtotal

                                                 _____**Total Points Lost**

Figure 11.3 Daily point record form

Play Materials

Makeup kits
Toy animals
Boats
Cars
Blocks
Badges
Marbles
Jump ropes
Gliders
Model airplane kits
Picture books
Painting sets
Crayons
Coloring books
Records
Colored chalk
Clay

Musical instruments
Paper
Mechanical toys
Dolls
Kites
Costumes
Balls
Puzzles
Comic books
Balloons
Playing cards
Games of all sorts
Bean bags
Yo-yos
Play dough
Noisemakers (whistles)

Menu Ideas for Older Kids

Make the tokens exchangeable for letter grades.

Buy tickets for skating, bowling, or athletic events, and have the kids earn these. (Very often one can get them donated.)

Make a certain level of performance in the token program prerequisite for a work-study job.

Write a contract at school in which the parents provide the reinforcers at home, based on tokens earned.

Use tokens that can be spent in a school store or lunchroom.

Involve the children. Let the kids have a part in setting up the menu. Ask them what they would like to have on it. Try to find special and unique ideas for the menu, now and then. Change the menu weekly by adding and subtracting some items. Use only ten to fifteen items at a time.

Step 3. Set Prices and Wages

With behaviors identified and reinforcers selected, prices and wages must be established to relate the two through tokens. The first task is to set the hourly wage. With elementary students, five cents an hour is adequate. With junior high students, ten cents an hour will do the job. With high school students, you may need to go as high as twenty-five cents an hour.

In setting prices, begin by setting store items at retail price. Activities are priced in relation to the hourly wage. School-time activities (free time, recess, activity center) are priced at the hourly wage for each five minutes. Out-of-school activities are priced at the hourly wage for each twenty minutes.

Next, you have to decide how many tokens you need to give the average child per hour. This depends in part on how many different behaviors you want to reinforce and the stage in training. Go over your list of behavior objectives and see what would be reasonable. If you need to give out 5 tokens per hour, and the hourly wage is five cents, then 1 token equals one cent. If you need to give out 10 tokens per hour, and the hourly wage is five cents, then 2 tokens equal one cent. Thus, by figuring out the tokens needed per hour, you are able finally to put prices on your menu in terms of number of tokens required for each item. Your menu might look like this if the hourly wage is ten cents or twenty tokens.

Reinforcer Menu

Activities	Price in Tokens	Store items	Price in Tokens
20 minutes in activity center	80	Two lines of bowling ($1.00)*	200
Go home 30 minutes early	120	Candy bar (10 ¢)*	20
Go on picnic (2 hours)	120	Model car (75 ¢)*	150
15-minute game period	60	School emblem (15 ¢)*	30
5 minutes extra recess	20	Soft drink (15 ¢)*	30

*These numbers would not be on your menu. They just illustrate here how price in tokens was determined.

Adjustments. Follow the law of supply and demand in making adjustments over time. Increase the prices of popular items, and reduce the prices of slow moving items. Gradually make it harder to earn tokens by requiring more work for fewer tokens.

Response Cost. Once a token system is operating well, it is possible to charge for misbehaviors. Tell the children that certain undesired behaviors will cost 2 or 5 tokens each time they occur. The children will have to decide if they want to spend their tokens in this way or some other way.

Step 4. Selecting Tokens

Select a token that is readily given, handy, and will cause a minimum of interference with the child's ongoing behavior.

Possible Tokens

Marks on the blackboard
Marks on a paper or card on the child's desk

Plastic chips that go on a ring
Poker chips
Pennies

Gold stars
Numbers on a paper
Marks on a ladder with 50 steps
Marbles in a jar

A counter with a light flash or buzzer
Tickets
Punches on a card

Step 5. Using Tokens

At the start with young children, establish the value of the tokens by handing out one to each child and then requiring the children to use the tokens to get some treat. After a couple of pairings like this, they will get the idea. With older children, instructions alone may be all that is necessary.

When giving out tokens, tell the children what they have done to earn them. Focus on their behavior, not the tokens. In fact, it is a good practice to talk about the tokens as little as possible.

When giving tokens for academic work, be sure the work is checked and corrected *before* the tokens are given.

Initially the exchange can occur daily, but with older children, weekly is enough. Use the exchange to let the kids know they are improving and doing a good job. The evidence is there in the tokens or points they have earned. This is also a good time for the teacher to reevaluate the procedures to see what is not working for which children. If children have not earned tokens, there is something wrong with the system, not the kids.

Step 6. Record Keeping

To monitor and evaluate your system, you need to keep records of the points each child earns and spends each day and the daily carry-over. A chart like the one in figure 11.3 can be used on a daily basis. Then you can keep the weekly summary on another chart, shown in figure 11.4.[3]

A note. Parents should be kept well-informed about any special reinforcement procedures. Hold a session with them before starting and explain what is being done and why.

Informal Token Systems

It is often necessary to devise more effective reinforcement systems for single children in the classroom. Here are some procedures that have worked.

1. Jimmy hit other children and did not complete class assignments. The teacher worked out a procedure with his mother so that Jimmy took a note home each day he worked hard and was cooperative. With a note Jimmy could watch TV for a specified period that evening. Without a note he could not.

2. Aaron was a fourth-grade boy from a deprived background. He would not get down to work in class, preferring to dawdle or play with his friends. It was often reported that he hit younger children coming to and from school.

Aaron earned check marks on the board, one check for every ten minutes of good working behavior. If he earned ten checks, he could spend thirty minutes in the kindergarten supervising younger boys in the use of carpentry tools. The younger children could use the tools only when he was there, so they appreciated his coming. Aaron learned to work in the classroom, and work cooperatively with younger children.

Teacher's Weekly Summary Point Record
Starting Date _____

Child Names	Jimmy	Mary	Jane	Tom	Aaron
Pts. Carried Over	__	__	__	__	__
Pts. Earned	+__	+__	+__	+__	
Pts. Lost	-__	-__	-__	-__	-__
Day Total	__	__		__	
Pts. Spent	-__	-__	-__	-__	-__
Pts. Carried Over					
Pts. Earned	+__	+__	+__	+__	+__
Pts. Lost	-__	-__	-__	-__	-__
Day Total	__	__	__	__	__
Pts. Spent	-__	-__	-__	-__	-__
Pts. Carried Over	__	__	__	__	__
Pts. Earned	+__	+__	+__	+__	+__
Pts. Lost	-__	-__	-__	-__	-__
Day Total				__	__
Pts. Spent	-__	-__	-__	-__	-__
Pts. Carried Over	__	__	__	__	__
Pts. Earned	+__	+__	+__	+__	+__
Pts. Lost	-__	-__	-__	-__	-__
Day Total	__	__	__	__	__
Pts. Spent	-__	-__	-__	-__	-__
Pts. Carried Over	__	__	__	__	__
Pts. Earned	+__	+__	+__	+__	+__
Pts. Lost	-__	-__	-__	-__	-__
Day Total	__	__	__	__	__
Pts. Spent	-__	-__	-__	-__	-__
Pts. Carried Over					

Figure 11.4 Weekly point record form

3.   In one school, the problem of how to manage the children's rowdiness, fighting, and running when leaving school was solved by training the patrol boys to pass out colored chips to children who were well-behaved. The class with the most chips each week got a pennant for its door.

4.   Jack earned an X on the board for each half day he did not fight in class. Initially four X's earned a party for the whole class, and Jack became the means of a treat for everyone. Later he worked for ten X's, and so forth.

5.   A number of teachers have had their class earn recess by showing good working habits. The general procedure is to determine about how long the available work time is and divide that by an average recess duration. Have the whole class then earn recess time each day. For every five to fifteen minutes of good working, one or more minutes of recess is earned. The formula should be set so that improved working will earn a slightly longer recess than is currently available free. Some teachers have found this effective, while the contrary procedure of counting black marks that lead to losing recess often failed. The points-for-recess procedure can also be used with a single child in the class.

6.   Kenny was sent to see the social worker every time he had a tantrum or fought in class. Tantrums and fighting seemed to increase. After a discussion, the teacher and the social worker decided that Kenny would have to earn time with the social worker by showing progressively improved classroom behavior. Tantrums and fighting decreased rapidly.

7.   Some teachers find it difficult to control what boys or girls do in the bathroom. Often the children are messy, destructive, and hurtful to others. For young children, direct supervision by the teacher or aide can help teach good bathroom behavior. For older children, you might want to assign a group leader to each half of the boys and each half of the girls. The group leader could report daily on which children followed the bathroom rules. Points might be awarded daily on the basis of the report. The points could be traded in for a treat or small party every so often. Obviously, such a procedure should only be used when there are definite problems to overcome.

Many teachers have asked if setting up a system for one child does not lead to other children misbehaving to get a reward. This has not been seen. Usually a simple explanation that Jimmy needs special help is enough. If there were a problem, however, the system can be arranged (as it was for Jack) so that the special child earns a treat for the whole class. Then all are motivated to help the target child do better. The reinforcement system must be suited to the child and the situation.

Maintaining Gains While Getting Off a Token System

There are two common situations to consider. In the first situation, the class is your own; you have things running smoothly and want to eliminate the token system. You plan to keep the children motivated with praise, occasional special events, and perhaps grades. In the second situation, the children come to your special class for remedial work or specific help. The goal is to return them to regular classes as soon as feasible. In both cases, you will need to know how to fade out a token system. For children in a special class temporarily, it will be helpful to work with the regular classroom teacher in planning the return to regular class.

Fading Out a Token Program

When the objectives of a special reinforcement system have been met, it is possible to shift in steps to more typically available classroom reinforcers. Social reinforcement is continued, but made more intermittent. The number of points that can be earned each day is gradually reduced, about 5 percent every few days. Store items are slowly dropped from the reinforcer menu, but activities are kept. Points are given out only at the end of the day, rather than after each work period. Eventually, the children are working for praise, grades, pride in their accomplishments, and an occasional special activity planned by the teacher. Throughout the fade-out period, really let the students know how pleased you are with their progress. "You have really learned to work on your own, without the point system. You should be proud of yourselves!"

Returning to a Regular Class

Hill Walker, Nancy Buckley, and their colleagues have studied a variety of procedures for maintaining, in a regular class, gains made in a special class. The interested student is strongly urged to study their findings in detail (see unit 11, reference 3). The highlights are:

1 Using fading procedures, as described above, to make a special class more like a regular class, they found the following with five children:

   Before treatment, 39 percent appropriate behavior in regular class
   During treatment, 90 percent appropriate behavior in special class
   After treatment, 66 percent appropriate behavior in regular class

   The behavior on return to regular class was quite variable and seemed partly a function of skill level. The children with lower skills still had more trouble.[4]

2 Training the teacher in the regular classroom in the appropriate use of reinforcement principles proved to be very successful.[5] The five children in this study showed:

   34 percent appropriate behavior at the start in their regular classes
   95 percent during the latter stages in special class
   87 percent on follow-up

   A month prior to the return of the children, each classroom teacher was asked to participate in a program to help keep the gains of the "special" children going. They agreed and signed a contract. The contract provided for: (a) training the teacher in classroom management procedures, (b) weekly monitoring of teacher and the target child, and (c) course credit for the teacher, with her grade based on how well the target child maintained gains. The gain had to be maintained above 75 percent to earn an A. All five teachers made it.

The classroom observations produced other interesting findings. A comparison of the five teachers' behaviors in baseline and follow-up showed these results:

	Baseline	Follow-up
Attends to total behavior	11.2%	14.2%
Attends to appropriate behavior	5.6%	13.1%
Attends to inappropriate behavior	5.4%	2.1%

Initially the teachers divided their time between appropriate and inappropriate behavior. After training they focused on appropriate behavior.

These same children were followed up in the next academic year. No attempts were made to work with their new teachers on maintenance. The children averaged 80 percent appropriate behavior. A control group who had received a similar treatment, but whose teachers were not trained in behavior principles, showed only 64 percent appropriate behavior during next year follow-up. The teacher training procedure thus proved very successful in maintaining the gains after the token program ended.

summary

Strong reinforcer systems are sometimes needed for poorly motivated students. When this is the case, a token or point system should be considered. Token systems have proved themselves highly effective in reducing problem behavior and in increasing academic learning. Keep in mind, however, this caution—Don't use it if you don't need it.

In designing a token system, the first step is to specify the behaviors that earn tokens. Chart your general goals, then get down to specifics appropriate for each child.

1 Specify quality as well as quantity.
2 Gradually increase your behavioral requirements so the children work for longer periods without reinforcement.
3 Focus on reinforcing improvement.
4 Consider writing out daily assignments for each child where appropriate.

The next step is to build a reinforcer menu. Consider special activities and games, foods, and play materials. With older children you might write a contract at school with reinforcers provided by parents.

In setting prices and wages, decide on an hourly wage. Then set prices so that at first store items are priced at the retail price, each five minutes of an in-school activity costs the hourly wage, and each twenty minutes of an out-of-school activity costs the hourly wage. To specify prices in tokens rather than cents, you need to decide how many reinforcers you should give in an hour to do the job for your class. Once this is decided, the rest falls out by simple arithmetic. Adjustments can be made to your price schedule according to the law of supply and demand. Also, gradually increase the work requirements for earning tokens. "Charging" for infrequent misbehaviors (a response cost procedure) can be considered after a token system is established.

The tokens should be handy, readily given, and noninterfering. Points, electrical counters, and plastic chips may be useful, depending on the setting. When giving out tokens for academic work, require a work-check and corrections *before* the tokens are given. The exchange should be planned to show the kids how they are coming along and how pleased you are. Charts and records simplify the management of a token system and let both teacher and students know where things stand.

Informal token systems may be devised for a single child or a small group. A number of illustrations of such systems were given.

When it comes time to end a special reinforcement system, careful plans must be laid for the transition. If you are going to keep the kids in your class, slowly fade out the components of the token system. If the children are to be returned to another class, follow the fade-out procedure, but also train the receiving teacher in good reinforcement procedures. Without such training, your efforts may be wasted.

broadening your perspective

Tokens for Not St-St-St-tutt-er-ing

As a variety of studies show, token reinforcement is useful in speech therapy. Roger Ingham and Gavin Andrews demonstrated this effectiveness with thirty-nine men averaging twenty-five years in age. The men were hospitalized for up to twenty-one days in Sydney, Australia, for the speech therapy.

Two behaviors were identified to earn reinforcers: syllables spoken per minute and percentage of nonstuttered syllables. The patients could earn tokens for improving over a baseline level and lose them for a poorer performance. Tokens were required to earn meals and luxuries in the hospital. The criteria were gradually increased as performance improved in order to shape normal speech behavior. The major treatment procedure was a forty-five minute rating session, which occurred nine times a day between 7 A.M. and 9 P.M. During rating sessions, the men were required to speak a prescribed number of syllables to others in their group. Raters recorded the speech behavior.

Treatment was divided into three phases. First, for twenty-one recording sessions (two and one-third days), the token system was used by itself. In the next stage, the token system was combined with delayed auditory feedback. This technique is designed to teach new speech habits by slowing down speech (vowel sounds are held and smooth transitions are made between speech sounds). The delay training starts with a 250-millisecond delay, and then the delay is faded out in steps as stutter-free speech is achieved at each delay level. In the third phase, the men faced situations in which they normally had shown a high rate of stuttering. These included conversations with strangers, sales people, prospective employers, telephone callers, and even "ladies of pleasure" in a well-known locality of Sydney. The men obtained 1000-syllable cassette recordings of their speech in each situation, and tokens were given.

The findings from a series of experiments within this treatment model are these:

1　In the token-only phase, the use of token reinforcers reduced the mean number of syllables stuttered (over twenty-one sessions) from 10 percent to 6 percent. Mean syllables spoken per minute increased from 125 to 150.
2　When token rewards were given for reinforcement and penalties (fines) were given for poorer performance, the percentage of stuttering was lower than if only rewards were used.
3　Doubling the token reward cut error rate in half.
4　If tokens were given noncontingently (just for completing the rating session), performance was poorer than when tokens were made contingent on improved performances.
5　During the second stage where delayed auditory feedback was used with contingent tokens, it took fifty-three rating sessions on the average to fade out of the delay while maintaining stutter-free speech. With noncontingent tokens, it took seventy-two rating sessions on the average to complete the fadeout.
6　Tokens were used in the third stage, but no formal experiments were reported.
7　Follow-up studies indicate that sixty-five of the men treated were free of stuttering nine months later. Some relapses did occur, so a maintenance program was added to help those with relapses.[6]

Reducing the Delusional Talk of Schizophrenic Patients

One of the more prominent behaviors of chronic psychotics is delusional speech or "sick talk." While we do not understand always how delusions get started, we do know that such talk gets a lot of attention, which may be a key factor in maintaining behavior we label psychotic. Wincze, Leitenberg, and Agras used a token economy to modify the delusional behavior of ten schizophrenics who had been hospitalized an average of twelve years. Characteristic delusions were: "Mr. Beam is torturing me with electricity," "I am the Lord. I was born in the year 1," "Big Lady had an electric gun on me,"

"The Mafia is trying to kill me because I know who killed Kennedy," "I'm Queen Arlene, the fourth crown queen of North America."

Each patient's verbal behavior was recorded during training sessions with a therapist, during conversations with the nursing staff on the ward, and during interviews with a psychiatric resident not familiar with the study. During the training sessions, direct probes of the delusional area were made using 15 questions drawn from a pool of 105 created separately for each patient.

The experimental conditions were as follows:

1 *Baseline.* Noncontingent tokens given at the beginning of the day or on request.
2 *Feedback.* In training sessions, lights indicated correct and incorrect (delusional) responses to probe questions. Also patients were told why an answer was correct or not, for example, "That is not correct. Jesus Christ lived almost 2000 years ago."
3 *Tokens.* Tokens could be earned for nondelusional talk and correct responses. At first this occurred only in training sessions; later tokens were given in training sessions and on the ward.

Tokens could be exchanged for meals, extra dessert, store items, cigarettes, time off the ward, TV time, game room time, visitors, books, magazines, time in bedroom from 8 to 9 A.M., and any other activity reinforcing for a particular patient.

The results showed that *feedback* was effective in reducing the delusional behavior of five out of ten patients by at least 20 percent. The *token program* drastically reduced delusional talk in six of nine patients during training sessions. (One subject did not go through the token condition.) The average change from initial baseline to token condition was from a mean of 82 percent delusional talk to 28 percent delusional talk for nine patients. Delusional talk on the ward did not change as a function of use of tokens in training sessions. When tokens were also given on the ward, four out of seven patients showed some improvement, and two definitely showed *more* delusional talk. These latter two patients showed little change in training sessions. The psychiatrist detected no changes in the patients that corresponded to experimental changes.[7]

Consistent with earlier work by Ayllon and Haughton,[8] and Meichenbaum,[9] this study shows that delusional talk can be rather quickly modified by reinforcement contingencies, although success was not achieved in every case. Furthermore, the change was rather narrowly restricted to the training conditions. Further work is needed to show ways to produce more generalized changes.

Analysis of Components in a Token System

Hill Walker, Edward Fiegenbaum, and Hi Hops carred out a most remarkable analysis of the effects of different components in a token reinforcement system. The design allowed for the introduction and evaluation of one component at a time. Five children were involved in the experimental classroom. The procedures are described in detail in *Token Reinforcement Techniques* by Walker and Buckley.[3] There were ten phases to the experiment, which lasted four and a half months.

1. *Baseline in regular classroom.* Prior to placement in the special class, each child was observed for 20 six-minute observations in his regular class during one week.

2. *Baseline in experimental classroom.* Another one-week baseline was taken in the experimental classroom. An attempt was made to give children the kind of attention they were getting from the teacher in the regular class.

3. *Social reinforcement.* The children were given praise about thirty times a day for appropriate behavior. No attention was given to inappropriate behavior.

4. *Social plus token reinforcement.* The students could earn a maximum of 35 points and a minimum of 20 per day. All children continued to receive thirty praise statements a day from the teacher, usually when the tokens were given. The teacher praised by telling the children what they had done to earn tokens and then giving the tokens.

Phases 5 and 6 were identical to 3 and 4 respectively.

7. *Social reinforcement plus tokens plus response cost (cost contingency).* In this phase the tokens could be lost for not attending, talking back to teacher,

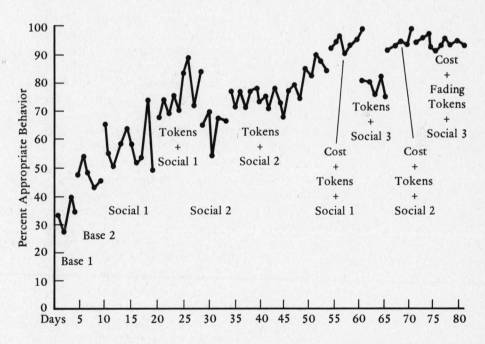

Figure 11.5 Analysis of the effects of different components of a token reinforcement program

talking out of turn, being out of seat, disturbing others, fighting, swearing, and so forth. The tokens were points on an electrical display board. Fines were levied by marking a response cost card on the child's desk (to inform him), turning out his light on the board, and subtracting the points from his counter.

Phases 8 and 9 were identical to 4 and 7 respectively.

10. *Social plus response cost plus fading tokens.* During this last two weeks, the conditions were the same as phase 9 except that the number of points that could be earned was reduced from 35, in steps, down to 11 for the last two days. Social reinforcement continued and fines could be levied.

The results of the study are given in figure 11.5. In this figure, each data point represents the average percent of appropriate behavior (interval method) shown by the five children each day. Social, tokens, and cost all added to the effectiveness of the program. Also, as indicated by baseline 2 versus baseline 1 comparisons, just coming to the special class also helped to increase appropriate behavior.

Achievement Place

Achievement Place is a home-style community-based treatment facility for court-referred teenagers, run originally by Ellery Phillips and Montrose Wolf. Achievement Place operates with a token economy. The daily routine is similar to that in any home. The boys get up at seven, clean up, eat, and get ready for school. They have regular assigned chores to be completed. After school they do their homework. Then, they can watch TV, play games, or have other privileges if they heave earned the tokens required.

The target behaviors that earn or lose points are indicated in table 11.1.

The points were tallied on three-by-five-inch cards that the boys always carried with them. Privileges could be earned for a week at a time. At the end of each week, the boys could trade the points for the next week's privileges. Table 11.2 shows some of the privileges that could be earned.

The economy was set up so that a boy could earn all of the basic privileges if he did all that was expected of him. Some privileges were auctioned off to the highest bidder each week. For example, the "car privilege" allowed the winning bidder his seating choice in the car for a week. Various house managership positions were also auctioned off.

Many experimental studies have been carried out within the economy. For example, one study showed that the fines were quite important in reducing aggressive statements. When they were removed, aggressive statements went up. When they were replaced, aggressive statements went down. Another study showed that a manager system for cleaning the bathroom was more effective than a group contingency. In the manager system, one boy is responsible for assigning tasks, checking each of them, and awarding points or fines. In the group contingency, all the boys were responsible; if 75 percent of the weekly tasks were completed, they earned points. Fines were levied below that.

TABLE 11.1 BEHAVIORS AND THE NUMBER OF POINTS THAT THEY EARNED OR LOST

Behaviors That Earned Points	Points
1) Watching news on TV or reading the newspaper	300 per day
2) Cleaning and maintaining neatness in one's room	500 per day
3) Keeping one's person neat and clean	500 per day
4) Reading books	5 to 10 per page
5) Aiding house-parents in various household tasks	20 to 1000 per task
6) Doing dishes	500 to 1000 per meal
7) Being well-dressed for an evening meal	100 to 500 per meal
8) Performing homework	500 per day
9) Obtaining desirable grades on school report cards	500 to 1000 per grade
10) Turning out lights when not in use	25 per light

Behaviors That Lost Points	Points
1) Failing grades on the report card	500 to 1000 per grade
2) Speaking aggressively	20 to 50 per response
3) Forgetting to wash hands before meals	100 to 300 per meal
4) Arguing	300 per response
5) Disobeying	100 to 1000 per response
6) Being late	10 per min.
7) Displaying poor manners	50 to 100 per response
8) Engaging in poor posture	50 to 100 per response
9) Using poor grammar	20 to 50 per response
10) Stealing, lying, or cheating	10,000 per response

TABLE 11.2 PRIVILEGES THAT COULD BE EARNED EACH WEEK

Privileges for the Week	Price in Points
Allowance	1000
Bicycle	1000
TV	1000
Games	500
Tools	500
Snacks	1000
Permission to go downtown	1000
Permission to stay up past bedtime	1000
Permission to come home late after school	1000

Over the past six years, Achievement Place has proved to be a very successful alternative to juvenile-home placement for problem boys. It has also provided a laboratory where more effective procedures in the design of the treatment environments could be studied.[10]

The Home-Point System

Token systems can be used in any home to help children learn to be more responsible. Christophersen and others at the University of Kansas have reported a number of home-points systems. Following is an example.

There were three children in the family. Each was put on a point system. George, aged nine, had problem behaviors at school and home. He had been skipping school, was sassy, and did not follow directions at home. Dollie, aged eight, had mild cerebral palsy and was in a class for the educable retarded. At home she was hyperactive and occasionally had tantrums.

TABLE 11.3 AVAILABLE PRIVILEGES AND SPECIFIED BEHAVIORS

	Licenses Available	Price in Points
	Basic privileges	60
	Drive-in movie	200
	Picnic	50

	Behaviors That Earned and Lost Points	Points Earned or Lost
George	1) Make beds	10
	2) Hang up clothes	10
Keith	3) Empty trash	20
	4) Make bed	20
Dollie	5) Feed cat	20
	6) Bathe	20

Behaviors That Earned Points	Points Earned
1) Sweep rug	10
2) Clean bathroom	20
3) Answer telephone	15

Behaviors That Lost Points	Points Lost
1) Bickering	10 Each occurrence
2) Teasing	10
3) Whining	10

Keith, aged five, whined too much. Table 11.3 shows a partial list of the behaviors that could earn and lose points in the system set up for this family.

After baseline observations were made, the parents were given instructions on how to set up and operate the point system. Phone contacts and a home visit helped to get things going right. Total training time was about ten hours.

During baseline, George rarely cleaned his room and never fed the dog. With the point system, he did these chores daily. During baseline Keith never took out the trash, and Dollie did not clean her room or feed the cat. With the point system, these tasks were done each day. The introduction of fines practically eliminated George's bickering, violation of a bedtime quiet rule, and teasing. A multiple-baseline design was used with George. One behavior was put on the fine list, then two weeks later another, then two weeks later the third. In each case the behavior improved only when the fine contingency was applied.

For Dollie, a similar multiple-baseline study showed fines effective in eliminating whining, bickering, and jumping on furniture. For Keith, fines eliminated his whining, bickering, and violation of the bedtime quiet rule.[11]

self-test

1 When children have learned that schoolwork usually results in failure, it may be necessary to use strong, obvious, and _____ reinforcers for each appropriate response.

2 Token reinforcement systems are one practical way to introduce _____ reinforcers into the classroom.

1 immediate

3 The use of rewards for learning is often interpreted as a form of _____.

2 stronger

4 The first step in designing a token system is to specify the _____ that earn tokens.

3 bribery

5 In specifying behaviors that earn tokens, be sure to specify _____ as well as quantity.

4 behaviors

5 quality

6 It is convenient to consider three classes of _____ reinforcers: activities, foods, and play materials.

7 In setting prices and wages, the first task is to set the _____ _____.

6 backup

8 Once a token system is operating well, it is possible to also _____ for misbehaviors.

7 hourly wage

9 When the objectives of a special reinforcement system have been met, it is possible to shift to more _____ _____ classroom reinforcers in steps.

8 charge,
  fine

10 If the children are to be returned to a regular class, follow the _____ procedure, but also train the receiving teacher in good reinforcement procedures.

9 typically
  available

10 fade-out

NUMBER RIGHT _____

exercise 1 programed practice

1 Many children have been taught that schoolwork leads to _____ and punishment.

2 Turned-off children may need strong, obvious, and _____ reinforcers for each appropriate response.

1 failure

3 Token reinforcement systems are one practical way to introduce _____ reinforcers into the classroom.

2 immediate

4 In a token reinforcement system, points or some _____, like poker chips, are given as the immediate reinforcer.

3 stronger

4 tangible

5 Later, these are _____ for reinforcing activities, edibles, or play materials.

6 In the O'Leary and Becker study, the tokens were _____ written on the page of a notebook taped to each child's desk.

7 Presentation of points was paired with _____ from the teacher.

8 Gradual changes were made so that the children had to work for _____ periods before points were given and had to wait four days to _____ them.

9 Reinforcing consequences can be used to teach responsible behavior if the appropriate _____ reinforcement procedures are followed.

10 A concern of some teachers is that if more basic rewards like toys and candy are used, the children will not learn to learn for its _____ sake.

11 This is just not the case. Conditioned reinforcers are established by following a _____ stimulus with a known reinforcer. If learning activities are followed by reinforcers, they will become _____ reinforcers, and learning can take place for its own sake.

12 Never use a _____ motivational system than you need to get the job done.

13 The first step in the design of a token system is to specify the _____ that earn tokens.

14 Most academic tasks can be treated as _____ behaviors and some kind of ratio schedule can be used. "For each ten arithmetic _____ completed, checked, and corrected, you can earn 1 token."

---

5 exchanged

6 points, numbers

7 praise

8 longer; exchange, trade

9 differential

10 own

11 neutral; conditioned

12 stronger

13 behaviors

14 countable; problems

15 Most social and study skills can be handled by requiring a fixed _____ of performance according to some criterion. "For each ten _____ of working on-task without an unexcused interruption, you can earn 1 token."

16 For behaviors that earn tokens, be sure to specify _____ as well as quantity—so many tokens for so many _____ responses or corrected responses.

17 If your concern is with study skills *and* academic performance, place a _____ on each.

18 Be sure to reinforce _____.

19 It is convenient to consider three classes of _____ reinforcers: activities, foods, and play materials.

20 With behaviors identified and reinforcers selected, prices and _____ are established to relate the two through _____.

21 The first task is to set the _____ _____.

22 In setting prices, begin by setting _____ items at retail price.

23 School-time _____ are priced at the hourly wage for each five minutes.

24 Out-of-school activities are priced at the hourly wage for each _____ minutes.

25 Increase the prices of popular items and _____ the prices of slow-moving items.

15 interval;
   minutes

16 quality;
   right

17 contingency

18 improvement

19 backup

20 wages;
   tokens

21 hourly wage

22 store

23 activities

24 twenty

25 reduce,
   decrease

26 more;
    fewer

27 charge

28 tell;
    behavior

29 before

30 records

31 single

32 work; recess

33 six

34 increased;
    earn, buy;
    decreased

26 Gradually make it harder to earn tokens by requiring _____ work for _____ tokens.

27 Once a token system is operating well, it is possible to also _____ for misbehaviors.

28 In giving out tokens, _____ the children what they are doing to earn them. Focus on their _____ and not the tokens.

29 In giving tokens for academic work, be sure the work is checked and corrected _____ the tokens are given.

30 Keep _____ of the points each child earns and spends each day and the daily carry over.

31 Often teachers have to devise a reinforcement system for a _____ child in the classroom.

32 The general procedure for having a class earn its recess is to figure how many minutes of work earn a minute of recess by dividing _____ time by average _____ time.

33 If recess is usually fifteen minutes long and you have 1½ hours of work time before recess, then _____ minutes of work time would earn one minute of recess time.

34 Kenny went to see the social worker every time he had a tantrum in class. Tantrums _____ in frequency. Kenny then was required to _____ time with the social worker by behaving well in class. The tantrums and fighting _____.

35 If the usual methods of reinforcing behavior do not work, the teacher should

_____ her procedures in order to find effective _____.

36 When the objectives of a special reinforcement system have been met, it is

possible to shift to more _____ _____ classroom rein-

forcers in steps.

37 The special elements of the program are gradually _____ out.

38 If the children are to be returned to a regular class, use the _____

procedure, but also train the _____ _____ in good rein-

forcement procedures.

35 change;
    reinforcers

36 typically
    available

37 faded

38 fade-out;
    receiving
    teacher,
    regular
    classroom
    teacher

exercise 2

Practice in Devising Token Systems

Use the answer sheets that follow to write your solutions to the problems presented. Explain how you would handle the problem, and support the procedure you would use by relating it to reinforcement principles or to the rules about designing token systems. Bring solutions to discussion group.

1 Devise a token reinforcement procedure for dealing with the following problem:

Jimmy is a first-grade boy who gets along well with his peers and is achieving well in reading and language classes. His problem centers around the arithmetic class. During the arithmetic class he talks with his friends, leaves his seat, and in general ignores the subject matter. When asked to join the group or participate in the arithmetic studies, he simply refuses; however, if kept in for special study sessions, he seems to have no difficulty covering the material. He is currently behind the rest of his group and getting further behind every day.

2 Devise a token reinforcement procedure for dealing with the following problem:

Marsha is a bright, verbal child in the second grade. She is having no difficulty completing her assigned tasks, but is constantly in trouble in the classroom because she is so rowdy. She has a large repertoire of tricks that amuse her friends and she attracts much attention by her disruptive behavior. Praise for appropriate social behavior seems to have little effect. She has been in trouble at least once a day the past week because of her behavior in the restroom. One day she plugged up the sink and ran water all over the floor. Another time she splashed water on her classmates. Once she dropped a roll of paper down the toilet. Yesterday she soaked her hair, and then, after pulling it down in front of her face, she ran around pretending to be a witch who would eat the other children.

3 Devise a token reinforcement procedure for dealing with the following problem:

Mary's problem is easy to overlook. She is somewhat withdrawn. She never gets into trouble on the way to school, at recess, or in the classroom. She speaks very softly and often does not answer a question unless it is directed to her a second or third time. This failure to respond is particularly noticeable in the reading group where Mary would (if permitted) go through the entire period without making a sound. She is falling behind the rest of her group in reading.

4 Devise a token reinforcement procedure for dealing with the following problem:

Doug is superactive. He doesn't sit still at all. Casual observers quickly label him hyperactive and possibly brain-damaged. Medical examination has revealed no physical abnormalities, but none of the usual classroom procedures seem sufficient to keep Doug working on a task in his seat. Although he was initially working at the same level as most of his peers, he is currently behind and getting further behind daily.

5 Describe the current operation and problems of some classroom you are familiar with. Then design a token reinforcement system for that classroom. Use the outline for answers to problems 1 to 4, and type out your report to turn in to your group leader. If necessary, think about visiting a special education classroom, or a regular class, to develop the observations you will need to complete this report.

Answer Sheet—Problem 1

1 Specify the behaviors that earn tokens: _____

_____

_____

2 Describe the backup reinforcers or how you would determine them: ____

_____

_____

3 Describe how you determined prices and wages: _____

_____

_____

4 Describe your tokens and why they were selected: _____

_____

_____

5 Summarize your instructions to the class or child about the system: _____

_____

_____

6 Describe the records you will keep: _____

_____

_____

7 Indicate the steps to be taken to get off the special system later: _____

_____

_____

Answer Sheet—Problem 2

1 Specify the behaviors that earn tokens: _____

_____

_____

2 Describe the backup reinforcers or how you would determine them: ____

_____

_____

3 Describe how you determined prices and wages: _____

_____

_____

4 Describe your tokens and why they were selected: _____

_____

_____

5 Summarize your instructions to the class or child about the system: _____

_____

_____

6 Describe the records you will keep: _____

_____

_____

7 Indicate the steps to be taken to get off the special system later: _____

_____

_____

Answer Sheet—Problem 3

1 Specify the behaviors that earn tokens: _____

_____

_____

2 Describe the backup reinforcers or how you would determine them: _____

_____

3 Describe how you determined prices and wages: _____

_____

_____

4 Describe your tokens and why they were selected: _____

_____

_____

5 Summarize your instructions to the class or child about the system: _____

_____

_____

6 Describe the records you will keep: _____

_____

_____

7 Indicate the steps to be taken to get off the special system later: _____

_____

_____

Answer Sheet—Problem 4

1 Specify the behaviors that earn tokens: _____

_____

_____

2 Describe the backup reinforcers or how you would determine them: ____

_____

_____

3 Describe how you determined prices and wages: _____

_____

_____

4 Describe your tokens and why they were selected: _____

_____

_____

5 Summarize your instructions to the class or child about the system: _____

_____

_____

6 Describe the records you will keep: _____

_____

_____

7 Indicate the steps to be taken to get off the special system later: _____

_____

_____

discussion questions

1 Describe the components of a token reinforcer system.

2 Indicate when such systems might be used and when they should not be used.

3 Explain why the use of special reinforcers is not bribery.

4 Describe the six main steps in designing a token system.

5 What would you do to maintain the gains of a token system while eliminating it in your own class?

6 How would you maintain gains from a token system in a special class when it comes time to return the children to their regular class?

7 Give examples of token systems existing in the business sector of our society.

8 Describe a number of places where token systems might be used to help people learn more appropriate behavior.

9 Be prepared to describe to the group your solution to the problems in exercise 2.

project 4

An Experimental Token Program

Name _____

Date Due _____

Section _____

Part A. Baseline

Follow the procedures of project 3, part A, in unit 7.

Part B. Experimental Token Program

1 Specify the behaviors that earn tokens: _____

_____

_____

2 Describe your backup reinforcers and how you determined them: _____

_____

3 Describe how you set prices and wages: _____

_____

_____

4 Describe your tokens and indicate why you selected them: _____

_____

_____

5 Summarize your instructions to the class or child about the system (use an

extra page if needed): _____

_____

_____

6 Describe the records you will keep: _____

_____

_____

7 Discuss your proposed system with your group leader before starting it.

8 Use the report forms provided to record your results.

Recording Sheet

Name _____

Observer _____ Teacher _____

Subject _____ Date _____

Time _____ School _____

Observed Behavior: _____

Minute	Observation Intervals (Ten Seconds Each)						Comments
	1	2	3	4	5	6	
1							
2							
3							
4							
5							
6							
7							
8							
9							
10							
11							
12							
13							
14							
15							
16							
17							
18							
19							
20							

Project Report Form

Child's Name _____ Observation Time _____

Target Behavior _____ Setting of Observation _____

_____

Daily Data

Baseline		*Experimental*	
Date	Percent On-Task Behavior	Date	Percent On-Task Behavior

1. ____ _____ 6. ____ _____

2. ____ _____ 7. ____ _____

3. ____ _____ 8. ____ _____

4. ____ _____ 9. ____ _____

5. ____ _____ 10. ____ _____

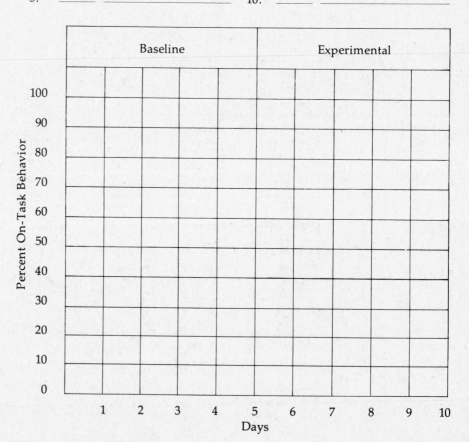

unit 12

Point-Contract Systems for Junior High and High School Students

objectives

When you complete this unit you should be able to—

1 State the four main features of a teacher-student contract.
2 Describe the differences between the term-course contract, the learning-center contract, and the home-school contract.
3 Explain why an explicit, effective instructional program is essential to a term-course contract.
4 Describe Keller's system for "personalized instruction" and outline its essential components.
5 Give five points from research related to studies of "personalized instructional" systems.
6 Give an example of the use of a home-school contract.

lesson

Point-contracts are specialized token reinforcement systems in which a written contract details the performance requirements and possible consequences. The students agree to meet certain requirements, and the teacher (or a parent) agrees to provide certain rewards if the requirements are met. The contracts function very much like those that are the basis for most adult exchanges of services and goods. A contract has four essential parts and a possible bonus clause:

1 Specification of responsibilities, or the performances to be reinforced.
2 Specification of privileges, or the rewards to be earned.

3 Specification of sanctions for failure to live up to the contract.
4 Specification of a monitoring method.
5 Specification of possible bonuses for going beyond contract requirements.

There are at least three settings in the junior high and high school where point-contract systems hold promise. First, the subject-area teacher who has students for one period a day can use the contract to provide structure, motivation, and continuity. Second, a learning center or team-teaching staff can use contracts to individualize instructional objectives and keep track of a large group doing different things or small groups doing the same thing. Third, the school counselor can arrange contracts with several teachers and parents of students who need special help.

The Term-Course Contract

The single-subject-area teacher has the greatest potential use for point-contract systems, especially if the students can select the course. In most schools today, options can be arranged. If students elect one of four offerings in a subject area and sign a contract with that teacher, this is likely to have two benefits. The teacher will work harder at doing a good job; otherwise students will no longer elect the course. The students will be committed to study an area of their choosing. It will be harder for the students to put the blame for a poor performance on the teacher or the "stupid" subject area. A contingency is placed on both the teacher and the student.

Contracts and detailed course descriptions should be available during registration periods. The contract should spell out what the students will be expected to do to earn what kind of grades and course credits. In case of failure to meet a contract requirement, the primary sanction might be loss of credit, rather than a failing grade. The option to try again without penalty would be available.

Instructional Objectives

Before writing a contract to meet the criteria stated above, a teacher must decide how to provide instruction effectively and evaluate mastery fairly. Ideally, with current knowledge of instruction, it should be possible for each student to earn an A through a full mastery of the material. A number of successful approaches use programed materials and teaching machines, as well as traditional textbooks. To make a body of material accessible to students, break the course down into units and set clear performance objectives for each unit. Then, select a teaching mechanism (programed text, teaching machine, ordinary text with study questions, small group discussion, specially prepared exercises requiring student performance, and so on). Then test for mastery of the unit (oral or written) and reteach if the objectives are not met.

The research literature on teaching methods (mostly with college students) offers some interesting ideas to the junior high and high school teacher. Much of this research centers around a system first described and tested by Fred Keller and used at the University of Brasilia in 1964. Keller describes his system as follows:

The way the system operates can best be understood, perhaps, if you will try to imagine for a moment that you are once again a college freshman. Assume that you have just arrived, along with about a hundred other students, at the first meeting of a course in elementary psychology, with laboratory. This is a one-term course, with seventy-five minute class meetings scheduled for Tuesday and Thursday mornings (a Wednesday afternoon and Saturday morning period will soon be added in response to student demand).

Since this is the first meeting of the class, you probably arrived late and missed some of the Professor's opening remarks (and a little cup of coffee, if you're in Brazil), but one of the assistants greets you pleasantly and gives you a mimeographed hand-out, from which I shall now quote:

This is a course through which you may move, from start to finish, at your own pace. You will not be held back by other students or forced to go ahead before you are ready. At best, you may meet all the course requirements in less than one semester; at worst, you may not complete the job within that time. How fast you go is up to you.

The work of this course will be divided into thirty units of content which correspond roughly to a series of homework assignments and laboratory exercises. These units will come in a definite numerical order, and you must show your mastery of each unit, by passing a "readiness test" or carrying out an experiment, before moving on to the next.

A good share of your *reading* for this course may be done in the classroom, at those times when no lectures, demonstrations, or other activities are taking place. Your classroom, that is, will sometimes be a study hall.

The lectures and demonstrations in this course will have a different relation to the rest of your work than is usually the rule. They will be provided only when you have demonstrated your readiness to appreciate them; no examination will be based upon them; and you need not attend them if you do not wish. When a certain percentage of the class has reached a certain point in the course, a lecture or demonstration will be available at a stated time, but it will not be compulsory.

The teaching staff of your course will include proctors, assistants, and an instructor. A *proctor* is an undergraduate who has been chosen for his mastery of the course content and orientation, for his maturity of judgment, for his understanding of the special problems that confront you as a beginner, and for his willingness to assist. It is he who will pass upon your readiness tests as satisfactory or unsatisfactory. His decision will ordinarily be law, but if he is ever in serious doubt, he can appeal to the classroom assistant or even the instructor, for a ruling. Failure to pass a test on the first try, the second, the third, or even later, will not be held against you. It is better that you get too much testing than not enough, if your final success in the course is to be assured.

Your work in the laboratory will be carried out under the direct supervision of a graduate laboratory assistant, whose detailed duties cannot be listed here. . . . There will also be a graduate classroom assistant, upon whom your proctor will depend for various course materials (assignments, study questions, special readings, and so on), and who will keep up to date all progress records for course members. The classroom assistant will confer with the instructor daily, aid the proctors on occasion, and act in a variety of ways to further the smooth operation of the course machinery.

The instructor will have as his principal responsibilities: (a) the selection of all study material used in the course; (b) the organization and the mode of presenting this material; (c) the construction of tests and examinations; and (d) the final evaluation of each student's progress. It will be his duty also to provide lectures, demonstrations, and discussion opportunities for all students who have earned the privilege; to act as a clearing-house for requests and complaints; and to arbitrate in any case of disagreement between students and proctors or assistants. . . .

All students in the course are expected to take a final examination, in which the entire term's work will be represented. With certain exceptions, this examination will come at the same time for all students—at the end of the term. . . . The examination will consist of questions which, in large part, you have already answered on your readiness tests. Twenty-five percent of your course grade will be based on this examination; the remaining 75 percent will be based on the number of units of reading and laboratory work that you have successfully completed during the term. . . . .

Together with this description and a few items of information concerning course machinery, staffing, and study materials, you are handed your first work unit—your first assignment—and listen to a few inspiring words from your instructor. He outlines the rules of the game once more, for those who didn't read them or didn't believe them; he expresses his complete faith in your maturity and willingness to work for what you get; he promises you a square deal; he tells you of his great expectations; and he ends by suggesting that you drop the course at once if the prospects don't appeal.

Along with the unit assignment, you receive a set of *study questions* and some advice on how to use them. These questions will vary in number with the degree of their generality and the type of reading that they cover, but they are designed to include every point that your instructor thinks essential in the reading assignment (and to exclude, perhaps, some items that he thinks are of lesser merit).

You are now on your own in the course, although you may not really believe it. You are somewhat disturbed by your "freedom," the amount of testing that you see ahead, the talk about "excellence" and "perfection," the apparent absence of lectures to clarify your reading, and the general strangeness of everything. On the other hand, there are the positive features of noncompulsory lecture attendance, going at your own speed, and getting your first A or B. You decide to hang on, at least until the drop-out deadline.

The course description tells you exactly what steps to take from this day on. First, you are to study your assignment until it is fully mastered—until you are sure that you can cope successfully with all the study questions of the unit. You can do this work at home, in your dormitory, or in the classroom (which was recommended by the instructor). Others will be studying in the classroom, and the studyhall proctor will always be on hand to help if you have trouble with any part of the assignment. Besides, the study hall will be the source of announcements and new materials for the course. You decide to work at home.

When you are ready for testing, you report to your study-hall proctor, who doesn't seem surprised to see you, or ask you where you have been. He sends you immediately to the testing room or asks you to wait a moment until a place is ready. (The number of students to be tested at one time will depend upon the current availability of proctors for grading, and a pile-up of students waiting to be tested is preferable to a pile-up waiting to be graded).

When you get to the testing proctor, you will receive one of the four or more test forms for the unit on which you have been working. He will also hand you your blue book, one or two pages of which you will use in answering your test questions. In ten or fifteen minutes, when you have completed your answers, you will return your test form to the testing proctor. He will record the event and send you, with your blue book, into the proctor's room next door, for grading. There you will find, in a special cubicle or at a special table, the grading proctor to whom you have been assigned for the duration of the course, to whom you will always report except on those occasions when a substitute may be necessary.

The next step is the important one. The proctor, with you seated beside him, will grade your readiness test. First, he scans the test quickly, checking each wrong answer with his pen. If there are too many of these, the grading operation stops right there and you are advised to study further before coming to be tested and graded; this test won't be counted. (You will also be told not to come back until a certain time has elapsed—say at least thirty minutes. This is not only to encourage studying, but also to keep you from "shopping around" among test forms or gaining familiarity with all the available questions).

However, if you have made but two or three errors, you will be given a chance to defend your answers. If your defense is impressive and if a restatement of the questions evokes satisfactory replies, your proctor will add an O.K. to his earlier check marks to indicate a change of grade. If your defense turns out to be inadequate, he will discuss the matter with you, recommend the restudy of certain points, and send you away with the promise that your failure will not weigh against you, either then or in the future. In case all the answers were initially correct or deserve an O.K., he will probably congratulate you, record your success, and send you back to the study hall for your next assignment. If time permits, he may ask you why you answered one or two questions as you did, just to probe the depth of your understanding or to get acquainted. He keeps your blue book when you leave, and will pass it along to the assistant or the instructor at the end of the period, for inspection and recording.

This sequence of events will be repeated for the remaining units of the course, with review assignments and laboratory exercises introduced at appropriate times along the way. The number of tests that you will require for each unit may vary considerably, but the average may be no more than two. When the last one has been passed, you can arrange the date of your final examination. Beyond that, you are free to turn to other matters or, ideally, to begin another course of study under a similar program of advancement.

This learning situation is in some respects similar to that which one meets in the field of programed textbooks, teaching machines, and computer-based instruction. There is an initial analysis and organization of subject matter; there is great concern for the terminal behavior aimed at in each student; there's the provision for individualized progression, as each basic step is mastered; and there is a feedback to the instructor which enables him to improve the program.

In this case, however, the steps are not "frames" in a "set"; they are more inclusive, and better described as homework or laboratory assignments. The "response" is not simply the completion of a prepared statement by filling in a work or phrase; it is the resultant, you might say, of many such responses, and better described as the understanding of a principle, a formula, a concept, or a technique. Advance within the program is not based simply upon the appearance of a confirming word or presentation of the next frame, but involves a *personal interchange between the student and his peer or his better.*

The use of a programed text, a teaching machine, closed-circuit television, or a computer is quite possible within such a system. It may even be desirable. (One of the textbooks was programed in the course I've just described). But such devices are not at present to be equated with the course itself.[1]

Several studies on mastery of material have compared a teaching program such as Keller's with the more traditional textbook-lecture approaches. Bill Sheppard and Harold MacDermot[2] used a modified Keller system in teaching Psychology of Learning. Students were assigned five to fifteen pages of text that they had to explain in detail to a listener (a student who had completed the unit). If both were satisfied with the student's performance, the unit was recorded as passed, and a new unit started. If not, the student studied more and returned for another checkout. Compared to the traditional method, more students dropped the self-paced personalized instruction—15 percent versus 6 percent. However, on both objective and essay tests, the students in personalized instruction performed significantly better. They also rated the course more positively. Similar results are reported by James McMichael and Jeffery Corey.[3]

A key feature of the Keller method is the requirement for much written and oral *responding* by the student, *with evaluation*, prior to entering a final test situation. Several studies support the importance of these features. For example, one study varied the number of units checked by a proctor. Exam performance was better with proctoring, and the more units proctored, the faster the student progressed.[4] In another approach, Alba and Pennypacker[5] used student-manager teams. The managers were students trained to give feedback. For a given unit, the checkout consisted of a number of statements on cards with blanks to be filled in. The student could give an answer and get immediate feedback from the manager, who had the answer on the back of the card. A performance criterion (percent right) had to be met before the next unit could be attempted. The group following these response requirements did better than those following traditional procedures.

Some other important components of such systems are study questions, grades contingent on previously specified levels of performance, and a performance criterion. When study questions covering the major points of each unit are provided, test performance is better. When grades can be earned for specified levels of performance, performance is higher.[6] When the performance criterion for passing a unit is set high, performance is higher.[7] If 95 percent is required to pass a unit test, this performance is more likely to be achieved than if the passing level is 75 percent. Another concern in using a performance criterion is the specification of a performance level at which remediation is required. For example, if performance falls below 90 percent, no points are earned. The student is required to redo the unit until the criterion of 90 percent is met. Bostow and O'Connor[8] showed that a required remediation procedure like this increased group performance by one-half of a letter grade.

The use of self-pacing, while desirable in many cases, is not necessary. The contract can specify given requirements to be met prior to certain dates (for example, the dates of the midterm and final exams).

The Contract

With a clear understanding that it makes little sense to write a contract if the course of study does not involve specific objectives and ways of achieving them, we can now look at a sample. This contract is set up on the assumption that most class periods will be used for checkouts, short lectures and demonstrations, self-paced study, and quizzes. If class is used primarily for lecture, then a special discussion-checkout session would be required.

The student's part of the contract tells how points can be earned, what they can be exchanged for, and what will happen if they are not. The teacher's part of the contract tells what the teacher will be responsible for and that he intends to be fair.

In setting a relationship between grades and points, the key is to be reasonable, *but do not set the standard too low*. In the example, we have used approximately 85 percent of possible points for A, 75 percent for B, and 65 percent for C. It would be just as good to use 90 percent, 80 percent, and 70 percent. But keep in mind that these values are unrealistic unless the test items clearly fit with instruction, and the criteria for projects can be readily met by most students.

Contract

For the Student

I wish to learn more about _____ .

I understand that I can earn points toward a grade by doing the unit assignments in order and by meeting the following requirements:

1 Passing unit checkouts (18 units in course)

    Units 1 to 9 are to be completed by _____ .

    Units 10 to 18 are to be completed by _____ .

10 points for each checkout passed at 90% correct or better (I understand that if I fail a checkout the first time, I can retake it without penalty, after at least 30 minutes additional study. I also understand that I must pass the checkout before starting a new unit.)

2 Doing a term project (theme, report, etc.) consisting of _____ _____ .

up to 50 points (Criteria for grading will be provided to me before I start.)

3 Taking the midterm quiz Date _____

up to 50 points

4 Taking the final quiz Date _____

up to 70 points

    Total possible points

350 points

I understand that my grade will be determined as follows:

    I can earn an A with 300 or more points.

    I can earn a B with 260 or more points.

    I can earn a C with 220 or more points.

I understand that I will receive no grade or course credit if I earn less than 220 points.

Signature of student _____ Date _____

For the Teacher

I agree to help you learn more about _____ .

I will provide you with appropriate lectures, demonstrations, text assignments, and study questions. The checkouts and examinations will be based on the key ideas and procedures highlighted in the study questions. I will provide you with any additional assistance you may require. I will award points and grades according to the schedule given above.

Signature of teacher _____ Date _____

Figure 12.1 A sample contract

The Learning-Center Contract

In unit 10 we described procedures used in the Anne Arundel County Learning Center by Shlomo Cohen to individualize instruction for dropouts and provide motivation for learning. Any school learning center can do the same. To earn certain credits, grades, privileges, and other rewards, the students agree to do some units of study and be checked out on them.

To work efficiently, the learning center must have sequentially programed materials and placement testing so students can begin at a level they are ready for. Then the teacher can negotiate a contract with the student for the week or month, depending on individual needs.

Figure 12.2 shows a contract from the Corrective Reading Program,[9] which is designed for the poor reader in grades four to twelve. The students come for daily lessons in the learning center and are taught in groups of five to eight. The lesson involves a teacher presentation of new word-attack skills (ten minutes), group reading designed to give practice on the skills being taught, and individual checkouts on the reading. Charts are provided to show graphically each student's progress and to keep track of points. Contracts are renegotiated each two weeks. A teacher's manual provides detailed guidelines for implementing the point-contract system.

The Home-School Contract

A number of counselors have tried various contracts in which school performance and attendance is reinforced by the parents at home. In unit 10 in the

...AND BOTH PARTIES AGREE TO...

Reading Contract: For the student

I want to learn to read better. I understand that I will earn points for working hard. I will try to earn as many points as I can each day.

I understand that I can earn points in the following ways:

1 Work-Attack Skills (0–5 points)
I can earn points for the following the signals and reading words correctly.
If I make no mistakes, I can earn 5 points.

2 Group Reading
0–4 errors   _____ points
5–8 errors   _____ points
9–12 errors   _____ points
Over 12 errors   _____ points

3 Studying the Stories
If I study the stories while others are being checked out, I can earn 2 points.
If I do not study the stories while others are being checked out, I earn 0 points.
If I prevent others from studying the stories during checkout, I lose 2 points.

4 Individual Checkouts
I can earn points for first reading as follows:
0–1 errors   _____ points
2–3 errors   _____ points
4–5 errors   _____ points
6–8 errors   _____ points
I can earn points for second readings as follows:
0–1 errors   _____ points
2–3 errors   _____ points
4–5 errors   _____ points
6–8 errors   _____ points

I understand that the points I earn each day will count toward my weekly grade:
_____ points earn an **A** grade.
_____ points earn a **B** grade.
_____ points earn a **C** grade.

I understand that the points I earn can also be exchanged for (fill in if applicable): _____

I understand that if I fail to keep my part of the contract, the teacher has the right to take steps to insure the group's progress.

For the Teacher

I will award points as specified in this contract. I will give you the maximum number of points for following the rules as set up in the contract.

It is my responsibility to teach everyone in the group. If you disrupt another person's lesson, I will exclude you from the group. You may get back into the group only by following the rules set up in this contract.

I will make an effort to help you make up points in individual checkouts when you are absent for legitimate reasons.

Any rule changes must first be presented in a new contract.

Teacher's signature   *Student's signature*

_____   _____

Date _____

Figure 12.2 A sample reading contract

Contract

DATE   February 12, 1971

CONTRACT   # 1

1) Bartholomew may earn 25¢ for each task that he completes in reading. He may earn up to $2.50 per week. To pick up his money, Bartholomew should bring a note to the office from the reading teacher stating how many tasks he has completed.

This contract will expire February 26, 1971, at which time it may be renegotiated.

I, Bartholomew, agree to the terms of the agreement as stated above.

_____

Bartholomew

We, the undersigned, agree to the terms of the contract as stated above.

_____   _____

Father   Mother

(Contract #2 same as above, negotiated March 1, 1971, expired March 19, 1971)

Figure 12.3 Contract negotiated between Bartholomew and his parents

study by Bailey, Wolf, and Phillips, the daily report card from school provided privileges at home (Achievement Place). MacDonald, Gallimore, and MacDonald[10] used a contracting procedure in Honolulu to increase daily attendance by children who were chronically truant. Specially-trained attendance officers made "deals" so students could earn after-school and week-end privileges at home by attending school. One "deal" used time with a girl friend as the reinforcer. The contracts were very successful in increasing attendance.

Contracts between home and school were also a part of the Anne Arundel Learning Center program. For example, with the simple contract shown in Figure 12.3, Bartholomew increased his average number of reading tasks completed from .05 per day to 2.0.[11]

summary

Point-contracts are specialized token reinforcement systems in which the performance requirements and consequences are written out and agreed to by both parties. The contract should specify responsibilities, privileges, sanctions, possible bonuses, and monitoring procedures. Three kinds of possible contracts were illustrated: the term-course contract, in which credits and grades are the consequences; the learning-center contract, in which a fuller range of backup reinforcers can be used; and the home-school contract set up by counseling personnel, in which behavior and progress at school earn privileges and rewards at home.

A term-course or learning-center contract can only be effective if there is a clearly outlined program of instruction and procedure for accomplishing it. A good example of these two points is the Keller "personalized instruction" system. It requires teaching materials broken down into units, a specified teaching mechanism, and specified response requirements for the students.

The research literature supports the efficacy of the Keller method over traditional lecture methods, and also establishes the importance of providing performance practice (not just silent reading), study questions, contingent grades, and a high performance criterion. It seems likely that many of these procedures will be used in middle and high school settings in the near future.

self-test

1 A contract has four essential parts: specification of _____, specification of _____, specification of _____ for failure to live up to the contract, and specification of a _____ procedure.

1 responsibilities, privileges; sanctions; monitoring

2 Before writing a contract, a teacher must decide how to provide and evaluate _____ effectively.

3 Characteristics of successful approaches include breaking the course down into _____ and setting clear performance _____ for each.

4 Then, a _____ mechanism is selected to get the objectives across.

5 A key feature to the Keller method is the requirement of much written and oral _____ by the student, with _____ prior to a final test situation.

NUMBER RIGHT _____

2 instruction

3 units;
  objectives

4 teaching

5 responding;
  evaluation

exercise 1 programed practice

1 Point-contract systems are specialized _____ _____ systems in which a written contract details the performance requirements and possible consequences.

2 A contract has four essential parts: specification of _____, specification of _____, specification of _____ for failure to live up to the contract, and specification of a _____ procedure.

3 The subject-area teacher who has a group of students for one period a day can use the contract to provide structure, _____, and continuity from day to day.

4 The learning-center staff or a team-teaching staff can use contracts to _____ instruction.

1 token
  reinforcement

2 responsibilities;
  privileges;
  sanctions;
  monitoring

3 motivation

4 individualize

5 parents

6 grade;
  credits

7 instruction

8 A

9 units;
  objectives

10 teaching

11 mastery

12 Fred Keller

13 better

14 positively

15 responding;
  evaluation

16 manager

5 The school counselor can arrange contracts with several teachers and _____ for students who need special help.

6 A term-course contract should spell out what the students will be expected to do to earn what kind of _____ and course _____.

7 Before writing a contract, a teacher must decide how to provide effective _____ and evaluate it.

8 Ideally, with current knowledge of instruction, it should be possible for each student to earn an _____ through a full mastery of the material.

9 Characteristics of successful approaches include breaking the course down into _____ and providing clear performance _____ for each unit.

10 Then, a _____ mechanism is selected to get the objectives across.

11 A test of _____ is then given (oral or written) and a mechanism for reteaching is provided if the objectives are not met the first time.

12 Much current research centers around a system using the above procedures first described and tested by _____ _____.

13 On both objective and essay tests, the students in Keller's "personalized instruction" perform _____ than those in conventional instruction.

14 They also rate the course more _____.

15 A key feature to the Keller method is the requirement of much written and oral _____ by the student, with _____.

16 Another approach to getting student responses going used student-_____ teams to give checkouts.

17 **Some other important components of such systems are the use of study**

_____, making _____ contingent on acceptable levels of

performance, and the use of a performance _____.

17 questions;
  grades;
  criterion

18 **It makes little sense to write a contract if the course of study does not involve**

rather specific _____ and ways of achieving them.

19 **In setting a relationship between grades and points, the key is to be reason-**

18 objectives

able, but do not set the _____ too low.

20 **In a learning-center contract, the students agree to do some units of study**

and be _____ _____ on them to earn certain credits,

19 standard

grades, and privileges.

21 **To operate efficiently, the learning center has to have _____ mate-**

rials and placement testing so that students can be placed in the materials at a

20 checked out

level they are ready for.

21 programed

discussion questions

1 State the four main features of a teacher-student contract.
2 Describe the features of a term-course contract.
3 How would a learning-center contract differ from a term-course contract? Why?
4 How would a home-school contract differ from school-based contracts?
5 Why is an explicit, effective instructional program essential to a term-course contract?
6 Describe Keller's system for "personalized instruction," and outline its essential components.
7 Cite the outcome of research related to study of Keller's personalized instructional system, and discuss its implications for design of a contract system. (Be able to do this for each outcome mentioned.)
8 Give an example of the use of a home-school contract.
9 Discuss the structure of *this* course in relation to point-contract systems

unit 13

Punishment: When To, How To, and Why Not To

lesson

We have delayed the detailed examination of punishment for two reasons. First, if you use reinforcement effectively, you usually do not have to use punishment. And second, the most effective approach to weakening behavior depends on the use of reinforcers, both presenting them and taking them away.

As noted earlier, stimulus events that follow a behavior and weaken its future probability are called *punishing stimuli*. There are two types. Type 1 involves the presentation of events that we generally refer to as painful or aversive. These include loud noises, excessive heat and cold, various odors, excessive pressure on the body, intense light in the eyes, electric shock, and so forth. Type 2 punishers involve taking away or cutting off reinforcers. *Response cost* procedures, such as fines or loss of privileges, involve taking away reinforcers. *Time out* involves cutting off reinforcers and access to them. The use of punishing stimuli is called *punishment*.

The two types of punishment can be related to the two types of reinforcement as follows:

Effect on Behavior	Procedure	
	Present Stimulus	*Terminate Stimulus*
Strengthens	Positive Reinforcement (candy)	Negative Reinforcement (getting out of the rain)
Weakens	Punishment type 1 (spanking)	Punishment type 2 (fine)

As you know, neutral stimuli, when followed by reinforcing events, develop reinforcing properties. They become conditioned reinforcers. In a similar way, when neutral stimuli are followed by punishing events, they develop punishing properties—that is, they weaken responses that they follow. They become *conditioned punishers*.

Is Use of Punishment Immoral?

Probably no area of behavioral psychology has generated more emotion, confusion, and misunderstanding than the topic of punishment. Some people believe that any use of punishment under any circumstances is immoral. Some believe it is all right to punish children severely as long as you don't slap them in the face. Some equate any form of isolation procedure with prison, regardless of benefits to the child. Some believe we should eliminate the word *punishment* from the English language, as if that would somehow make people more loving.

But consider this: For three years a child has been kept in a strait jacket whenever unattended (nighttime, for example) to prevent him from gouging his flesh and cutting an artery. Now suppose that by applying a mild electric shock (no more painful than a hypodermic needle) every time the child begins to gouge himself, this behavior could be eliminated in three days. Which is the moral thing to do—to use punishment to eliminate a behavior that completely restricts this child's possibilities for normal development, or to cuddle him and be kind to him each time he begins to hurt himself?

Remember Peter? His mother punished him by placing him in his room with the door closed until he was quiet for five minutes. She used this only six times the first week and his behavior changed dramatically. A positive relationship with his mother became possible after his demanding and aggressive behavior was punished. Did the result justify the method used?

When the long-term effects of using punishment are far more beneficial than not using it, the moral person will do what is best for the child and use punishment. It would be immoral *not* to do everything possible to help children learn what is necessary in order to live freely in our society. There are few mothers of two-year-olds who question the use of punishment when it keeps their child from being hurt or killed by automobiles, knives, gas, or fire. Punishment, in itself, is not immoral, even though it may be used in ways that are harmful to children or adults.

Is Punishment Effective?

Teachers have been told that they should not use punishment because it doesn't work and that it produces only temporary suppression of behavior, not real change. But current research shows that punishment is very effective. There are many stimulus events that can be shown to weaken behavior. The belief that punishment is ineffective arises from misinterpretation of early research. In early studies, the rate of punished behavior decreased during the period of punishment (temporary suppression), but increased to the prepunishment rate after the punishment was removed. Now suppose we used the same logic on the effects of reinforcement. As long as a behavior is reinforced, it is maintained at a high rate. When the reinforcement is removed, the rate eventually returns to its prereinforcement level (extinction). By this logic, behavior followed by reinforcement is temporarily enhanced, but it isn't really changed. The fact of the matter is that operant behavior is a function of consequences. As the consequences change so does the behavior. But this does not mean consequences are not effective. The question becomes one of learning how to use consequences to maintain behaviors over time.

Azrin and Holz have reviewed the current status of punishment research, and they conclude that punishment has an effect on behavior opposite from reinforcement.[1] Most of the principles of reinforcement are readily transferable to the analysis of punishment, except the goal is weakening, rather than strengthening, behavior. For example, punishment is more effective when it is intense or given in greater quantity, as is reinforcement. Also, punishment is more effective when it is given immediately.

There is no question that it is possible to use punishment to produce strong and lasting effects on behavior. *However, that does not mean it should be used.* Other matters need to be considered in deciding when and where to use punishment.

Why Is Punishment Usually to Be Avoided?

Punishment involves presenting aversive stimuli (type 1 punishers) or withdrawing reinforcing stimuli (type 2 punishers). Use of type 1 punishers is usually to be avoided, not because they don't work, but because of undesired side effects. Parents and teachers want to teach children to come to them for help in solving problems. This goal is inconsistent with the major side effect of using type 1 punishers: *people learn to avoid and escape sources of punishment.*

Escape behavior is reinforced (negatively) because it gets one away from a punishing stimulus. When you take your hand off the hot stove, the burning stops. *Avoidance behavior* is reinforced (negatively) because it gets one away from a conditioned punishing stimulus. The conditioned punisher is usually a signal (S^D) that punishment is near. Get away from the conditioned punisher, and you avoid the punishing stimulus. Sight of the hot stove preceded getting burned last time. Next time you see the stove, you stay away from it. When a child is punished excessively, he will learn to avoid not only the spankings (unconditioned punishers) but the people who did the punishing and the places where it occurred (conditioned punishing stimuli).

A number of names have been used to describe the avoidance and escape behaviors *taught to children* through punishment at home and at school. Here are a few of them:

Name	*Avoidance or Escape Behavior*
Cheating	Avoiding punishment for being wrong
Truancy	Avoiding or escaping the many punishments that go with school failure, poor teaching, and punitive administrations
Lying	Avoiding the punishment that follows doing something wrong
Sneaking	Avoiding being caught misbehaving
Hiding	Avoiding being caught
Murdering	Escaping from a punishing person by destroying him

A Model for Aggression.   Another reason for avoiding the use of physical punishment is that it shows a child how to be aggressive to others. Children imitate what they see adults doing. Children whose parents are aggressive in the use of punishment are more aggressive with other children.

SPARE THE ROD AND SPOIL THE CHILD.

How Is Punishment Used Effectively?

Effective punishment must do these things:

1 Prevent avoidance and escape from the source of punishment
2 Minimize the need for future punishment
3 Not provide a model of aggressive behavior

Peter's mother used punishment effectively. She eliminated Peter's objectionable behavior while improving her relationship with him. Let's look at the procedures she used in the context of the three points just mentioned.

1. *Preventing Avoidance and Escape from the Source of Punishment.* Instead of spanking Peter, which might drive him away from her, his mother used time out as the punishment. By taking away reinforcers (attention, in this case), his mother set it up so that Peter had to come back to her to get reinforcement. Furthermore, his mother was not paired with strong, painful, or fear-inducing stimuli. Peter wanted to return to his mother because she was a source of reinforcement rather than a source of punishment.

Generally, withdrawal of positive reinforcers is an effective form of punishment *as long as there are clear-cut steps provided for earning the reinforcers back.* Peter could earn his mother's attention back by being quiet for five minutes.

The use of time out and withdrawal of privileges gets around the problem posed by avoidance and escape behavior. Another way is to insure that the child cannot escape the punisher. This is only possible with very young children or with the use of drastic techniques, such as confinement. The teacher seldom has this kind of control.

Peter's mother also gave him much attention and affection for cooperative behavior. Although Peter did not like being in his room, he did like being with his mother, and this fact was capitalized on in devising the procedure to change his behavior.

2. *Minimizing the Need for Future Punishment.* Peter's mother used two procedures to minimize the future need for punishment. First, she gave a warning signal. "Stop that" became a conditioned punisher by being paired with time out. Eventually, the warning signal alone was sufficient to get Peter to behave. Second, his mother reinforced behavior incompatible with objectionable behavior. If Peter was being cooperative he could not be demanding. If he was being affectionate he could not be aggressive. Objectionable behavior was replaced by an alternative way of getting his mother's attention, which was more satisfying to his mother and better for Peter's development.

3. *Avoiding the Use of an Aggressive Model.* The withdrawal of reinforcers rather than the use of aversive stimuli insures that an aggressive model is not provided to the child.

Thus, effective punishment relies on reinforcement of behavior incompatible with the punishable behavior and removal of reinforcers contingent on misbehavior (type 2 punishment). Also, to make punishment effective, you should follow these rules:

1. *The punishment should be immediate.* Take away the points or start the time out when the punishable behavior begins.

2. *When reinforcers are taken away, be sure to define a way to earn them back.* "You may rejoin the group after you are quiet for five minutes." "You may go to gym tomorrow if there is no fighting between now and then."

Consider the case of Claire. She was a bright sixteen-year-old who was about to be expelled from high school for delinquency (truancy, poor grades, and incorrigibility at home).

At the time help was sought, Claire was staying at home but threatening to run away. There was no father in the home. Her mother had taken away (as punishment) all money, use of the telephone, and dating privileges. The treatment plan worked out with Claire and her mother was as follows: one note from school each day (signifying attendance at all classes) earned Claire telephone privileges for that day; four notes during the week earned one weekend date; five notes earned two dates. This plan worked beyond belief even though Claire's mother was very skeptical at first. When Claire was simply punished by loss of privileges, she showed no improvement. It was not until a definite way to earn the privileges back was provided (by showing responsible behavior) that a change became evident.[2]

Peter earned back his mother's attention by being quiet for five minutes. Claire earned back telephone and dating privileges by attending school regularly. Claire's plan worked so well that the notes were eliminated within a few months with no loss of attendance.

3. *Use one warning only.* The first time a punishable behavior occurs, give a warning. The next time, back up your warning signal with a cost contingency or time out.

4. *Stay calm* and matter-of-fact when administering a punishment. Don't fuel the fire with personal anger. You are trying to teach responsible behavior. Show that behavior yourself.

5. *Be consistent.* Be sure the undesired behavior is not reinforced now and then.

Isolation Is Not Time Out

One is likely to associate time out with isolating a child from other people for a while. But isolation is not necessarily time out, nor is time out necessarily isolation. As noted before, time out refers to *time out from positive reinforcement*. If the classroom is not reinforcing, taking the child out of it cannot be a time-out punishment. In fact, placing a child in the hall or sending him to the principal may be reinforcing if special attention is given or peer status is enhanced. For the autistic child, isolation may be reinforcing. *Isolation is not time out. Time out consists of cutting off the possibility of all reinforcement for a period of time.* This may be done *in* the classroom with a chair in the corner, as long as the rest of the class is trained to ignore the child being punished. Time out might consist of taking away the child's programed reader for the rest of the reading period, because he was looking up the answers and writing them in. Just sitting with nothing to do for twenty minutes while everyone else is learning can be a time-out punishment.

When Should Punishment Be Used?

There are two circumstances under which punishment may be required because direct reinforcement approaches are likely to fail. The first is when behavior is so *frequent* that there is little or no incompatible behavior to reinforce. Head banging, rocking, and other behavior frequently associated with autism may require punishment until attention to other stimuli can be established. The authors have used time out with a very aggressive kindergarten child who failed to respond to several approaches using reinforcement. The teacher was not able to find enough cooperative behavior to reinforce. Time out quickly stopped the child's hitting and pushing, but he still had to be taught how to play cooperatively with other children.

The second circumstance where punishment may be required is when the problem behavior is so *intense* that someone might get hurt, including the child himself. Intense aggression, self-destructive behavior, and tantrums may require punishment. Such behavior may cause irreparable damage to the child himself or to others. Under such circumstances, punishment is a justifiable alternative.

Technical Note on Multiple Functions of Stimuli

Stimulus events can serve different functions with respect to different responses. In discussing the criticism trap, we noted that the teacher's saying "sit down" served a conditioned reinforcing function for standing (a preceding response) and a cuing or discriminative function for sitting (a following response). In discussing chaining, we emphasized that the stimuli between two responses in a chain have both reinforcing and discriminative functions.

Stimuli associated with aversive conditioning can also have multiple functions. For example, if the words *no* or *don't* or *stop that* are followed by punishment, they can serve as a conditioned punisher for the response that precedes them and as a warning signal (S^D) for the response that follows them (and reduce the likelihood of further punishment). For example, Peter starts to push his sister, and his mother says, "Stop that." He stops pushing and walks away from his sister. "Stop that" could serve a punishing function for pushing and have a discriminative function for stopping pushing and walking away.

summary

Punishment is an effective method of changing behavior. However, because the person punished learns to avoid and escape the punisher, this is not usually a preferred method. There are problems for which the use of punishment is the most humane solution. They usually involve very intense or very frequent objectionable behavior. When punishment must be used, take care to insure its effectiveness and to minimize the development of avoidance behavior. Effective punishment is given immediately. It relies on withdrawal of reinforcers and provides clear steps for regaining them. To make punishment effective, use a warning signal, carry it out in a calm matter-of-fact way, accompany it with reinforcement for behavior incompatible with the behavior being punished. Be consistent and insure that the undesired behavior does not receive reinforcement.

broadening your perspective

If the teacher is to use punishment at all, some kind of response cost (point loss) system is to be preferred. In unit 11 we illustrated the effectiveness of fines (point losses) as used in Achievement Place and in the home-point system. The studies that follow are not intended to provide models for regular classroom teaching, but to give you a fuller understanding of the hows and whys of punishment in more unusual teaching situations.

Self-Destructive Behavior

Ivar Lovaas and James Simmons studied the problem of self-destructive behavior by working with three profoundly retarded children (two aged eight and another eleven) who showed severe self-destructive behaviors.

John showed minimal social behavior. He did not imitate or talk, and he was not toilet-trained. Since the age of two, he had shown self-destructive behavior. He used his fists and knuckles to bang his temple and forehead, producing bruises and contusions. At seven years, he was hospitalized by his parents. For six months prior to the experiment, he had restraints on his legs and arms continuously. There were multiple scars all over his head. He kicked and screamed, and was generally out of control.

Linda's social behavior was very much like John's, and in addition she resisted affection. At the start of the experiment she had many scabs on both ears, her left ear was bleeding, and her legs were badly bruised. She had been kept in restraints much of the time for more than a year and a half.

Gregg had spent most of the previous two years in restraints. He had been hospitalized for eight years. He did not walk or talk. His head and face were much scarred.

Lovaas and Simmons studied two procedures for eliminating the self-destructive behavior of these children. In the first study John and Gregg were placed in a room by themselves without restraints or attention for ninety minutes a day to see if self-destructive behavior would extinguish. John hit himself 9000 times over eleven days before he quit. Gregg hit himself more than 900 times a session at the start. This gradually dropped to a low of thirty after sixty sessions. Extinction worked but it proved costly in terms of time and hurts. It could be fatal with some children. Also, the effects did not generalize to other situations. Self-destructive behaviors still occurred in other settings.

In contrast, when an electric shock was delivered by a hand-held, battery-operated prod, self-destructive behavior was reduced drastically. For John, it took only twelve brief shocks over four sessions to stop self-destructive behavior in one setting. John quickly learned which attendant shocked him and stopped his self-destructive behavior with that attendant only. When the second attendant also used shock, the self-destructive behavior stopped with him also. As John showed less self-destructive behavior, he also whined less and avoided the attendant less. Being freed from restraints also brought many new positive experiences to John.

Similar dramatic changes in the behavior of Linda and Gregg occurred when mild shock was used. In all cases, there was no broad generalization to persons or places. It is probably necessary to provide punishment in many situations with many persons to achieve generalized control.

An additional study was made with Gregg, to look for some of the variables that maintained his destructive behavior. First, the experimenters tried deprivation of attention for twenty-four hours. This had no effect. Then they did the reverse and gave him continual attention for twenty-four hours. This had no effect. Next they gave Gregg "understanding and sympathy" for thirty seconds after each third time Gregg hit himself. For two out of three study periods, this attention reinforced self-hitting. For one period, it did not. Next, they looked for stronger reinforcers. In the last study, the attendant took Gregg out of his crib after each fifth hit for thirty to sixty seconds. He would comfort him and allow him to play with drawers, doors, and blocks. The rate of self-hitting increased drastically under this "understanding" approach to treatment.

In summary, these studies show that there are situations in which punishment using shock may be the most humane thing a concerned human being can do for another; and in contrast, tenderness and sympathy may be dangerous to life.[3]

Self-Stimulation and Discrimination Learning in Autistic Children

Characteristic behaviors of children called autistic are rhythmic body rocking, hand waving, hair twirling, and arm flapping. When these are going on, the children seem oblivious to their environment. Robert Koegel and Andrea Covert showed how a punishment procedure prepared the children for instruction.

Two children aged five and seven participated. A discrimination learning experiment was set up: the children were to press a bar whenever a red light went on and a noise sounded (S^Ds). If they responded within ten seconds, they received a candy. If they did not respond in ten seconds, the light and noise went off and they got no candy. So the children had to learn to discriminate when to respond.

During baseline, subject 1 showed self-stimulation about sixty percent of the time and made correct responses about twenty percent of the time (random responding). Subject 2 showed no correct responses and showed self-stimulation about twenty percent of the time. A punishment procedure was then introduced to suppress self-stimulation. This consisted of sharply saying "No," and if necessary, slapping the child briskly on the hands when he began self-stimulation. With punishment, self-stimulation went to zero, and correct responding rose to over 90 percent in the trials for both children. Thus, the use of punishment to suppress self-stimulation made new learning possible.[4]

Time Out and Bedwetting

Enuresis or bedwetting can be annoying, particularly in a five-year-old. At the University of Tennessee Psychological Clinic, Vey Nordquist worked with Michael, whose parents brought him to the clinic because he tantrumed a lot and wet his bed four or five times a week. The treatment strategy was to see if bedwetting would be eliminated when another class of behaviors changed. Home observations established that Michael was very oppositional. When parents asked him to do something, he refused; when they tried to insist, he had a tantrum. Disruptive and oppositional behavior received a lot of parental attention, but Michael was left alone if he was playing quietly. This suggested that the parents were giving differential reinforcement for misbehavior.

The parents were trained to reinforce Michael's cooperative behavior and

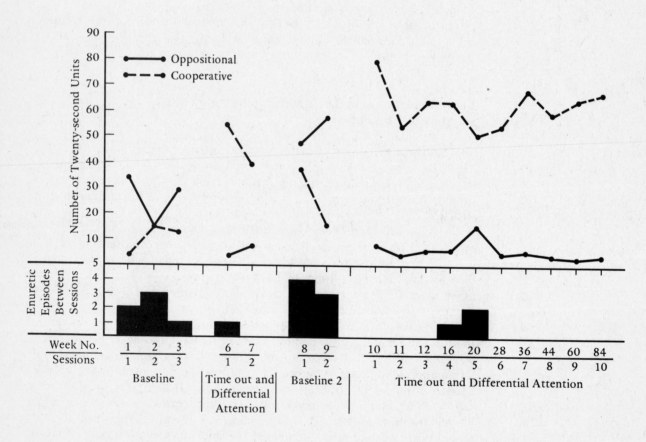

Figure 13.1 David's oppositional and cooperative behavior over baseline and treatmemt periods and the number of enuretic episodes recorded by parents between each session.

to use time out for oppositional behavior. Time out consisted of placing him in a corner in his bedroom and leaving him for ten minutes. Observers recorded thirty-minute samples of Michael's behavior in his home each week, during which time out was not used. Parents recorded bedwetting daily. Figure 13.2 shows the results for oppositional behavior and bedwetting. When time out and attention to cooperative behavior was used, cooperation increased, oppositional behavior decreased, and bedwetting decreased. The effects were maintained over an eighteen-month period.[5]

The explanation for this is not obvious. One good idea, however, comes from the work of Robert Wahler.[6] His data suggested that the use of time out increased the parents' effectiveness as social reinforcers. It could be that this increased effectiveness allowed parental reinforcement for a dry bed to work, although it had not in the past.

Use of Time Out in Speech Therapy

There are many ways to use time out. Leija McReynolds used time out in a one-to-one training situation with Paul, a five-year-old with no functional speech. He had been diagnosed as having brain damage. Paul was being trained to imitate sounds. He was fed ice cream for right responses and given praise. During one phase of training he started jargon talk, which consisted of unintelligible vocalizations, and it gradually increased to two or three times a minute. Then the time out procedure was introduced. The teacher took the ice cream and turned around in her chair with her back to Paul. She remained in this position until jargon talk had stopped for thirty seconds. Thus, time out (punishment) started with jargon talk and ended (reinforcement) with the stopping of it. Jargon talk stopped in twelve minutes of training. A similar time out procedure was effective in increasing the number of correct responses made. When sounds in word chains that had been imitated correctly before were now imitated incorrectly, time out was initiated and remained in effect until the correct imitation was given.[7]

A Comparison of Time Out and Response Cost

Burchard and Barrera compared the effects of two durations of time out and two levels of token fines on the antisocial behavior of mildly retarded adolescents. A thirty-minute time out or a thirty-token fine was more effective than a five-minute time out or a five-token fine, with the exception of one subject. One subject responded more favorably to the lower-level punishments. The higher-level punishments became increasingly more effective over time, whereas the lower values did not. For a given level of punishment, time out and fines were equally effective.[8]

self-test

1 Type 2 punishment involves _____ _____ or cutting off reinforcers.

1 taking away

2 Type 2 reinforcers are those previously called _____ reinforcers.

2 negative

3 When neutral stimuli are followed by punishing events, they become _____ punishers.

3 conditioned

4 When behavior is no longer reinforced it returns to its prereinforcement rate. When behavior is no longer punished, it returns to its _____ rate.

4 prepunishment

5 Punishment should be used when the objectionable behavior is so _____ that there is nothing to reinforce or so _____ that someone may be hurt.

5 frequent; intense

6 It is best to avoid type 1 punishment because of _____ side effects.

6 undesired

7 When a child is punished excessively, he will learn to avoid not only the spankings, but the _____ who gave them.

7 people

8 Effective punishment must be used in a way that _____ the future need for punishment.

8 minimizes, reduces

9 Objectionable behavior will decrease when the teacher makes a practice of reinforcing behavior _____ with the objectionable behavior.

9 incompatible

NUMBER RIGHT _____

exercise 1 programed practice

1 If you use _____ effectively, you usually do not have to use punishment.

1 reinforcement

266   UNIT 13

2 punishing

3 presentation

4 taking away

5 response cost

6 negative

7 presentation

8 punishing

9 conditioned

10 temporary

11 yes

12 prepunishment

13 punishment

14 punishers

2   Stimulus events that follow a behavior and weaken the future probability of such behavior are called _____ stimuli.

3   Type 1 punishment involves _____ of aversive events.

4   Type 2 punishment involves _____ _____ or cutting off reinforcers.

5   Time out and _____ _____ are both examples of type 2 punishment.

6   Instead of talking about positive and _____ reinforcers, we might also talk about type 1 and type 2 reinforcers.

7   Type 1 reinforcers would involve _____ of rewarding events.

8   Type 2 reinforcers would involve stopping of _____ events.

9   When neutral stimuli are followed by punishing events, they become _____ punishers.

10 Teachers have been told that they should not use punishment because it produces only a _____ suppression of behavior, not real change.

11 Is punishment really effective? Yes. No. (*Circle one.*)

12 When behavior is no longer reinforced, it returns to its prereinforcement rate. When behavior is no longer punished, it returns to its _____ rate.

13 Most of the principles of reinforcement are readily transferable to the analysis of _____.

14 Just as reinforcers are more effective when they are immediate and intense, so are _____.

15 It is possible to use punishment to get strong and _____ effects on behavior. However, other matters must be considered in deciding when and where to use punishment.

16 Some people believe that any use of punishment under any circumstances is _____.

17 It is best to avoid type 1 punishment because of _____ side effects.

18 One major side effect of punishment is that we learn to _____ and _____ sources of punishment.

19 Behavior that gets one away from an aversive stimulus is called _____ behavior.

20 Escape behavior is learned because it is _____ reinforced.

21 Behavior that gets one away from a conditioned punishing stimulus is called _____ behavior.

22 When a child is punished excessively, he will learn to avoid not only the spankings, but the _____ who gave them and the _____ where they were given.

23 Cheating, lying, and sneaking are all learned _____ behaviors.

24 Children imitate adult behavior. They also imitate the _____ behavior of the punishing adult.

25 Effective punishment must _____ avoidance and escape from the source of punishment.

26 Effective punishment must be used in a way that _____ the future need for punishment.

---

15 lasting

16 immoral, evil

17 undesired

18 avoid; escape

19 escape

20 negatively

21 avoidance

22 people; places

23 avoidance

24 aggressive

25 prevent

26 minimizes, reduces

27 model

28 confine

29 withdraw, take
away, remove;
punishment

30 earning,
getting

31 warning

32 conditioned

33 incompatible

34 reinforcement

35 time out

36 frequent

27 Effective punishment should not provide a _____ of aggressive behavior.

28 One way around the problem of avoiding or escaping from the source of punishment is to _____ the person being punished. However, the teacher does not have this kind of control.

29 Another way to prevent avoidance and escape behavior is to _____ reinforcers. That is, the teacher can use the procedure of making reinforcers unavailable as a kind of _____.

30 Withdrawal of positive reinforcement can be effective as long as there are clear-cut steps provided for _____ the reinforcers back.

31 Using a _____ signal before punishing a child will help to minimize the future need for punishment.

32 The warning signal will come to act as a _____ punisher for the behavior it follows and, for most occasions, will be sufficient to replace the actual punishment.

33 A second procedure useful in reducing the future need for punishment is the practice of reinforcing behavior _____ with objectionable behavior.

34 Isolation is not necessarily time out. Time out consists of cutting out the possibility of all _____ for a period of time.

35 If placing a child in a room by himself does not cut off all reinforcement, it cannot be called _____ _____.

36 If a behavior is so _____ that there is little or no incompatible behavior to reinforce, punishment may be required.

37 The second circumstance under which punishment may be required is when the problem behavior is so _____ that someone might get hurt, including the child himself.

38 The case study about the sixteen-year-old girl (Claire) demonstrated that loss of privileges alone was not effective in getting her to change. It was not until a definite way to _____ the privileges back was provided that a change became evident.

39 A stimulus like "stop that" that is followed by punishment now and then can have two stimulus functions. It can serve as a _____ stimulus for preceding responses, and as a _____ for following responses that decrease the chances of punishment.

37 intense

38 earn, get

39 punishing;
   signal,
   warning,
   discriminative
   stimulus

discussion questions

1 Define two types of punishment.

2 Explain how a conditioned punisher is established.

3 What is meant by saying that a reinforcer is effective?

4 What happens when a reinforcer no longer follows a response?

5 Why did scientists think that punishment was not an effective way to weaken behavior?

6 Reinforced behavior returns to its prereinforcement strength when it is not reinforced any longer. What happens to punished behavior when it is not punished any longer?

7 Extend the principle of immediacy to punishment: why are responses punished immediately weakened more than responses punished after a delay?

8 Explain the difference between escape behavior and avoidance behavior.

9 How is avoidance behavior learned?

10 Why should teachers avoid using punishment?

11 Analyze cheating, truancy, lying, and sneaking as effects of the use of punishment to control the behavior of children.

12 Give two key procedures involving reinforcers that are central to weakening undesired behavior.

13 Give five additional procedures for using punishment.

14 Explain what is meant by time out.

15 Is isolation always time out?

16 Give four different procedures that could be considered time out.

17 What is response cost?

18 By analogy, what would a type 2 reinforcer be?

19 Give two situations in which the use of punishment may be necessary.

20 Explain why in Claire's case the punishment that her mother used did not work.

21 Explain the multiple functions of stimuli such as "stop it" that have been paired with punishment.

22 How do the Lovaas and Corte studies support the morality of using type 1 punishment?

23 What are some apparent positive benefits of the use of time out by parents?

24 What factors influence the effectiveness of time out?

25 Which is more effective, time out or response cost?

unit 14

Teaching Self-Confidence and Self-Esteem

objectives

Many school children today are *taught* failure; others are alienated from their own families and ethnic histories by what they are taught at school. These educational effects are especially prevalent in the ghettos, but they are not restricted to any geographical or ethnic group.

To combat this situation, many reform-minded educators, sociologists, and psychologists conclude that educators should quit teaching subjects and focus all efforts on making children happy, confident, loved, and respected. Many assume that if a child is given self-esteem, he will be able to do anything.

This unit challenges the common assumptions about the place of self-esteem and related attitudes in learning. It provides a conceptual and procedural basis for teaching children to like themselves, to like school, and to persist in the face of failure through more *effective teaching of basic skills.*

lesson

An attitude is a subjective construct referring to how someone feels about some class of stimulus events. It is subjective simply because an observer cannot see the feelings of another. We determine the attitudes of others by inference. We infer a positive attitude from friendly approaches, smiling facial expressions, and words of support for the object of the attitude. Similarly, a negative attitude is inferred from avoidance or attack behavior, facial grimaces, and words expressing dislike for the object of the attitude.

It is very important to note that positive attitudes are inferred mainly from behavior that is strengthened and maintained by reinforcing stimuli, or approach behavior. Also note that negative attitudes are inferred mainly from behavior that is strengthened and maintained by aversive stimuli, or avoidance or attack behavior. If children are trained to approach and talk positively about some class of stimuli, we say they have positive attitudes toward it. Similarly, if children are trained to avoid or attack and talk negatively about some class of stimuli, the children are said to have negative attitudes toward those stimuli. Attitudes are unseen *products* or *results* of learning encounters with reinforcers and punishers, not *causes* of learning or failing. They are established as by-products of the teaching of approach and avoidance behavior.

Self-confidence and self-esteem have to do with attitudes toward one's own capabilities and oneself as a person, respectively. These attitudes are taught through instances that make one appear capable or not, likable or not. It is unlikely that anything can be taught to a child without also teaching him attitudes toward himself or the learning task. It is also unlikely that we can teach self-esteem or self-confidence without teaching the child to do some tasks well and reinforcing him for that.

Each teaching instance provides an opportunity for teaching attitudes as well as capabilities. For example, the teacher says, "Tell me the word and I'll show you the picture. Listen: mmmmaaaannnn. Say it fast. What word is that? Good. You're really smart. What are you going to see in the picture?" This presentation is teaching a number of attitudes that relate the child to the teaching encounter. For example: "There is a payoff for responding correctly;" "school work is fun;" "the teacher is nice;" "I got to see the picture because *I am smart*." Attitudes toward the teacher, the material, the significance of schoolwork, and the child's adequacy are taught through the presentation of a variety of instances.

Attitudes can be taught directly or accidentally. When they are taught accidentally, there is a possibility that the teacher will not teach what she wants to. She may want to motivate the child to work harder; but instead of reinforcing working harder, she scolds the child and gives him a great deal of attention for not working hard. When he tries to work, she acts as if she *expects* such behavior. The child learns that there is no payoff for working hard, and he gives up. The teacher then infers that he has a poor attitude toward school work or low self-esteem.

Consider another example. The teacher holds up an apple and says, "This is red." She then presents the apple to a child and says, "What is this?" The child answers, "Apple." The teacher then says, *"Look at it.* Is it red?" The child shrugs and looks down. The teacher did not intend to demonstrate to the child that he is a failure, that he is dumb, or that learning is a punishing experience; however, her presentation very likely helped to teach these attitudes. She presented the child with an instance of failure in the learning situation. If she presents a number of similar instances, the child learns to expect failure in new learning situations and tries to avoid them. As noted in unit 13, one consequence of repeated punishment is learning to avoid and escape from sources of punishment. Failure experiences often function as punishment.

The extent of an attitude is a function of the *number of instances* used in the teaching. This point will become clearer after the principles of concept teaching are covered later in volume 2 of this series.

Some Procedures for Teaching Self-Confidence and Self-Esteem

There are a number of important elements in teaching procedures that help to form confident children who like school and themselves. First, the children must receive praise and other demonstrations that they are capable, successful, smart, and so forth.

Second, the model the teacher presents is also very important. This model, itself, must be an instance of "I can do it," "I can succeed if I work hard," "I am smart," and "learning is fun." The teacher is able to show the children through his behavior what he wants them to learn.

Third, it is essential to have a suitable academic program—one in which they can learn and succeed with a low error rate. Such a program should provide frequent demonstrations that the child is smart and capable. It should also teach the skills required for living successfully in a technological society. Without a basic competence in language arts, science, mathematics, physical skills, and interpersonal skills, it is highly unlikely that any sense of competence or esteem established in school will last for long outside the classroom. There is good reason to believe, in fact, that academic failure is a major cause of low self-esteem in our society. The unproductive use of punishment is the second major cause.

Two specific attitudes can be taught systematically as a part of the program for promoting self-esteem. These attitudes are "persistence pays off" and "I know when I am right."

Teaching Persistence

In many new learning situations the child has to stay with the task long enough to eliminate responding to the wrong stimuli and zero in on the right ones. This takes some trial and error. If he has not learned that persistence leads to success, he may quit before there is a chance to succeed and be reinforced for doing so. Children need to learn to behave according to the rule "if I keep trying, I will succeed."

The program for teaching persistence requires *reinforcing success trials following error trials* on new learning tasks. A concept or rule about persistence should also be taught so that transfer of persistence to any new task is readily accomplished by labeling it another instance of the rule. The procedures are as follows:

1. Each time one of the children in the group is having difficulty on a new task, the teacher focuses on reinforcing working hard. "Tommy's working hard. You watch. He's going to catch on. If you work hard, you'll get it." Reinforcement is given for working in the face of failure. "He'll learn this. He's a smart boy." The teacher introduces the same routine if one of the other children in the group makes fun of the child who is having trouble. "Wait a minute. He's working hard. And he's going to show you. He'll get this stuff."

2. In the early stages of training persistence on difficult tasks, be sure other tasks at which the child can succeed are also provided. Avoid too much failure early in the program, because the child might quit before he succeeds. When the child successfully fulfills the task requirements, the requirements are increased. Also, in the early stages, praise and attention for working hard are given frequently; then they are gradually made more intermittent.

3. When the child demonstrates that he has finally mastered the skill, the teacher relates his performance to the rule. The teacher triumphantly announces, "What did I tell you? I told you he would get it. He kept working hard and now he's got it. He's a smart boy. He knows that if you work hard you'll get it." The teacher demonstrates to all the children that they have witnessed an instance of the rule, "If you work hard, you'll get it." The teacher should make sure that he or she provides reinforcement for persistence by making a fuss about the child's new accomplishments. The teacher may also provide the child with some kind of tangible reinforcer. Tangibles are particularly effective for children who have not had a great deal of experience with learning from adults in a formal situation. For the more sophisticated child, these are often not necessary.

Unless the child is taught to persist long enough to succeed, the teacher does not have the instances needed to show the child he is competent. Once this has been accomplished, the teacher works on teaching the child to evaluate responses and to be confident about his own responses.

Teaching Confidence in One's Own Judgment

1. This program begins with simple fooler games, as introduced in unit 10. The teacher indicates that she is going to "catch" the children unless they are careful. She then announces that she will do something: "I'm going to name animals. Listen: tiger, elephant, dog, table, horse—" If the children do not react, she acts gleeful. "I tricked you. Lisa thinks that a table is an animal. Tyrone thinks that a table is an animal. That's silly." When the children catch the teacher's mistake, she presents the confidence routine: "Good thinking. Karl knew what was right, and I couldn't fool him by saying something else."

2. As the children become familiar with a variety of fooler games, the teacher begins to introduce foolers out of context. She is careful never to introduce foolers in the presentation of a new teaching task, because she wants the children to trust her in these situations. However, after the chil-

dren have mastered a basic skill, such as adding, the teacher may ask the children, "What's six plus two? Yes, eight." She then writes on the board, $6 + 2 = 9$. If the children don't catch the mistake, she acts amused. If they do catch it, she presents the confidence routine: "They knew what was right. I couldn't fool them."

Note that these tasks are also good for programing attention. If a child fails the task because he fails to attend, the teacher can point out the importance of attention: "If you don't watch and listen, I'll catch you every time."

3. After the children have begun to work with foolers, the teacher can introduce a variation. "I'm going to try to teach you something that is really hard, and you might not be able to get it. I'm probably the only one who can do it." The teacher then presents a new task that will probably be learned with little difficulty. The teacher acts surprised. "How did you do that? I thought I could catch you, but I couldn't. You learned this the right way. You're too smart for me." This routine demonstrates to the children that if they attack new learning situations the right way, they will succeed, even beyond the expectations of the teacher.

For a fooler program to succeed, the material must be carefully sequenced so that the children are successful enough times for them to become confident about their ability. If they consistently fail in fooler tasks, the demonstrations will not be instances of the concept we wish to teach.

Robert Is Taught to Like Himself, School, and Reading

In this case study, no conscious attempt was made to teach Robert self-esteem. The goal was to teach him to behave in class and to read. The teaching of self-confidence and self-esteem was a natural by-product of effective teaching in which lots of reinforcement was used.

Robert was six years old. He was the older of two children; his parents were divorced; his father was going to college after having served in the Air Force. Robert was attending first grade in a class of twenty-three children. Robert came to our attention in February when his teacher and principal asked for help. His teacher reported that he was a "holy terror." For six months the teacher had attempted to control his behavior, but he was getting worse. Robert caused so much trouble in the classroom that other children were unable to do their work. Much of the teacher's time was spent keeping Robert out of trouble.

When he was observed in the classroom, he was rarely found to pay attention when teaching was going on. During baseline observations, he was off-task 87 percent of the time. Robert spent much of his time moving around the room or halls, talking inappropriately, crawling on the floor, or daydreaming. He spent up to thirty minutes a day in the principal's office. Robert scored an IQ of 93 on the Stanford-Binet. The average IQ in his classroom was 116. In mid-March just before a tutoring program was started, he scored the 1.4 grade level in reading on the Wide Range Achievement Test and had a Language Age of 6 years and 4 months on the Illinois Test of

Psycholinguistic Abilities. In six months of school he had completed only three preprimers in the Ginn basic reading series. The rest of the class was nearly through the first year of the program.

Robert's teacher had taught school for more than ten years. She was found to spend much of her time responding to disruptive behavior with reprimands, scolding, and explanations of what children should not do. When asked to specify what she wanted changed and what her goals for Robert were, she made a list of sixteen different kinds of behavior she *did not like*, but she had difficulty in saying what she expected of Robert in a positive way.

This experimental study focused first on helping the teacher learn to use praise and other reinforcers in the classroom and to ignore disruptive behavior. This took a little doing, but it was accomplished. Robert's off-task behavior dropped from 87 percent to 51 percent. Then for six weeks, a special tutoring program in reading was provided for him. He was given twenty-one hours of tutoring in thirty sessions. The tutoring was carried out by a college junior in psychology who had no prior experience in remedial reading work. The procedure used was developed by Staats and Butterfield.[1]

The tutoring materials consisted of 358 vocabulary words from the first grade Ginn program written on three-by-five cards, and story passages pasted on five-by-eight cards. The tutoring started at a place where Robert could read all of the words and worked progressively through the first year program. Before each new story, Robert read the new words from the three-by-five cards. If he was right on the first presentation, he earned two points for each word. If it took several trials and help from his tutor to read the word, he earned one point. When he read all the words correctly, the story was presented on a series of five-by-eight cards. He earned four points if he read a story card on first presentation with no errors. If the unit was read correctly on subsequent presentation, he earned two points. Later, he also earned points for answering comprehension questions and completing workbook assignments in class or at home. Robert also earned ten points if he wore his glasses. In the past, he had usually left them at home.

When Robert earned points, he was praised, He was told how well he was doing. The points were recorded as marks on cards that were divided into fifty squares. For fifty points he received a ten- to fifteen-cent prize, for one hundred points a thirty-cent prize, and for two hundred points a fifty-cent prize.

In the classroom, his teacher's use of praise and criticism changed remarkably. She became very positive in supporting appropriate classroom behavior. Over the six weeks of tutoring, Robert's off-task behavior in the classroom declined to 20 percent. In the tutoring sessions, he earned $5.50 in prizes. On a pretest, Robert had read 63 percent of the words in the first-year Ginn program correctly. After tutoring, he read 93 percent of the words correctly. His reading score on the Wide Range rose to grade level 2.0. He gained six months in six weeks. His Language Age on the Illinois Test of Psycholinguistic Abilities also rose six months.

He progressed rapidly in class. He began to talk about catching up with other kids. He sometimes explained proudly to his tutor that he worked on his assignments at home as well as at school. He wore his glasses to every tutoring session except one, and began wearing his glasses in class.

Robert was taught more than reading. He was taught that he was competent and that he could succeed. He learned to like reading and to like school. The best evidence for this came during summer school. His mother had registered him only for reading from 8:00 to 10:00 in the morning. When 10 o'clock came the first day, he begged to stay at school. On the second day he broke into tears when his mother tried to take him home. His teacher told him she would be glad to have him stay if his mother and the principal approved. His mother said Robert himself would have to ask for permission from the principal. This was a child who had spent a good part of the previous year in the principal's office. Robert did it. The principal later reported that Robert "appeared to be quite frightened. Tears were still on his cheeks, and he seemed to have difficulty talking." But he did it. Attending school had become a positive thing for Robert. During that summer and the following year, he was very well-behaved in class.[2]

implications

The child who has self-confidence is more likely to stay with a problem and show interest in new learning situations. But such a child is not a good learner because of first being taught self-esteem and confidence. He has been reinforced for learning many tasks and has learned, as a result of his accomplishments that he is a capable and likable person.

Any effective teaching program can include procedures for simultaneously teaching children a variety of attitudes about learning, about school, and about themselves as learners. Without an effective teaching program, the task is difficult, if not impossible. Those who emphasize self-esteem as a primary goal in child development probably have the cart before the horse. Viewing self-esteem as the *goal* misses the point that self-esteem is the *product* of good teaching. One cannot teach attitudes about learning without presenting instances of learning tasks. One cannot teach self-esteem without presenting instances of accomplishment.

self-test

1 self-esteem,
   self-confidence

2 approach

3 attitudes

4 failure

5 praise;
   successful

6 model

7 success

8 judgment

9 product, result

1 This unit challenges the importance of _____ as a cause of learning.

2 Attitudes are inferred mainly from _____ and avoidance behavior with respect to classes of stimuli.

3 Each teaching instance provides an opportunity for teaching _____ as well as capabilities.

4 If the teacher presents a number of instances in which the child fails, the teacher is demonstrating to the child that he is a _____.

5 To develop and maintain self-confidence, the child must receive _____ and other demonstrations that he is capable, _____, smart, and so forth.

6 The teacher should be a _____ of the behavior she wants the children to learn.

7 The persistence program allows for the reinforcement of _____ trials following error trials on new learning tasks.

8 Fooler games are used to teach children to trust their own _____.

9 Viewing self-esteem as a goal misses the point that self-esteem is a _____ of good teaching.

NUMBER RIGHT _____

exercise 1 programed practice

1 Many school children are _____ to be failures.

2 This situation has led some professionals to conclude that we should quit worrying about teaching children and focus all efforts on making them _____, confident, _____, and respected.

3 This unit challenges the importance of _____ as a cause of learning.

4 An attitude is a subjective construct referring to how someone _____ about some class of stimulus events.

5 Attitudes are inferred mainly from _____ and avoidance behavior with respect to classes of stimuli.

6 It is important to note that _____ are inferred from behavior that is strengthened and maintained by reinforcers or punishers.

7 Attitudes are the unseen products or _____ of learning encounters with reinforcers and punishers, not _____ of learning.

8 _____ is an attitude that can be taught through tasks in which being capable is prompted and reinforced.

9 Each teaching instance provides an opportunity for teaching _____ as well as capabilities.

10 When the teacher is not aware that she is responsible for the _____ a child is taught, there is a great possibility that she will not teach what she intends to teach.

11 If the teacher presents a number of instances in which the child fails, the teacher is demonstrating to the child that he is a _____.

1 taught

2 happy;
loved

3 self-esteem,
self-confidence

4 feels

5 approach

6 attitudes

7 results;
causes

8 Self-confidence

9 attitudes

10 attitudes

11 failure

12 Failure often functions as a _____.

13 One consequence of repeated punishment is learning to _____ and escape from the source of punishment.

14 The breadth of an attitude (the number of instances included in the class of events a feeling is directed toward) is a function of the group of _____ used in teaching the attitude.

15 To develop and maintain self-confidence the child must receive _____ and other demonstrations that he is capable, _____, smart, and so forth.

16 The teacher should be a _____ of the behavior she wants the children to learn.

17 A suitable _____ _____ in which each child can succeed is also essential. Otherwise the teacher is hard-pressed to demonstrate that the children are _____ and capable, and that learning is fun.

18 _____ _____ is a major cause of low self-esteem in our society today. The unproductive use of _____ is another major cause.

19 The attitudes that "_____ pays off" and "I know when I am _____" can be taught in a systematic way. These attitudes are important components in building self-esteem.

20 The persistence program allows for the reinforcement of _____ trials following error trials on new learning tasks.

12 punisher

13 avoid

14 instances

15 praise; successful

16 model

17 academic program; smart

18 Academic failure, Poor teaching; punishment

19 persistence; right

20 success

21 The persistence program also teaches the concept, "If you keep _____ _____, you will succeed."

22 Unless a child is taught to persist long enough to succeed, the teacher will not have the _____ she needs in order to show the child he is competent.

23 Fooler games are used to teach children to trust their own _____.

24 The fooler procedure is used only when the children can do the tasks quite well. The teacher makes intentional _____ for children to catch.

25 Later she uses a variation in which she says essentially, "This is really hard. You may not get it." When the children do get it, she acts _____ at how smart they are.

26 The case of Robert illustrates how competence, self-confidence, and self-esteem are increased as by-products of effective teaching in which much _____ is used.

27 In being taught to _____ better by means of a token reinforcement program, Robert was also taught that he was capable, smart, and likable, and that school was a pretty nice place.

28 The change in the teacher's behavior from criticism of misbehavior to _____ for appropriate behavior was probably very influential in forming Robert's new attitudes about school.

29 Viewing self-esteem as a goal misses the point that self-esteem is a _____ of good teaching.

21 working hard

22 instances, examples

23 judgment

24 mistakes, errors

25 surprised

26 reinforcement

27 read

28 praise

29 product, result

30 You cannot teach self-esteem in the abstract. Attitudes about self and learning are taught by presenting _____ of learning tasks.

31 A person who is confident and feels positive about himself has been _____ for learning many tasks and has learned, as a result of his achievements, that he is a _____ and _____ person.

30 instances

31 reinforced;
   capable, smart;
   likable

discussion questions

1 Explain why an attitude is subjective.

2 Explain how it is possible to infer attitudes from behavior.

3 Describe a procedure for teaching a child that he is a failure in school.

4 Specify three general procedures likely to produce attitudes of self-esteem and self-confidence.

5 Outline a procedure for teaching persistence.

6 Outline a procedure for teaching confidence in one's own judgment.

7 Describe the procedures used to get Robert to like himself, school, and reading.

8 Explain why those who emphasize self-esteem as a teaching goal have the cart before the horse.

unit 15

Fear, Dependence, and Withdrawal

objectives

The next two units consolidate the behavior principles already discussed by applying them to a range of common problems exhibited by school-age children.

After completing this unit you should be able to—

1 Discuss procedures for respondent (or reflex) conditioning.
2 Relate the respondent conditioning model to emotional conditioning processes.
3 Indicate why a teacher using good reinforcement techniques need not be concerned about emotional development in most cases.
4 List the procedures available to the teacher for eliminating fearful behavior.
5 Explain how behavioral consequences maintain behavior that is often attributed to emotional problems, such as dependency and anxiety.

lesson

Classes of Response—A Review

As first discussed in unit 2, responses can be divided into two classes: *respondent* or *reflexive behavior*, which is elicited by preceding stimuli; and *operant behavior*, which is controlled by consequences. Responses controlled by consequences are also called voluntary behavior, intelligent behavior, and operations.

284

Unconditioned Stimuli

In order to teach his students about reflexive behavior, the senior author suddenly shouted very loudly in the classroom. Many of the students jumped. They were momentarily upset. Their breathing changed, their hearts beat faster, and some even perspired. What they felt was a reflex reaction to a sudden strong stimulus. *Reflexive behavior is elicited (made to happen) by preceding stimuli.* It is not influenced by consequent events——rewarding or punishing. If reflexive behavior is punished, it does not occur less often. Reflexes or respondents are not controlled by consequences as operant behavior is. Reflexes are controlled by specific preceding stimuli. They involve the actions of the glands (salivary and adrenal glands, for example) and the smooth muscles (stomach, colon, pupils, heart, diaphragm, and so forth).

The preceding stimuli that make reflexes happen are called *unconditioned stimuli.* Food in the mouth elicits saliva. A loud, sudden noise elicits a startle reaction. Painful stimuli elicit the *activation syndrome*, which includes an increased heart rate, an increased breathing rate, the secretion of adrenalin, and the release of sugar to the blood. The activation syndrome prepares one for an emergency reaction requiring intense muscle effort. Emotional reactions represent various combinations of reflexive reactions.

Conditioned Stimuli

If a neutral stimulus precedes the presentation of an unconditioned stimulus, that neutral stimulus will come to elicit the same reflex response elicited by the unconditioned stimulus. The neutral stimulus becomes a conditioned stimulus. This basic principle has been used in this text since unit 5, where it was pointed out that neutral stimuli can become conditioned reinforcers if they are *closely followed* by effective reinforcers. In unit 13 the same principle was the basis for saying that when children are punished, they learn to escape not only the punishment, but also the punisher and the place of punishment. Finally, in unit 14 we pointed out that attitudes involve feelings, which are best understood as conditioned or unconditioned emotional responses.

A Model of Respondent Conditioning

Watson and Rayner provided the first clear demonstration of conditioning a fear in a child. The first step was to demonstrate that a loud noise (a hammer striking a steel bar near the child's head) produced a fear reaction consisting of jumping or puckering his lips, trembling, and violent crying. They also determined that showing the child a white rat produced no reaction. Next the presentation of the white rat was closely followed by the loud noise. After

Model

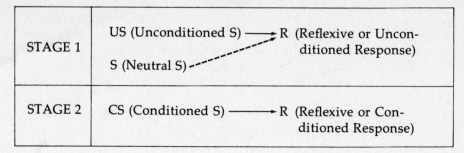

Time ⟶

Example

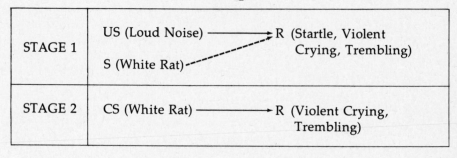

Time ⟶

Figure 15.1 A model of respondent conditioning

a couple of pairings, the eight-month-old boy was found to cry in terror and tremble in the presence of the white rat.[1]

In this example, the fearful response of the child to the white rat was conditioned by following the presentation of the white rat with a loud noise. After a few pairings of this sort, the white rat alone came to elicit the fearful response without the loud noise. The child had been taught to be afraid of the white rat. Feelings of love, sexual attraction, appetites, hate, disgust, and sadness may be conditioned in a similar way.

Figure 15.1 presents a model of the respondent conditioning process. In stage 1, the neutral stimulus S_1 occurs, then the unconditioned stimulus S_2 occurs and elicits the respondent. In stage 2, the formerly neutral stimulus (now the conditioned stimulus) directly elicits the respondent.

STAGE 1

Whistle is blown.	Prince, a German Shepherd is taught to come and sit.	He is given a dog biscuit.	He salivates.
Respondent Model Whistle is a neutral stimulus.		The biscuit is an unconditioned stimulus for salivating.	Salivation is a reflexive (or unconditioned) response.

$$S \qquad\qquad US \longrightarrow UR$$

Operant Model Whistle will become a discriminative stimulus.	With appropriate prompting, coming, and sitting becomes an operant response.	The dog biscuit is a reinforcer for coming and sitting.	

$$S^D \longrightarrow R \longrightarrow S^R$$

STAGE 2

(after many repetitions): Whistle is blown.	Prince comes and sits and salivates.	He is given a dog biscuit.	He salivates more.
Respondent Model Whistle is conditioned stimulus for salivating.	Salivating is a conditioned response.	The dog biscuit is an unconditioned stimulus for salivating.	Salivation is an unconditioned response.

$$CS \longrightarrow CR \qquad US \longrightarrow UR$$

Operant Model Whistle is a signal for coming and sitting.	Coming and sitting is an operant response.	The dog biscuit is a reinforcer for coming and sitting.	

$$S^D \longrightarrow R \longrightarrow S^R$$

Figure 15.2 Interrelations of operants and respondents

Interrelations of Operant and Respondent Models

In review unit 9, we introduced the idea of stimulus functions. We have also suggested that a given stimulus, such as food, can have different functions with respect to different responses. For example, food can *reinforce* a response that it follows, and it can *elicit* the respondent salivation. Figure 15.2 gives an example of the simultaneous conditioning of an operant (coming and sitting) and a respondent (salivation) with food serving both a reinforcing function (for coming and sitting) and an eliciting function (for salivation). Note also that the preceding stimulus, whistle, serves both a *discriminative* function and an *eliciting* function after conditioning.

Ways to Eliminate Fears

Teachers work primarily at strengthening behavior that operates on the environment—that is, voluntary or operant behavior. Furthermore, if teaching is carried out in a way that emphasizes reinforcement, success, and competence, there is little need to worry about the affective or emotional development of the child. He will be taught positive attitudes and feelings at the same time he is taught learning tasks. The effective use of reinforcers will automatically eliminate negative attitudes and feelings *and* build positive attitudes and feelings. There are times, however, in dealing with emotional problems such as fear, when knowledge of the principles of reflex conditioning can be useful.

Extinction

There are two ways in which the reaction to a conditioned stimulus can be changed. First, one can keep presenting the conditioned stimulus without pairing it with the unconditioned stimulus. The reflex reaction to the conditioned stimulus will slowly weaken. This process is called *extinction*. It parallels the extinction process for operant behavior, wherein a response weakens when it is no longer followed by reinforcement. Note that the conditioned stimulus has to be presented; the mere passage of time is not enough to weaken the reflex reaction. To eliminate the fear of the white rat, the rat would be presented to the child many times, unaccompanied by the loud noise. Eventually, the presence of the rat would not be fearful to the child. The fear would be extinguished.

The principle of extinction also applies to positive conditioning. If conditioned reinforcers such as praise are to maintain their effectiveness, they occasionally need to be followed by unconditioned reinforcers; otherwise, extinction will occur.

Counter-Conditioning

The second way to eliminate a reaction to a conditioned stimulus is to condition an incompatible reaction to the same stimulus. This is called *counter-*

conditioning. Mary Jones described the procedures she found effective with a boy named Peter in eliminating a fear of a rabbit. The two methods of greatest value were showing him a number of other children playing with the rabbit, and gradually bringing the rabbit closer while Peter was being fed. In the first case, the rabbit was paired with the positive reactions of other children. In the second case, the rabbit was paired with an unconditioned stimulus—food. In both cases, a new positive reaction that was incompatible with the fearful reaction was associated with the conditioned stimulus, the rabbit.[2] You might be interested to know that this study was first reported in 1924.

For counter-conditioning to be effective, it is important to use procedures that keep the fearful reaction from occurring. In the above example, the rabbit was *gradually* brought closer to Peter. A conditioned stimulus at a distance does not elicit as strong a reaction as one that is close by. When the fear-arousing stimulus is presented in graded steps while positive unconditioned or conditioned stimuli are paired with it, the fearful reactions are less likely to occur, and the new reactions are more likely to be associated with the conditioned fear stimulus.

Note that if the teacher or parent reinforces closer and closer approaches to the feared stimulus, all the conditions are present for effective counter-conditioning of the fear. In other words, it is possible to change fears by changing the avoidance behavior (operants) that go with them rather than by focusing on the respondents. Avoidance behavior can be changed to ap-

THE COACH SAYS YOUR FEAR OF LINEMEN SHOULD BE COUNTER-CONDITIONED BY SATURDAYS GAME.

proach behavior if the right reinforcement is given at the right time. As avoidance is being changed to approach, the fear is counter-conditioned.

Any problem involving emotional conditioning can usually be more clearly formulated and dealt with in terms of the related operant behavior. The reason for this is that the operant behavior can be observed and can provide clear feedback on the progress of the change program. Often respondents are not visible and, therefore, there is no way of knowing whether they are being changed.

Examples of Behavior Problems and Their Solutions

The following are documented case studies that illustrate a variety of change procedures used for fearful, dependent, and withdrawn children.

Karl Overcomes His Fear of School

Many children cry wildly when their mothers leave them at school. Usually, if they are left alone for a few minutes, the crying is quickly extinguished, and other responses take over. In some cases when the conditioning is very strong, or the reinforcement of crying and screaming has been high, other steps are required to eliminate the fearful reactions.

Patterson described a procedure to overcome Karl's reluctance to stay at school. Karl was seven when he was brought to the University of Oregon Clinic on referral from the school nurse. In his first few days in first grade, he had shown a reluctance to stay at school. By the second week, he would stay only as long as his mother remained in the room. He had had similar troubles in nursery school and had always tried to accompany his mother when she left for home. Attempts to punish, bribe, and cajole failed to keep him in school.

In the first clinic session Karl did not want to go with the therapist. His teeth chattered; he clenched one fist and had a firm grip on his mother with the other. He was brought to the playroom with his mother. She sat by the door as the therapist set up a doll-play situation in which the doll, Henry, was being taken by his mother to see the doctor. After structuring the situation, the therapist would ask how Henry felt in the doctor's office without his mother, or what Henry was going to do. Karl was given candies if he said Henry was not afraid and showed "big boy" behavior. Mother was soon moved out of the playroom. Other situations were presented, such as Henry's mother leaving him at home while she went to the store, or his mother staying home while Henry walked toward school.

At the end of the first session, Karl's mother was encouraged to praise him for remaining in the playroom. She was also to encourage other independent behavior at home and report on it at the next session. Karl listened to this interchange with interest.

In the next eleven sessions, situations were presented in which Henry was slowly taken closer to school and eventually was staying there. Karl began expressing positive feelings about staying at school. He continued to receive candy. The fear-arousing stimuli were being associated with adult reactions and candy. At the time of session eleven, he made his first actual trip to school with his visiting teacher, who had been helping him at home with his reading. Over the next two weeks, he gradually stayed longer and longer in school, until finally he was staying all day by himself. He was given much praise for his bravery, and he soon announced that he would return to school full time, which he did.

Three months later, a follow-up showed a dramatic improvement in Karl's classroom adjustment—and no fearfulness.[3]

Comments. Karl's fear of leaving his mother was eliminated by reinforcing closer and closer approximations to the desired behavior and verbalized feelings. This use of graded steps is another example of the principle of shaping described in unit 7. Note that the process began with imaginary situations involving Henry, a doll. The fear-arousing stimuli were psychologically kept at a distance at first, and then they were slowly brought closer and closer as Karl showed he could handle them.

Dependent Behavior

Karen, age six, would not get up, dress herself, and eat her breakfast in time for school unless her mother was nagging or helping every step of the way. Her mother reinforced her "help me" behavior in part because she thought that was what mothers were for and in part because she was afraid Karen would be late for school.

Since the tasks were ones Karen could do, the problem was handled by (1) getting Karen an alarm clock and telling her she was responsible for getting ready for school; (2) stopping all nagging; and (3) praising her for her success.

Karen's teacher was informed about what was being done and was asked not to give her extra attention if she came late. Her mother kept records of her progress.

Karen was late for school six times in the first two weeks, but only once in the second two weeks. In the next six weeks, Karen left home a little late about once a week, but hurried to school on time. Her mother was pleased with the change in their relationship. She said, "This is now her problem, not mine. The whole situation is very much improved." Karen was very proud of herself on the days she left for school early, and she received praise for this.

Comments. When the parent or teacher continues to do things for a child after the child could be taught to do them for himself, the child is being reinforced for not growing up, for being dependent on adults. If the teacher views immature behavior as a sign of anxiety, insecurity, or slowed development, and then smothers the child showing such behavior with affection and attention, it is very likely to encourage the behavior.

Regressive Crawling

Francis Harris illustrated how teachers inadvertently kept an undesired behavior going because of their misinterpretation of it. Mary was a three-
year-old girl attending nursery school. Mary spent over 80 percent of her
morning crawling like a baby. At first, her teachers thought she was showing
regression because there was a new baby in her home. They tried to give
Mary sympathetic attention, especially when she crawled. They would also
suggest activities that required her to stand. None of this helped. When the
teachers began to ignore the crawling and to give her constant attention
when she was standing, normal behavior became predominant within a
week. When the teachers went back to attending crawling, it quickly returned to an 80-percent level. Then, once again, reinforcement of standing
and extinction of crawling corrected the situation. Within a week no special
attention for standing was required because Mary was engaging in regular
nursery school activities.[4]

An Adult-Oriented Child

Ann was four and from an upper-middle-class family. She reacted freely
with adults but did not play with children. She was not withdrawn or
frightened. As time went on, she spent more and more time just standing
and looking. Often, she retired to a make-believe bed in the play yard to
sleep for a few minutes. Less than 15 percent of her time was spent playing
with peers. About 40 percent of her time was spent interacting with adults.

A program was devised to encourage more peer interaction. When Ann
was alone, she was given no attention by the teacher. If she came to the
teacher with another child, attention was given. If she came to the teacher
alone, minimal attention was given. When Ann was playing with another
child, the teacher would go to them and give them attention and play materials. For example, "You three girls have a cozy house. Here are some more
cups, Ann, for your tea party." If Ann began to leave the group while the
teacher was there, the teacher turned away from her and attended to the
other children. During the six weeks of this program, Ann's playing with
other children quickly increased to about 60 percent of the time, and interactions with adults dropped to under 20 percent. Isolated play dropped from
about 45 percent to 20 percent of the time. Attention from adults was slowly
faded out and the peer play continued on its own.[5]

Clingy Behavior

Another frequent classroom problem is the child who has to be by his teacher's side all of the time. Like Ann, such children are adult-oriented, but they
are not necessarily as verbal and engaging as Ann. There is a general rule
about dependent behavior: *Children who show dependent behavior are reinforced by social reinforcers from adults (attention, affection, praise, nearness).*

These same reinforcers can be used to strengthen independent behavior such as playing alone, exploring, playing with peers, learning skills, and working on tasks. The teacher suggests (prompts) small steps toward some independent activity, gives support to help the child take new steps on his own, and reinforces improvement. When the dependent behavior occurs, she appears to be busy with other things. "Big boy" and "big girl" behavior is praised and encouraged.

A Warning. When reinforcement for any behavior is withdrawn, there is initially some emotional upset. A teacher who no longer reinforces "help me" behavior is bound to encounter this. Therefore, you should be prepared to take some outbursts without giving in or getting angry. Ignore the behavior, and it will fade out in a short time. The first few outbursts are usually the longest. Stay with your change program and you will succeed.

Withdrawn Behavior

Withdrawal from adults, from peers, or from activities can have several bases. First, withdrawal can represent a fearful avoidance of persons or situations, in which case the procedures described earlier in this unit are relevant. Second, withdrawal can be the result of extinction of all behavior in that situation. When this is the case, some priming action is needed to get behavior going that can then be reinforced. Third, withdrawal can be due to not having been taught the appropriate social behavior in the first place. Some children have not been taught how to interact with others. In this case it is necessary to teach the appropriate social behavior.

A Withdrawn Girl. Linda was a nursery school child who was quite withdrawn. She showed little peer interaction or interaction with adults. Adults were not reinforcers for her. One teacher set about making herself Linda's special friend. She spent time with her, gave her things to play with, played with her, talked especially to her, and so forth. This made Linda more adult-oriented, and the teacher became a more effective reinforcer for her. The teacher could now use this new capability to reinforce child-oriented interactions. The steps were slow. The teacher had to set up many of the interactions, such as bringing other chilren to Linda's play area. The result was a striking change in Linda's interactions with others.[6]

Teachers who have switched from criticism to praise to establish good classroom control often report that it is not just the previously misbehaving children who benefit from the change. Formerly quiet children benefit as well, because the teacher now has time to reinforce their steps of progress and to draw them out with various prompts. Withdrawn children need someone to take the time to turn them on.

A Passive Boy. The inactive or passive boy is usually not fun for other boys to play with and is likely to be exluded from play groups. Mark was such a boy in an experimental nursery school. He showed little interaction with his peers.

The teachers decided to reinforce one particular activity to see what effect this might have on peer relations. Climbing on the jungle gym was the target behavior. Before the program was begun, frequency of climbing on anything was less than 5 percent of the time spent in the play yard. Social reinforcement was then given to Mark every time he climbed on the jungle gym. After nine days, Mark spent over 60 percent of his time outside climbing on the jungle gym. His peer interactions changed. He began talking more with peers, and he became a happy and active member of several boys' play groups.[7] By taking a key behavior and working on it, the teachers saw desirable changes in other behavior also.

summary

Respondent behavior is elicited by preceding stimuli. Stimuli that naturally elicit respondent behavior are called unconditioned stimuli. The responses controlled by unconditioned stimuli involve the reactions of the smooth muscles (heart, diaphragm, blood vessels, stomach, colon, pupils, and so forth) and glands (adrenals, salivary glands, and sweat glands, for example). Emotional reactions, such as fear, love, and hate, involve various combinations of respondent reactions.

Neutral stimuli that consistently precede unconditioned stimuli also come to elicit reflexive actions. Social reinforcers are made effective through this reflex conditioning process. Sexual arousal that occurs simply from looking at someone you love has been conditioned in a similar way. Fears are conditioned when formerly neutral events are followed by aversive (punishing) stimuli.

A conditioned stimulus can be neutralized by repeatedly presenting the conditioned stimulus without the associated unconditioned stimulus. This process is called extinction. Fears can be extinguished if the fear-arousing stimulus is repeatedly presented and no aversive stimulus occurs.

A conditioned stimulus can also be neutralized through counter-conditioning. In this process, the conditioned stimulus is made the stimulus for a response incompatible with the one now elicited. A gradual introduction of the feared stimulus while something positive is happening to the person is an efficient procedure for eliminating a fear. Another effective procedure is to reinforce closer and closer approaches to the feared stimulus.

Approaches to any emotional problem such as fear should be stated in terms of operant behavior and its consequences, since one can readily see operant behavior, such as avoidance. It is easier to see and deal with what is happening when you focus on operant behavior rather than emotional or reflexive behavior.

Fear of school often involves emotional reactions to leaving mother, rather than a fear of school itself. The case of Karl illustrated one approach to eliminating such a fear. He was first reinforced, through doll play, for more grown-up feelings and actions; then, step by step, he was reinforced for going to school and staying there.

The key to understanding dependent behavior such as pleading "help me," acting babyish, and clinging to adults for attention is to recognize that it is maintained by social reinforcers. These same reinforcers can be used to teach independent behavior. When reinforcers are withdrawn from a particular type of behavior, the teacher should anticipate an increase in that behavior at first and some possible emotional outbursts before extinction will occur.

A child's withdrawal from adults, peers, or activities can be due to a conditioned fear, prior extinction of all behavior in that situation, or the failure of someone to teach the appropriate social behavior in the first place. In each case, the solution involves the reinforcement of the desired interactions.

self-test

1 not

2 activation

3 reflexive,
respondent

4 unconditioned
stimulus

5 emotional

6 without;
extinction

7 counter

1 Respondent behavior is _____ influenced by rewards and punishments as operant behavior is.

2 Painful stimuli elicit the _____ syndrome.

3 Emotional reactions consist of various combinations of _____ reactions.

4 A neutral stimulus can become a conditioned stimulus if the neutral stimulus is followed by an _____ _____.

5 The effective use of reinforcers automatically provides positive _____ conditioning.

6 There are two ways of changing the reaction to a conditioned stimulus. The first is to present the conditioned stimulus repeatedly _____ presenting the unconditioned stimulus. This process is called _____.

7 The second way to eliminate a reaction to a conditioned stimulus is to use _____-conditioning.

8 Counter-conditioning of a fear can also be accomplished by _____

closer and closer approaches to the feared stimulus.

9 Discriminative stimuli in an operant model can also function as

_____ stimuli in a respondent model.

8 reinforcing

9 conditioned,
   eliciting

NUMBER RIGHT _____

exercise 1 programed practice

1 Watson and Rayner provided the first clear demonstration of conditioning a

_____ in a child.

2 In this study, presenting a white rat to a child was followed by a

_____ _____. After this was repeated a couple of times,

the boy was found to cry in terror and tremble when the _____

_____ was seen.

1 fear

3 Some responses are controlled by their consequences. Others are elicited by

_____ stimuli.

2 loud noise;
  white rat

4 Responses controlled by _____ are examples of operant behavior.

Responses elicited by preceding stimuli are examples of _____ be-

havior.

3 preceding,
  unconditioned

4 consequences;
  reflexive,
  respondent

5 Respondent behavior is _____ influenced by rewards and punish-

ments as operant behavior is.

5 not

6 Respondents involve the actions of the _____ and smooth muscles.

6 glands

7 The _____ _____ are an example of glands.

7 salivary glands,
  sweat glands,
  adrenal glands

8 stomach, colon, pupils, diaphragm, heart	8 The _____ is an example of a smooth muscle system.
	9 Preceding stimuli that make reflexes happen are called _____ stimuli.
9 unconditioned	10 Food in the mouth is an unconditioned stimulus that causes _____ to flow.
10 saliva	11 Painful stimuli elicit the _____ syndrome.
11 activation	12 The activation syndrome prepares one for an emergency reaction requiring intense _____ _____.
12 muscle effort	13 Emotional reactions consist of various combinations of _____ reactions.
13 reflexive, respondent	14 A neutral stimulus can become a conditioned stimulus if the neutral stimulus is followed by an _____ _____.
14 unconditioned stimulus	15 In the Watson and Rayner example, the white rat became a _____ stimulus for a fearful reaction.
15 conditioned	16 While emotions and feelings are very important in understanding people, teachers work primarily in terms of _____ behavior.
16 operant	17 When reinforcement is emphasized, good _____ development will accompany the learning of tasks.
17 emotional	18 There are two ways to change the reaction to a conditioned stimulus. The first is to present the conditioned stimulus repeatedly _____ presenting the unconditioned stimulus. This process is called _____.
18 without; extinction	19 The second way to eliminate a reaction to a conditioned stimulus is to use _____-conditioning.
19 counter	

20 Peter learned new reactions to a rabbit (a conditioned fear-arousing stimulus) by observing other _____ playing with the rabbit.

21 Another procedure that was effective in reducing his fear was to bring the rabbit _____ closer while Peter was being fed.

22 Counter-conditioning of a fear can also be accomplished by _____ closer and closer approaches to the feared stimulus.

23 It is possible to change fears by changing the _____ behavior that goes with them.

24 Karl was progressively reinforced for going to _____ and staying there by himself.

25 Karen's "help me" behavior was eliminated by stopping all _____, getting an alarm clock to cue her, putting the responsibility for getting ready on her, and _____ her for her successes.

26 If the teacher (or parent), viewing immature behavior as a sign of _____, insecurity, or slow development, smothers the child showing such behavior with affection and _____, the behavior is likely to persist.

27 Mary's regressive crawling was controlled by _____ from her teachers.

28 Most dependent behavior turns out to be maintained by _____ _____ from adults. Those same _____ can be used to strengthen independent behavior.

20 children

21 gradually

22 reinforcing

23 avoidance

24 school

25 nagging;
praising

26 anxiety;
attention

27 attention

28 social
reinforcers;
reinforcers

29 Withdrawn behavior can be due to a conditioned fear, _____ of all

behavior in that situation, or the _____ of someone to teach the

appropriate social behavior in the first place.

30 In each case, the key to change is to prompt interactions for which

_____ can be given.

31 The operant model of behavior is called an S-R-S model. The respondent

model is an _____-R model.

32 Because stimuli can take on _____ functions with respect to dif-

ferent responses, the possibilities for the simultaneous conditioning of oper-

ants and respondents exists.

33 Discriminative stimuli in an operant model can also function as

_____ stimuli in a respondent model.

34 In the example given, a whistle functioned as a discriminative stimulus for

coming and sitting and as an eliciting stimulus for _____.

35 Both discriminative and conditioned stimuli are formerly _____

stimuli. Also, both are _____ stimuli.

36 Unconditioned stimuli and unconditioned reinforcers differ functionally.

Unconditioned stimuli _____ respondents which come

_____ them. Unconditioned reinforcers _____ operants

which come before them.

37 In the example given, the dog biscuit had a _____ function for

coming and sitting and an _____ function for salivating.

---

29 extinction;
   failure

30 reinforcement

31 S

32 multiple

33 conditioned,
   eliciting

34 salivating

35 neutral;
   preceding

36 elicit; after;
   reinforce,
   strengthen

37 reinforcing;
   eliciting

discussion questions

1 Define and give an example of *operant behavior*.
2 Define and give an example of *respondent behavior*.
3 Explain what is meant by an unconditioned stimulus.
4 Explain what is meant by a conditioned stimulus.
5 Describe how Watson and Rayner conditioned a fear in a child.
6 Draw a model of respondent conditioning.
7 Illustrate how the initially neutral preceding stimuli in an operant or respondent model can take on functional relations to operants and respondents at the same time.
8 Illustrate how unconditioned reinforcers can be unconditioned stimuli at the same time.
9 Explain why the teacher using good reinforcement techniques need not be concerned about emotional development in most cases.
10 Describe two ways to eliminate fears and other conditioned reactions.
11 Describe the procedures used by Patterson to eliminate a child's fear of school.
12 Explain what different types of dependent behavior have in common.
13 Give a general rule for changing dependent behavior.
14 Give three reasons why children may exhibit withdrawn behavior.
15 What is the general procedure for changing withdrawn behavior?

unit 16

Conduct Problems

objectives

After completing this unit you should be able to—
1 Integrate the traditional labels for problem behavior with their behavioral formulations.
2 Discuss how conduct problems are learned.
3 Specify a variety of procedures for eliminating conduct problems.

lesson

The term *conduct problem* is a label given to intense, active, unlawful, or immoral behavior shown by children. In previous units a variety of examples have been presented along with procedures for modifying such behavior. In unit 3, Peter's mother was taught to change his objectionable behavior by using appropriate reinforcement and punishment. In this same unit, Elmer and Edward's teacher was taught how to change their overactive off-task behavior and get them on-task by using the "specify, ignore, and praise" approach. In unit 13, we suggested that a variety of conduct problems, such as lying, truancy, and cheating, are the means for avoiding or escaping sources of punishment. The case of Claire illustrated how a simple change in the punishment procedure, allowing her to earn back her lost privileges, produced a marked change in her truancy.

Conduct problems always involve a payoff for the undesired behavior. The child learns to get reinforcement, and he learns to avoid or escape from punishment. In this unit we will take a closer look at the origins of conduct problems and various approaches to changing such behavior.

Throwing Tantrums

In response to seemingly minor events some children will flop on the floor, pound their arms, legs, or heads, and scream and yell. Some may attack their parents, and others may hold their breath until they turn blue or even pass out. Temper tantrums begin with the minor emotional upsets that go with the loss of reinforcers. Suppose Joe is used to eating various snacks before dinner, and his mother decides to stop this. She says, "No, you must wait for dinner." Joe stamps his feet and cries that he's hungry, and his mother gives in. Imagine this process taking place many times. Mother tries to wait Joe out, but he comes on even stronger. She gives in again. Progressively, Joe is *reinforced* for more intense protest behavior. Intense forms of protest, or tantrums, are taught through withholding reinforcers and then giving in and providing them.

Tantrums are relatively rare in school; but when they do occur, the teacher should know their causes and the procedures to eliminate them. The basic rule is that the teacher should not let tantrums be followed by reinforcers. It is also important to reinforce behavior incompatible with tantrums. In one case, we worked with Diane and eliminated her intense tantrums in three weeks. Her chair was placed in the back of the room. She was told she would be held down by the aide if she began a tantrum. This was done about five times. The other children were told they could earn a treat now and then by paying no attention to Diane's tantrums. And, Diane was told she could earn checkmarks on the board toward a class party for each half-day of good behavior. Diane made great progress and soon became a cooperative member of the class.

The sad part of Diane's story was that she went to a different school the following year. When she tried the same tricks again, she found they paid off. The staff at the new school felt that she had a deep-seated emotional problem. They had her put on drugs as her behavior got worse and eventually shipped her off to a class for the emotionally disturbed. The teacher who had seen Diane flower socially after her tantrums were eliminated found this outcome most disturbing. No one would listen to her at a case conference held to discuss Diane's behavior. The idea that behavior problems can be caused by reinforcement and punishment had not been accepted widely enough at that time to save Diane.

A standard procedure for eliminating tantrums is to isolate the child in a room by himself, or with an unresponding adult, until the tantrum is over. This insures that the tantrum does not pay off. The worst thing that can be done in a tantrum-treatment program is to start a time-out procedure and then give in. You have to *outlast* the child, or you will only make the tantrum worse. Typically, the tantrum that goes with the first use of time out can last from thirty minutes to two hours. If the child is not given in to, the tantrum accompanying the next use of time out may last only ten to fifteen minutes. By the third trial, the tantrum should last under five minutes. After that, one may see only fleeting beginnings of tantrums that can be turned off with a gesture. The way in which the first tantrum is handled is the key to success. In all cases, the adults handling tantrums should be as matter-of-fact as possible.

Zimmerman and Zimmerman reported a case of tantrum behavior by an eleven-year-old boy in a residential treatment center. The tantrums usually occurred in the hall when the boy was being brought to class. The result was a crowd of staff members standing around the boy, who was kicking and screaming. The teacher observed this consequence one day and told the attendant to put the boy in the classroom at his desk and leave. The teacher then proceeded to ignore him until he quieted down. After two to three minutes, the boy's crying became quieter, and he looked up. The teacher said she would be ready to work with him when he was ready. He continued crying for another four or five minutes and then indicated he was ready to work. The boy worked cooperatively for the rest of the class period.[1]

When the environment permits it, ignoring the behavior (extinction) is a good approach to eliminating tantrums.

Negativism

Protest behavior ("I won't do it." "No." "I don't want to." "Do we have to?") generally results from children not being managed in a positive way. The behavior continues, because it pays off; that is, the teacher gives attention to the protests and now and then lets the children have their own way.

Negativism can be avoided for the most part by following the suggestions presented in units 10 through 13 on how to reinforce and punish. If the child is intently involved in some activity, do not insist that he suddenly leave it. Give him a warning before taking any action. One can also avoid negative reactions by giving a child (or a class) a choice of two alternatives: "Would you rather stay an extra five minutes and finish the exercise before recess, or go to recess now and have to finish it when you come back?" "You have a choice, you can line up quietly the first time, or we can try it again."

Often negative reactions are provoked by being too abrupt, too bossy, and too negative in approaching children. If strong negativism has already developed, check to see how much attention you are giving it. Do not be trapped into acting insulted by a disobedient, disrespectful child. Make interactions more positive, and consider ways of increasing the reinforcement for desired behavior.

Fighting—Hitting, Kicking, Biting

All children learn to hit, kick, and bite. They are taught to hit a baseball, kick a football, and bite a steak, but not to use these responses to hurt people (except maybe in self-defense). When they do, they are likely to be called aggressive.

Traditional views of aggression have focused on weak superegos, guilt feelings, or internal drives. Often these have led to circular explanations. A popular view is that frustration causes aggression.[2] If frustration is defined as the reaction to absence of an accustomed reinforcer, then the development of tantrums, explained earlier, is consistent with the frustration-aggression view. The intensified reactions that occur when a response is first put on extinction are sometimes viewed as aggressive. However, just withholding reinforcement is not enough to build aggressive behavior. In fact, these intensified reactions disappear if no reinforcement is forthcoming. The critical element in the development of most aggressive behavior is the *reinforcement of more intense response forms when they do occur.*

This point is well illustrated in a study by Walters and Brown. Second-grade boys were trained to hit a plastic clown. Some of them were reinforced for hitting hard, and some for hitting softly. Fifteen reinforced turns were given. Later that day the boys were observed playing three games with an untrained second-grade boy. In one game the object was to be the boy standing on a cross when the referee yelled, "Stop." The next game was a period of free play. In the third game, called Scalp, the object was to get a piece of tape from another boy's arm without losing your tape. Observers who knew nothing of the prior training rated the boys for aggressiveness from behind a one-way screen. The boys who had undergone high-intensity training were rated more aggressive than those who had undergone low-intensity training. Results were similar when the training was reversed——that is, when those who were first given low-intensity training were then given high-intensity training, they were rated more aggressive.[3]

In a study by Brown and Elliot, the aggressive behavior of a whole classroom of three- and four-year-old boys was changed dramatically by training the teachers to give attention to cooperative behavior and to ignore aggressive behavior. The changes were quite unexpected by the teachers who were intially skeptical. The effect on two highly aggressive boys was especially dramatic. These two boys became friendlier than the teachers believed possible.[4]

The procedures for eliminating fighting are these:

1 Be sure the fighting does not pay off. Do not give attention to the aggressive behavior. Do not let the aggression produce a consequence favorable to the aggressor.
2 If punishment is used, do not be a model of aggression yourself. Use withdrawal of reinforcement as your punishment and provide a way of earning the reinforcers back through cooperative behavior.
3 Reinforce cooperative behavior directly.
4 Use rules and prompts to teach behavior incompatible with fighting.

Verbal Abuse and Swearing

Name calling and swearing can be learned through the model of parents or peers. The behavior is probably reinforced by the upsetting effects it has on others and by the attention it receives. Quite often children say, "I hate you" to their mothers or teachers. If the adult overreacts to such comments by acting hurt or trying to find out what's wrong, the child may well learn to use such comments to get attention.

In general, the first and best approach to verbal aggression is to ignore it. Act as if it did not happen. Give attention only to acceptable verbal behavior.

Martha, a five-year-old girl, was "balky, verbally insulting, occasionally foul-mouthed, and prone to tell disjointed stories about violent accidents." The variables controlling her behavior were systematically studied.

For the first ten days, Martha's teachers maintained their ongoing pattern of responding to her. During this baseline period Martha exhibited very little cooperative behavior with other children (see fig. 16.1). For the next seven days, Martha was showered with praise, attention, and desirable material goods. Some psychologists might have predicted that this "unconditional love" might lead Martha to be more cooperative. It did not. Only in phase 3 of the study, when cooperative behavior was directly followed by attention, praise, and play materials, and her abusive verbal behavior was ignored, did Martha become more cooperative. When reinforcement for cooperation was withdrawn (phase 4), cooperation decreased. When the reinforcement was reinstated (phase 5), cooperative behavior again increased. Just being nice to Martha was not enough to eliminate her verbal aggression. Reinforcement had to be diverted from the aggression and given to incompatible behavior.[5]

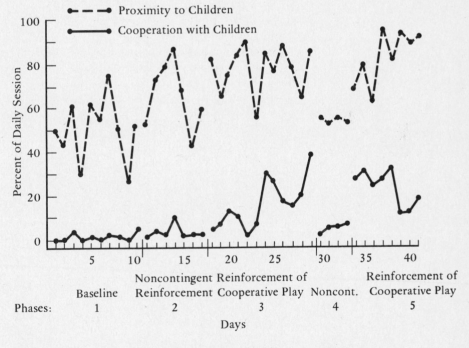

Figure 16.1 Daily percentages of proximity and cooperative play

Hyperactivity

Hyperactive is a fancy label for a child who is always on the go or who does not stay at one task very long. Hyperactive-behavior patterns are sometimes found in children who show evidence of neurological impairment, but this isn't always so; the presence of hyperactivity is *not* a reliable basis for inferring brain dysfunction.

The basic problem of the hyperactive child is that he has not been taught to work persistently or to stay with a task long enough to be successful. The solution is to find a way to reinforce persistence and time on-task. The following example from the work of G. R. Patterson is just one of many similar cases in which good reinforcement procedures produced dramatic changes.

Earl had a sad history. In early life he had been treated brutally by his parents and later by his grandparents. He had received a skull fracture when he was less than one year old. At four he had begun suffering from convulsions and motor incoordination. He had been adopted at the age of three, and for the next six years he had kept his new parents pretty busy. Earl was nine and in the second grade when Patterson became involved with him. He was hyperactive and doing poorly in school. In the classroom he was in continual motion. He often played "snowplow" with his desk. In many ways a small terror, he was controllable only when his teacher was present. He was very distractable and did little work. He was quite destructive to the classroom and aggressive toward his peers.

Earl's hyperactive behavior was reduced to a level lower than that of the other boys in the class by using the following procedure. The class was told that Earl had trouble learning because he did not pay attention. An "Earl box" was going to be used to help him. Each time he paid attention to his work for ten seconds, a light on the box on his desk would flash and a counter would move up one. For each flash he would earn candy (or pennies) that would be shared with the whole class at the end of the period. In this way his peers were encouraged not to distract him, and to support his progress. That is just what happened. His classroom behavior and performance improved, and he made new playground friends as well. Four months later Earl's parents indicated that his school behavior was still improved, that he was progressing in reading, and that for the first time other children were coming to his home to play with him.[6]

Stealing, Cheating, Lying, and Other Delinquencies

Stealing, cheating, lying, and other forms of delinquency often reflect the inadequacies of our current social system. No new principles are needed to understand why such behavior occurs. It occurs because immediate reinforcement is given and punishment is avoided. One immediate reinforcement for stealing is obvious: the child gets something he wants. He may also receive reinforcement from peers for his boldness or bravery. At the same time, our social system often fails to provide direct reinforcement for socially appropriate behavior. When children lack basic necessities, they are likely to learn to steal them. When children fail in school because of inadequate teaching, and when failure is punished, they are likely to learn to cheat. When children are not trained by the use of reinforcers, but are only punished for their misdeeds, they are likely to learn to lie.

As with other conduct problems, the solution is to make sure that the undesirable behavior does not pay off and to reinforce behavior incompatible with that which you wish to extinguish.

summary

Conduct problems are often more troubling to teachers and school administrators than academic failures. Somebody has misbehaved, and somebody has to do something about it. This unit has presented many instances of problem behavior in order to demonstrate that it always has a payoff and can be eliminated by changing what is rewarded.

People teach each other how to behave. Groups that have the power to reinforce or punish children (parents, peers, teachers, or school administrators) teach the behavior that is later labeled appropriate or inappropriate. To eliminate problem behavior it is necessary to provide children with what they need in order to live and learn without pain or punishment, and to reinforce behavior that is generally acceptable to the larger social sphere in which the child lives.

self-test

1 The basic rule for stopping tantrums is not to let them lead to a

_____.

2 The greatest danger in a tantrum-treatment program is to start to use time out

and then _____ _____.

1 payoff, reward

3 Negativism or balky behavior generally starts because children are not being

2 give in

managed in a _____ way.

3 positive

4 Negative reactions can be avoided by eliminating sudden _____ of activites and giving children a _____ of two alterantives.

5 The critical element in the development of most aggressive behavior is the reinforcement of more _____ response forms when they do occur.

6 The first approach to the elimination of verbal abuse is to _____ it.

7 Hyperactivity is not a basis for inferring _____ _____.

8 When children lack basic necessities, they are likely to learn to _____ to get them.

9 People _____ each other how to behave.

NUMBER RIGHT _____

4 interruptions;
  choice

5 intense

6 ignore

7 brain damage,
  brain
  dysfunction

8 steal

9 teach, train

exercise 1 programed practice

1 The term *conduct problem* is a _____ given to intense, active, unlawful, or immoral behavior shown by children.

2 Conduct problems are learned behavior. They are learned because they are _____.

3 Tantrums are taught by _____ reinforcers and then "giving in" (reinforcing progressively more _____ protest behavior).

4 The basic rule for stopping tantrums is not to let them lead to a _____. One should also reinforce behavior _____ with throwing tantrums.

5 A good approach to eliminating tantrums is to _____ the child. This

1 label

2 reinforced

3 withholding,
  withdrawing;
  intense

4 payoff, reward;
  incompatible

5 isolate;

insures that the tantrum does not _____ _____.

6 The greatest danger in a tantrum-treatment program is to start to use time out and then _____ _____. This procedure will _____ stronger tantrums.

7 Another way to eliminate tantrums is simply to _____ the child until the tantrum stops. This procedure is called _____.

8 Negative or balky behavior generally starts because children are not being managed in a _____ way.

9 Negative reactions can be avoided by eliminating sudden _____ of activities and giving children a _____ of two alternatives.

10 Also, the use of procedures that make the classroom a fun place and the teacher a reinforcing person will greatly reduce _____ reactions.

11 Negativism is often produced in others by being too abrupt, too _____, and too _____ ourselves.

12 The critical element in the development of most aggressive behavior is the reinforcement of more _____ response forms when they do occur.

13 Walters and Brown found that boys who were reinforced for hitting a plastic clown _____ were more aggressive in play with other boys than those reinforced for hitting _____.

14 Brown and Elliot found that the aggressive behavior of a whole classroom of young boys was greatly reduced when the teachers learned to _____ aggressive behavior and reinforce _____ behavior.

15 To eliminate fighting, be sure it does not _____ _____.

pay off

6 give in;
  reinforce,
  produce

7 ignore
  extinction

8 positive

9 interruptions;
  choice

10 negative

11 bossy;
   negative

12 intense

13 hard; softly

14 ignore;
   cooperative

15 pay off

16 If punishment is used for fighting, do not let the one who punishes be a _____ of aggressive behavior.

17 If swearing and name calling attract quite a bit of _____, there is a good chance the behavior will persist even if it is punished.

18 The first approach to the elimination of verbal abuse is to _____ it.

19 Martha's obnoxious verbal behavior was changed dramatically when her teachers no longer _____ _____ that behavior, but reinforced _____ behavior.

20 Hyperactivity is not a basis for inferring _____ _____.

21 The hyperactive child has not been _____ to work persistently at tasks.

22 Providing training in staying at a task, as in the case of Earl, will eliminate the _____ behavior.

23 Stealing is _____ reinforced by getting whatever is stolen. Stealing may also be reinforced by _____.

24 When children lack basic necessities they are likely to learn to _____ to get them.

25 When children fail to learn because of inadequate teaching, and when failure is punished, they are likely to learn to _____.

26 When children are not trained by the use of reinforcers, but are only _____ for their misdeeds, they are likely to learn to _____.

27 To eliminate conduct problems, make sure the undesired behavior does not

_____ _____, and reinforce behavior _____ with

that which you wish to extinguish.

28 We also need to make such behavior unnecessary by providing children with

what they _____ in order to live and learn without _____

or punishment.

27 pay off;
   incompatible

28 need; pain

29 teach, train

29 People _____ each other how to behave.

discussion questions

1 What kinds of behavior are covered by the term *conduct problem*?
2 What is common to the development of all conduct problems?
3 What are the common steps related to eliminating conduct problems?
4 How can a child be taught to throw tantrums?
5 Specify three ways to eliminate tantrums, and explain what is common to all these procedures.
6 Explain how negative behavior gets started and is maintained. Give an example.
7 Give one way of dealing with negative behavior.
8 Describe a study that supports the theory that reinforcement of intense response forms is critical for the development of aggressive behavior.
9 Specify one approach to eliminating swearing and name calling.
10 Define *hyperactivity*.
11 State how hyperactivity is related to brain damage.
12 Specify a procedure for dealing with hyperactivity.
13 In what way is our social system responsible for conduct problems such as stealing, lying, and cheating?

unit 17

Self-Management

objectives

When you complete this unit you should be able to—

1 Tell how behavioral principles can be used to help meet the objectives of a "free school" or an open classroom.

2 Describe the steps in teaching children about the long-term consequences of their actions.

3 Summarize the research in the effects of self-recording on behavior change.

4 Specify the procedures that seem to make self-evaluation and self-management of reinforcers effective in maintaining responsible behavior.

5 Give an example of how to study self-government systems experimentally.

6 Give an example of self-management using each of the following:
    eliciting stimuli
    discriminative stimuli
    reinforcing stimuli
    negative reinforcing stimuli
    punishing stimuli

7 Give an example of the use of deprivation-satiation conditions in self-management.

lesson

The freedom to manage one's own behavior can come only in conjunction with responsibility. The responsible person works toward long-term goals and respects the rights of others. These characteristics do not develop automatically.

The Colorado Springs Free School

The Colorado Springs Community School was begun in 1969 by a group of parents as an alternative to the local public school system. From the outset it was developed along the free school model. Children ranged in age from five to fourteen years old. Classes were voluntary for the children. Teachers, for the most part, tried to help the children organize activities by providing guidance, materials, and explanations when they were requested. Children had free run of the school and the surrounding area. There were very frequent field trips to local places of interest as well as more prolonged trips for camping. Children were not coerced into participating in any activities. They were encouraged to express their thoughts and feelings. Over the course of the year academic work became less and less frequent. The best efforts of a dedicated staff with a low student-teacher ratio were not sufficient to generate very much skill oriented behavior. Even more discouraging was the development of inconsiderate, rude, and abusive social behavior of the children toward one another and toward the adults. Children showed little respect for one another's rights to privacy, to work undisturbed, to their own property, or to be free from physical abuse. On occasion group meetings were held where these issues were discussed. The children would agree that many social and property abuses were undesirable for everyone concerned. However, these verbal statements had no effect on their subsequent actions. The school had become a place where nothing and no one was safe from destruction, even the building itself. Complete freedom from adult constraints had produced an environment where none of the children were free, even from fear for their own physical well-being.

We cannot be sure about the extent to which our experience applies to other free schools. However, it would not be surprising if the above factors have something to do with why so many free schools fail in a short time.

In planning for the next year the staff and some of the parents at the Community School began to rethink the issue of freedom within the school. First, it became evident that freedom is not a global entity. In fact, there seemed to be innumerable potential freedoms within a school environment. There were the host of freedoms associated with access to materials, activities, and areas, both within the school and within the community at large. Then there were the more personal freedoms such as the freedom of movement, of speech, of self-expression. There were freedoms associated with scheduling one's own activities, in one's own time, in a place of one's own choosing. There were also many freedoms which could be stated negatively: the freedom to leave a project momentarily without returning to find it destroyed or missing; the freedom to pursue a task without constant disruption; the freedom not to be continually abused or intimidated by fellow students as well as by adults. The list of potential freedoms seemed boundless.

Second, specific freedoms could be maintained only so long as they were accompanied by associated responsible behaviors. The Community School used many resources outside the school. However, when some of our children abused those resources we stood in danger of becoming less welcome guests. There have been many people who volunteered to conduct interesting projects at the school. However, when volunteers were verbally or otherwise abused they were less likely to volunteer their services in the future. When the destruction of property became rampant it was no longer possible to give children free access to equipment and materials. Thus, the abusive and destructive behavior of the children was eroding the freedoms within the Community School, and it was doing it in a way more certain than adult authority could ever do.

Another consideration was that all the children at the school were losing freedoms because of the irresponsible behavior of a minority of students. Even more frustrating was that the younger children were beginning to emulate the most aggressive, abusive, authoritarian behavior of their older peers. It seemed that the adults had relinquished their authority to the most aggressive children who were in turn shaping all the children to become progressively more insensitive toward each other.

The question that came sharply to focus from these discussions was how could a school develop and maintain the kind of responsible behaviors that would allow freedoms within the school to be maximized for all children. In the past we gave our children a school environment with a maximum of freedom from adult authority and assumed that their actions would rise to meet the occasion. They didn't. The opposite effect occurred and the result was a hostile, unproductive atmosphere. Therefore, we decided to try the opposite strategy. That is, we could award specific freedoms to individual children only as they began to demonstrate the appropriate responsible behavior.

Before attempting to put this new strategy to use on a school-wide basis we decided to try it first in a more limited way. The children had no previous systematic instruction in mathematics and their skills in this area were correspondingly limited. Therefore, we decided to examine the effect of making math class time available for students to use as free time dependent on their maintaining satisfactory rates in the acquisition of mathematics skills. . . .

When the freedom to leave class was made contingent on finishing one page of math their rate of work (problems/minute) almost doubled. A procedure in which children recorded their own progress in math on special charts generated much interest but little change in their rates of math progress. A third procedure in which students were required to pass a quiz each week in order to leave class early almost doubled the rate of work. Students in the older group were subsequently permitted to elect a condition in which they did not have to attend class at all if they passed two quizzes per week. Sixty percent of the older students elected to try this procedure. Their rate of work once again doubled. Those students were progressing at four times the normative rate of their public-school-age peers. With the onset of the last two conditions, students began to take initiative for their own academic progress. They began to come to class early to get a fast start. Students also began to voluntarily take some work home. They were beginning to demonstrate behavior that the teachers would call *responsible*.[1]

The Hinesburg, Vermont, Open Classroom

The Hinesburg School presented a unique challenge to the consulting teacher because it represented a philosophy of education traditionally considered antagonistic to a behavioral approach such as that used by the consulting teacher. This philosophy is based on the *open classroom* model exemplified in the British Primary Schools. In the open classroom model, large groups of children are provided with a variety of activity centers through which they may move freely and converse as they work. Typically, work projects are intiated and carried out by individuals or small groups. This flexible arrangement affords maximum interaction between children not possible in the traditional self-contained classroom.

The *open classroom* approach was new to the Hinesburg School. During the summer months both the principal and teachers had agreed to remove partitions between the previously self-contained classrooms in order to provide large open spaced areas for each group. Two and three member teaching teams were assigned from forty-eight to seventy-two children homogeneously grouped according to age.

The first referral for special education in the open classroom did not involve the typical *one* child and *one* teacher, but 64 children and three teachers. The teachers reported that until organization and management problems were remediated individual behavioral deficits could not be identified accurately.

The teachers stated their major problems as being related to time spent in moving from one activity to another, individualizing instruction, pupil motivation, and working effectively using a team teaching approach.

Procedure

With the help of consultants, the class was divided into thirds and each group was instructed as to which of the three entrances was to be used by that group. As each child entered the classroom he was required to check his attendance and request for milk and hot lunch on a chart devised by the consulting teacher. This procedure was specifically designed to reduce group time spent in nonacademic tasks.

Prescription packets were compiled daily for each child. These packets contained a prescription sheet listing the child's assignments as well as the areas of the room and the time for working on each assignment. These were helpful to the teacher in determining exactly where each child was in academic areas. Also contained in the packet were the previous day's corrected papers and *fun sheets*. This procedure was designed to reduce time spent in distributing work materials and moving to and from work areas.

A point system was established which allowed groups of five children to earn free time at the end of each academic block. The teacher directed one child in each group to record points for the entire group when they emitted specified behaviors.

Figure 17-1 represents a record of group time spent in nonacademic activities during a two-hour period on consecutive school days. During baseline conditions minutes of nonacademic time ranged from twenty-five to thirty-one minutes. As you can see, this is about one fourth the time spent in nonacademics. During the experimental condition when prescriptive packets, points and free time were instituted, minutes of nonacademic time dropped to under nine minutes. This level was maintained during subsequent postchecks taken at biweekly intervals. The consulting teacher aide recorded minutes of nonacademic time on one occasion during each condition.

The Open Space Environment facilitated frequent observation of the referred class by other teachers in the building. These teachers were anxious to develop similar procedures in their areas and requested our services.

Once the overall management problems were remediated, the teachers could then identify children with behavioral deficits. Thus, as a result of

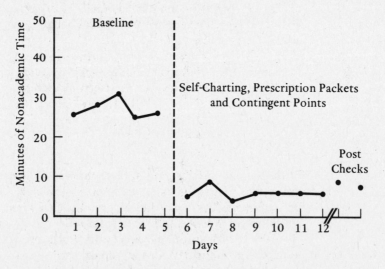

Figure 17.1 Minutes of group involvement in nonacademic tasks during two-hour sessions

the work in the referred classroom, teachers referred thirty individual children for consulting teacher services within the next few weeks.

Since this time, points have been removed and prescriptive packets are written together with the child on a weekly and contractual basis. It is no longer necessary to use free time as a reinforcer since children have become increasingly more involved in choosing and successfully carrying out their own programs.[2]

Learning To Be Responsible

As a part of being responsible, we learn to value longer-term reinforcers instead of immediate ones, and to consider the possible effects of our behaviors on others. Teaching these things is a continuous job of home, church, and school. One way is through courses in citizenship, good health practices, the control of pollution, sex and marriage, and so forth. Much can also be accomplished when the teaching adults discuss long-term consequences of behavior as the opportunities arise.

Within a point-contract system, a token reinforcement system, or an ordinary classroom, there are many opportunities for teaching the value of working to develop new skills, working cooperatively, and following rules for group living. When points are awarded for good work or when tokens are exchanged for backup reinforcers, the teacher has examples to use in teaching more general values.

In remedial reading, the following might happen:

Teacher: "You guys didn't think when we started that you could learn to read. But look, in four weeks of really hard work, you are all reading harder material with fewer errors, and you made criterion on seventeen out of twenty stories. Among you, you have earned a total of 480 points. Now I think that is just a little short of fantastic! It sure shows each of you that if you work hard at a task it will benefit you in the long run. Can you guys think of some other long-term benefits of learning to read better?" (This promotes a discussion of doing better in other courses, getting better jobs, and so on.)

In a class with behavior problems:

Teacher: "Before we have our special party today, I want to talk to you about how you have been doing since we started this point system. Before we started, you might remember things were a little chaotic in here. It was really hard for me to teach you. Since then, you have really changed. What are some of the changes you have noticed?"

Bob: "You are nicer to us."

Teacher:	"That's true, Bob. You have been so cooperative, I have wanted to let you know how much that pleases me."
Mary:	"The room is quieter, so it is easier to hear you."
Teacher:	"It's more pleasant for all of us when we follow the class rules. We can learn more and be more relaxed doing it."
Bill:	"We don't fight so much and tease like we did."
Teacher:	"I must say, you boys are really becoming more grown up. Do you know, when you stop hitting others, they are more likely to stop trying to get back at you. When you are nice to others, they are more likely to be nice to you."

In teaching long-term values, the first step is to talk about them so the students will learn to identify long-term consequences. Next, teach the students to identify conflict situations in which long-term consequences are important. As a situation arises, discuss it so the students can use what they have been learning to produce a responsible solution. Give them direct practice through role-playing moral dilemmas, having the students plan the school day (with teacher guidance), using various forms of student government, and setting up miniature situations that highlight value conflicts.

Research on Self-Management

The experimental analysis of responsible self-managed behavior is in its infancy. The available studies have a common theme running through them. *Children do not become responsible unless they are taught to be so.* Teachers who keep this point in mind can avoid the mistake of not monitoring, guiding, and supervising the value decisions of their students.

Self-Recording of Behavior

By recording your own behavior, you can sometimes change it, since the feedback can both remind you of what you are trying to change and reinforce you if it changes. The research literature suggests that junior high and high school students can be trained to use self-recording to help control their own behavior. For example, Marcia Broden[3] and others found that an eighth-grade girl in history class increased her study behavior when provided with slips to record how much she studied each day. Similarly, an eighth-grade boy decreased his talk-outs when provided with slips to record them each day. However, after a return to baseline, a second period of recording talk-outs was not as effective. The authors suggest that self-recording procedures should be combined with social reinforcement to be most effective.

Other studies suggest that children are not naturally accurate observers of their own behavior. Fixsen, Phillip, and Wolf[4] found, with boys in Achievement Place, that it was necessary to train them for observing their own behavior and to give points for concurrence with another observer, before accurate self-observations occurred. Even then, however, just doing self-reports did not significantly improve room-cleaning behaviors. In a similar vein, Santogrossi[5] and associates found that self-evaluation by adolescents in a psychiatric hospital did not decrease their disruptive behavior.

When self-evaluations are combined with a token reinforcement system, two groups of researchers report that adolescents not only reliably report their behavior, but make improvements and maintain them. In the first study, students recorded daily the number of correct responses they made to comprehension questions from SRA Reading Labs.[6] Accuracy increased for the class when there was self-recording and token rewards. In the second study, adolescents in a psychiatric hopsital school were shifted from teacher-evaluation to self-evaluation after the special class had been in operation for over three months.[7] The shift was made to prepare them to work more on their own without the token system. In making the shift, the teacher gave the following instructions:

> I am very pleased with how well you've been behaving in class lately, but it is important to learn to judge your own actions, without anyone's help. This is a very important part of becoming a mature and responsible adult. I think we can use the Special Reading Program and the token system as a way of helping to develop your ability to evaluate your own behavior.
>
> Beginning today I am going to ask you to give yourself your own ratings. You will decide how many tokens you deserve (or lose) based upon how you behaved during the rating period. In other words, I want you to determine the ratings the way I have been doing for the past weeks. You make your judgment based upon your own observation of how you followed the rules and tell me and the class how many tokens you deserve. Of course you will *earn* (lose) as many tokens as you say. Does everyone understand what I am talking about?

Given appropriate training, the students were able to report accurately their own behavior and maintain improvements.

Self-Management of Reinforcers

Lovitt and Curtiss[8] studied self-set contingencies with a twelve-year-old boy in a special class. When the boy, rather than the teacher, set the number of points for each academic task, he completed more tasks per minute. His rewards were usually higher than the teacher's, but a study to control for this magnitude-of-reward effect suggested that the critical factor was whether the student or the teacher set the payoff rules. Student-determined rules led to more work by the student.

In history lessons with ninth-grade girls, Glynn[9] found that test score accuracy was as high with self-determined token rewards as with experimenter-determined rewards. Also, each of these token reward procedures was better than two control procedures using no tokens or random tokens.

In another study, Glynn and associates[10] studied the effects of self-management procedures with a group of second-graders. After a training program in which the class could earn points if they were all on-task when checked by the teacher (on a random schedule), the program was turned over to the students. A tape recorder played intermittent beeps every one to five minutes. If the children were on-task when the beep occurred, they recorded a check mark. Checks could later be used for self-administered free time. This self-recorded and self-administered system was very effective in maintaining on-task behavior. With a somewhat different procedure, Bolstad and Johnson[11] also showed that control of an initially externally-managed token system could be turned over to the students without a loss in on-task behavior.

Experiments in Self-Government

Achievement Place has been used to experimentally study which forms of social design (governments) most readily teach youngsters to become responsible adults. At Achievement Place a semi-self-government system is used whereby the boys can vote to establish many of their own rules, monitor their own compliance, and conduct "trials" when violations occur. The boys participated more in the discussion of a violation when they had complete responsibility for setting the consequence of the "trial" than if the teaching parents set the consequence.[12] On the other hand, another study showed that the boys called fewer "trials" than the teaching parents did. A third study examined the various aspects of the management of routine household tasks.[13] The best system involved a peer-elected manager who had the authority to both give and take away points, depending on whether or not the other boys were meeting their obligations.

Self-Management: Learning to Control the Variables That Control You

So far we have looked at the problem of self-management as one of teaching students. In this section, the point of view shifts to the individual who wants to control his own behavior. Just how can we arrange conditions so we can change in a desired way? In the unit on the Criticism Trap, we faced one aspect of this question with the project on learning to praise more. We used the principles of behavior to change our own behavior (for example, reinforcement from feedback, prompting, and role-playing). To take a more systematic look at the problem, let us review the various principles of behavior and how they might be used in a self-management program.

Operant Control of Eliciting Stimuli

Many respondent behaviors can be controlled by the individual controlling the eliciting stimuli. For example, the actress who wants real tears at the right time might carry some ground-up onion in her handkerchief. Also, research has shown that each of us can think about eating certain foods, and our stomachs will produce the appropriate digestive juices. Most of us can make ourselves angry or sexually aroused by thinking about eliciting stimuli appropriate to our individual histories.

Behavior therapists have been using a procedure called *deep relaxation* for some time to help people learn to break the cycle of intense anxiety-eliciting tension. It involves tensing muscle groups one at a time, holding the tension for four or five seconds, and then letting go. A record is available that will help you learn this procedure on your own.[14] The tensing and letting go to the word *relax* slowly lets you learn to control relaxation and thus reduce tension. Later, relaxation is tied to deep breathing while counting to ten and saying, "Relax," each time you exhale. This allows you to get quickly into a relaxed condition when it is needed. When coupled with a procedure called systematic desensitization (a form of counter-conditioning), this deep relaxation procedure has been very helpful in removing anxieties, fears, angers, and other disturbing conditioned emotional reactions. Most persons who have experienced deep relaxation under the guidance of a therapist find a half-hour of relaxation is as refreshing as four hours of sleep.

Use of Discriminative and Reinforcing Stimuli

Throughout this text we have suggested ways the teacher can use prompts to help change his behavior: make the misbehavior of one child the cue to find someone else to praise; count your behavior; put up signs; give out tokens. Lists can help to organize a busy day.

Lloyd Homme[15] has suggested a set of self-management procedures combining use of discriminative stimuli with the Premack principle. Let's say that you are "down," and keep thinking about what depresses you. How can you change this? First, write out four or five happy thoughts—things, people, places, actions that make you smile or feel good. Next, you find several behavior chains, common in your daily routine, such as placing a telephone call, starting your car, or writing on the blackboard. Once you start a behavior chain, completing it is highly probable behavior. At the start you do not think a lot of happy thoughts, so, this is a low-probability behavior. When you start into a behavior chain, such as dialing a telephone number, set a rule that before you dial the last number you will think about one of the happy thoughts on your list for two seconds. Then, you finish the call and are reinforced by completing it. Making telephone calls provides discriminative stimuli for having happy thoughts, and then, happy thoughts are reinforced. Silly? Try it. Or, after you get into the car and insert the key, pause; tell yourself to relax while letting go all over. Then start the car. Or, as you start to write an assignment on the board, stop a second and think of something pleasant. Then finish the task.

Many approaches to improving study behavior involve a combined use of discriminative stimuli, shaping, and the Premack principle. For example, study in the same place each day and study only in that place, so it becomes discriminative for study. The radio and TV are somewhere else, you eat somewhere else, and so on. Possible conflicting behaviors are not allowed to occur there. Start out with a short study period at first—ten minutes, say. Then set up a contingency that after you complete studying, you can get a cup of coffee or a candy bar, call a friend, or do whatever is reinforcing for you. Each day you increase the study time until it is adequate for your needs. Chart the time studied each day.

Most weight-control procedures rely on a combination of discriminative stimuli, shaping, and reinforcement. Usually, eating should take place only in one place. The number of calories taken in is recorded. Careful weight records are kept. Usually, some procedures for getting reinforcement from others are advisable, such as making your chart public to close friends, including a "before" picture.

Using Negative Reinforcers

More and more we are designing our environments to control behavior with negative reinforcers. At first it was alarm clocks to get us up on time. Now it is seat belts that buzz until you buckle them, or buzzers that go on if you leave the keys in the car. As irritating as these devices are, they do get the job done.

Using Punishing Consequences

There are some powerful ways in which we can change our own behavior by entering into agreements that stipulate penalties for failure. For example, we know of one secretary who agreed to place $10 into a pot in her office, plus fifty cents for each day she did not smoke (the money normally spent for cigarettes). If she did not smoke for three months, she would get the full amount back, plus weekly luncheons on Friday. However, if she smoked, the money would be sent to the John Birch Society (an organization she opposed.) She stopped smoking for the period of the contract.

Making promises to others can have a similar effect. Failure to keep a promise can be punishing to those who have been taught the importance of keeping them.

Deprivation—Satiation

Reinforcers are not always equally effective. By planning certain activities to occur during periods of satiation, rather than deprivation, self-control can be enhanced. When you are hungry, it is hard to resist food. For example, if buying a lot of high calorie foods is a problem for you, don't go shopping just before dinner. Go after dinner. Similarly, if eating while cooking is a problem, prepare several meals when you are not hungry and place them in the freezer.

You can learn to use behavioral principles systematically to manage your own behavior toward desired goals. The task is difficult and full of traps. Very often, it is more effective to get someone else to cooperate with you in your change projects. The other person can help reinforce you for progress. In two-party conflicts, such as those in marriage, an outside behavioral counselor can be very helpful in planning a change strategy.

IT'S PART OF MY SELF-MANAGEMENT PROGRAM.

summary

Responsible self-management does not come automatically; it has to be learned. We earn various freedoms as we grow up by learning to respect the freedom of others. We are taught to think about the long-term reinforcing and punishing consequences of our actions. We are taught about relative values. Much of this learning is not easy, because distal consequences are not easily connected to current behavior. The teacher, the parent, the responsible adult needs to step in and teach children the long-term consequences of their behavior when potential conflict situations arise.

In teaching about long-term values, the first step is to talk about them— state a general rule about the consequences of certain kinds of behavior— so the students will learn to identify long-term consequences. Next, give practice in identifying situations where long-term consequences should be considered. Finally, give practice (in protected situations) in struggling with the consequences of different actions where values are in conflict.

The experimental study of self-management behavior is very young. One thing is clear from current research: children become responsible only if they are taught to be so. Studies have shown that when children record their own behavior (to increase or decrease), changes sometimes take place. But self-recording procedures are more effective if combined with praise from important adults. Self-recording and self-evaluation works well in token economies after the students have had training and experience. Students can also be taught to determine their own rewards in a responsible way. Current work is examining alternative designs for self-governing systems to find which most readily foster responsible behavior with the greatest freedom from adult authority.

Another approach to self-management is through a careful understanding of behavior principles. If we can find ways to control (change) the stimulus variables that control what we do, we can change our own behavior in desired directions. We can learn to control *eliciting* stimuli that upset us by learning to relax when we start to feel upset or by learning to think about pleasant things. We can use *discriminative* and *reinforcing* stimuli to prompt a change in our own behavior and to strengthen the new behavior. The use of such procedures (as taught by behavior therapists) have been effective in relieving unhappiness, improving study habits, stopping smoking, losing weight, and counselling married couples, just to mention a few possibilities. *Negative reinforcers* can be established through the use of mechanical devices (for example, the alarm clock) to help us manage ourselves more effectively. One can also make promises or enter into contracts to provide *reinforcement* and *punishment* to achieve a desired change. Finally, in self-management, we should keep in mind that reinforcers vary in effectiveness with deprivation and satiation conditions. Temptation can be avoided by doing certain risky things (like shopping when trying to diet) only under satiation conditions.

The task of self-management is not easy. It is best accomplished in cooperation with others who can help you achieve your goals.

broadening your perspective

Locking Up the Cigarettes

In the unit on punishment, we reported a study by Nate Azrin in which he attempted to use electric shock to get people to quit smoking. The people involved avoided the shock by quitting the experiment. He went back to the drawing boards and built a new device, using stimulus-control technology, to assist those who wanted to reduce smoking to a medically safe level (one-half pack per day, according to the Surgeon General's 1964 Report).

The principle involved discrimination learning. The subject learned that he could obtain a cigarette only when a ratchet sound occurred, indicating that the cigarette case was unlocked. Also, a clock on the face of the case indicated the delay interval was over. At all other times, reaching for a cigarette was placed on extinction because the case was locked. The basic human-engineering problem was to induce people to use the case. The solution was to start with a short period when the case remained locked. All seven participants agreed to a seven-minute locked period at the start, but they also said they would not participate if the case were locked for more than thirty minutes. Gradually, the case was locked longer between smokes. For some, this was done by the experimenter; for others, they could control the increase themselves. One subject dropped out because of travel commitments. Another found the case inconvenient to fit into his shirt pocket. The other five subjects stayed with it, and all reduced their smoking to under fifteen cigarettes a day. The initial smoking levels were 44, 41, 33, 28, and 21. The levels after seven to nine weeks when the case was *locked for an hour* between smokes were 15, 14, 15, 9 and 12 respectively. Participant observers and subject reports verified that only four violations occurred when cigarettes were obtained from others. The procedure of gradually increasing the nonavailability of a reinforcer is a relatively nonaversive (not upsetting) way of achieving self-control.[16]

Pill Prompting

Another self-management procedure is to have stimuli in your environment remind you when to do what. You might make a checklist, put up a sign, or set an alarm. A common medical problem is getting patients to take prescribed medicine on schedule. Azrin and Powell engineered a pill dispenser that would sound a tone when a pill was to be taken. When the patient turned the top of the device to shut off the tone, the pill came out into the hand.

The device was evaluated using normal adults (nurses) who were instructed to take inactive pills every half hour under three different conditions. In the first condition, they were given the usual pill bottle. The pills were not taken 16 percent of the time. In the second condition, the nurses used an apparatus that sounded a tone, turned itself off in three seconds, and did not deliver the pill. Pills were missed 11 percent of the time. In the third condition, the behaviorally-engineered dispenser was used and pills were missed only 3 percent of the time. The pill-taking prompter did its job.[17]

Make an Offer You Can't Resist—The Weight Control Contract

Seven women and one man between the ages of eighteen and thirty-three agreed to participate in a weight-reduction study. They first obtained a medical checkup and a physician's approval. The participants had to select their own diets or use one provided by their physician. Six agreed to lose twenty-five or more pounds, and one sixteen pounds.

A contingency contract was then written as a legal document before witnesses. The people entered into the contract to help themselves better manage their own weight. The contract provided for three kinds of contingencies: consequences for each two-pound weight loss or gain, consequences for meeting or failing to meet a two-week minimum goal, and consequences for meeting a terminal goal or for quitting before reaching the goal. The participants were asked to put up a number of personal objects they considered valuable (medals, trophies, jewelry, money). An individual contract specified how those objects could be earned back or lost as a penalty. Lost items would be donated to various charities. The contract also specified that the participants would be weighed at a specific time and place every Monday, Wednesday, and Friday, until the terminal weight was reached.

A baseline period was measured for each participant during which only the terminal contingency was in effect. In all cases except one, the participants gained or remained stable during baseline. The average gain for eight participants was .9 pounds per week. During the treatment conditions all three contingencies were in effect. In the first treatment period they lost an average of 2.1 pounds a week. During a brief reversal procedure, the average gain was 1.9 pounds per week. During the next treatment period, the average loss was 1.6 pounds per week. Six of the eight participants met the contract goals (and beyond). Two participants were terminated by agreement after losing 20 pounds each. The schedule of consequences had no further effect on weight loss. With two other subjects a reversal procedure was used wherein only the punishment clauses were not operative for twenty days. Weight increased during this period, showing the importance of the penalties.[18]

Changing Your Behavior With Your Marriage Partner

When a marriage is working, there is mutual reinforcement by the partners. The relationship is reciprocal. Each has rights and duties. When difficulties arise it is usually the case that each partner is giving reinforcement to the other at a low rate, and in fact, there is often a pattern of mutual coercion and withdrawal (using negative reinforcement until the other gives in).[19] The use of coercion often escalates until divorce is the only apparent alternative. As Stuart notes:

> A husband might wish his wife to express greater affection; following the failure of his amorous advances, he might become abusive, accusing his wife of anything from indifference to frigidity, abating his criticism when he receives the desired affection. The three flaws in this approach are: first, to the extent that he makes himself unpleasant, he is less likely to receive affection; second, to the extent that he is abusive or accusing, he debases his wife's affection and simultaneously reduces its reinforcing properties for himself; and third, to the extent that her affection is offered in compliance to his demand, it will appear to be appeasement rather than a gesture of genuine affection.

Stuart has examined a marriage counselling procedure that has these components:

1 Each spouse accepts the idea that the behavior of the other is a source of difficulty, rather than some "personality flaw."
2 They must work on the premise that to change the interaction, each partner must assume the initiative in changing his own behavior to break the mutual-coercion pattern.
3 Next, each spouse is asked to list three behaviors which he or she would like the other to *increase*. This gets off the negative focus.

4   These "three wishes" are placed on a Behavior Checklist, which is posted at home. Each spouse records the frequency with which the other performs the specified behavior. This provides a prompt and a record of change.

5   The final step involves working out some exchanges for desired behaviors. So much of this behavior by the husband can be exchanged for so much of that behavior by the wife. When reciprocity is still present, a simple charting of the goals can be effective. Where coercion is already great, a token exchange system may be needed to get the system going.

Stuart illustrates these procedures with a discussion of four cases.

Four couples have used the token system to modify each other's behavior. Individuals ranged in age from twenty-four to fifty-two and in education from high school diploma to doctorate. The couples were married for from three to twenty-three years and had a maximum of two children. Each of the couples sought treatment as a last-ditch effort prior to obtaining a divorce. In each instance, the wife listed as her first wish that her husband converse with her more fully, or at least that he not "close me out of his life even when he is at home." Considerable discussion was often necessary to identify what intensity level of conversation was positively reinforcing to the wife, and this was made clear and rehearsed during the treatment sessions. The wife was then instructed to purchase a kitchen timer which she could carry with her about the house. She was instructed to set the timer as soon as her husband entered and to give him one token when the bell rang after each hour in which he conversed at the criterion level. If he failed to behave at the criterion level by the end of the first thirty minutes of each hour, she had to notify him of this and offer constructive suggestions, cueing him as to how his performance could be improved upon. If she failed to do this, he had to be given a token even if he failed to perform adequately. If he so requested, at the half-hour cue time, the timer could be reset so that he could earn a token during the next hour (so that he waited sixty rather than ninety minutes before being rewarded).

The criterion level for conversation is naturally a negotiable factor. No one could be expected to talk to his wife constantly; if for no other reason, his children would not allow it. Therefore, conversational tokens can be earned for a wider range of responses ranging from intense conversation at one extreme to the wife's feeling free to interrupt her husband with a question at agreed intervals at the other extreme.

While tokens may have some intrinsic reinforcing properties in their own right (in addition to being associated with positive social responses when they are offered), they become more powerful when they function as contingencies for some other event. With the four couples cited, tokens were redeemable at the husband's request from a menu stressing physical affection. A different menu was constructed for each couple which took into account the base-line level of sexual activity, the desired level of sexual activity, and the number of hours available for nonsexual (in this instance conversational) interchange. Each of these couples had sex less than once per week (ranging from once in the year prior to treatment to once in the week prior to treatment), each desired sex an average of three times per week, and each had approximately five hours together on weeknights and fourteen hours on weekends, making a total of approximately fifty-two—fifty-four hours per week. Accordingly, husbands were charged three tokens for

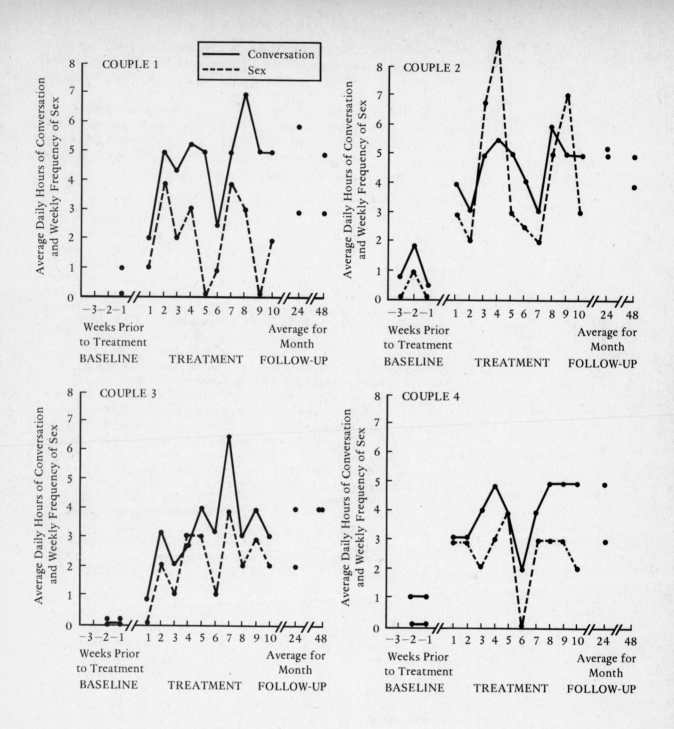

Figure 17.2 Average daily hours of conversation and weekly rate of sex of four couples, before, during, and after operant marital therapy

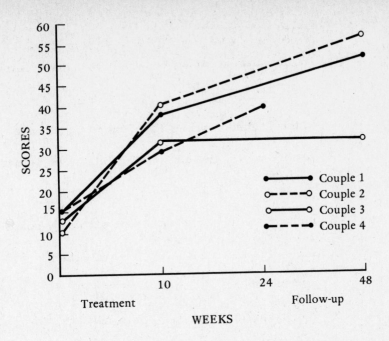

Figure 17.3 Marital satisfaction assessment inventory scores of four couples, before, at last session, and at follow-up

kissing and "lightly petting" with their wives, five tokens for "heavy petting," and fifteen tokens for intercourse. (These behaviors were not rehearsed during treatment sessions.)

Tokens earned and spent were recorded on the Behavior Checklist, which also provided data for continued graphing of interactional behavior. The performance of each of these couples is represented in figure 17.2 where it will be seen that the rates of conversation and sex increased sharply after the start of treatment and continued through twenty-four- and forty-eight-week follow-up periods.

At the start of treatment, at the conclusion of regularly scheduled interviews, and at the time of follow-up, each spouse was asked to complete a brief inventory measuring the extent of his own and his perception of his spouse's satisfaction in and commitment to the marriage. . . . The results are depicted in figure 17.3 where it can be seen that the rate of reported satisfaction increased in association with the reported behavioral changes. These changes enabled the couples to become more similar to nonclinic families on this dimension.

With each of these couples, all therapeutic sessions were held jointly. Sessions were held during the first four, the sixth, eighth, and tenth weeks, for a total of seven sessions. When it is considered that these couples were each on the brink of filing for divorce, this could be considered relatively inexpensive treatment. Follow-up contacts were held by phone or by mail, and all data, including that collected during sessions, were based on self-report.[20]

Keep in mind in thinking about managing your own behavior that others can help you out. That's what friends are for.

self-test

1 The responsible person knows about and works toward _____ - _____ goals.

2 In the Colorado Springs Free School, the abusive and _____ behavior eroded freedoms within the school in a way that no adult _____ could ever do.

3 In the Hinesburg open classroom, eventually points were unnecessary and _____ _____ were written together with the child on a weekly, contractual basis.

4 In teaching long-term values, the first step is to _____ about them so the students will learn to identify long-term consequences.

5 The available studies on self-management have a common theme: children do not become responsible unless they are _____ to be so.

6 When self-evaluations are combined with a _____ _____ system, adolescents not only reliably report their behavior, but show or maintain desired improvements in behavior.

7 It is also possible to look at self-management as a problem in learning to use _____ _____ to change your own behavior.

8 Lloyd Homme has suggested a set of procedures to be used in self-management combining use of _____ stimuli with the Premack principle.

9 Very often, it is more effective to get _____ _____ to cooperate with you in your change projects.

NUMBER RIGHT _____

1 long-term

2 destructive;
authority

3 prescriptive
packets

4 talk

5 taught

6 token
reinforcement

7 behavior
principles

8 discriminative

9 someone else

exercise 1 programed practice

1 responsibility

2 long-term

3 free

4 irresponsible

5 demonstrate

6 quizzes

7 initiative;
   responsible

8 open

9 motivating

10 self

1 The freedom to manage one's own behavior can come only in conjunction

with _____.

2 The responsible person knows about and works toward _____-

_____ goals.

3 In the Colorado Springs Free School, complete freedom from adult con-

straints produced an environment where none of the children were

_____ even from fear for their own physical well-being.

4 All the children at the school were losing freedoms because of the

_____ behavior of a minority of students.

5 It was decided to award specific freedoms to individual children only as they

began to _____ the appropriate responsible behavior.

6 Older students in the math group could elect a condition in which they did

not have to attend class if they passed two _____ per week.

7 Students began to take _____ for their own academic progress.

They were beginning to demonstrate behavior that the teachers would call

_____.

8 The _____ classroom approach was new to the Hinesburg School.

9 The teachers' major problems were moving from one activity to another,

individualizing instruction, _____ students, and working effec-

tively in a team-teaching approach.

10 Charts and _____-recording by the students reduced the time spent

on attendance.

11 Prescription packets were compiled, listing the child's _____ as well as the area and time for working on each assignment.

12 A point system allowed groups of five children to earn _____ _____ at the end of each academic block.

13 Eventually _____ were unnecessary and prescriptive packets were written together with the child on a weekly and contractual basis.

14 In teaching long-term values, the first step is to _____ about them so the students will learn to identify long-term consequences.

15 The next step is to teach the students to identify conflict _____ in which long-term consequences are important.

16 Direct practice can be accomplished through _____-_____ moral dilemmas, having the students plan the school day, using various forms of student _____, and setting up miniature situations to highlight _____ conflicts.

17 The available self-management studies have a common theme: children do not become responsible unless they are _____ to be so.

18 Broden suggests that self-recording procedures should be combined with _____ reinforcement to be most effective.

19 Other studies suggest that children are not naturally _____ observers of their own behavior.

20 When self-evaluations are combined with a _____ _____ system, adolescents not only reliably report their own behavior, but show or maintain desired improvements in behavior.

---

11 assignments

12 free time

13 points

14 talk

15 situations

16 role-playing;
government;
value

17 taught

18 social

19 accurate

20 token
reinforcement

21 Lovitt and Curtiss found that when the child sets the number of points for each academic task, he completes _____ tasks per minute.

22 Achievement Place has been used to study which forms of social design (_____) most readily teach youngsters to become responsible adults.

23 It is possible to look at self-management as a problem of using _____ _____ to change your own behavior.

24 Many _____ behaviors can be controlled by the individual controlling the eliciting stimuli.

25 Behavior therapists have been using a procedure called deep _____ to help people learn to break the cycle of intense anxiety-eliciting tension.

26 Lloyd Homme has suggested a set of self-management procedures combining the use of _____ stimuli with the Premack principle.

27 By setting a rule that before you dial the last number when making a call you will think about something pleasant, you can get _____ for happy thoughts by completing the call.

28 Many approaches for improving study behavior involve a combined use of _____ stimuli, shaping, and the Premack principle.

29 First, study in the same place each day and only in that place, so it becomes _____ for study.

30 Then set up a _____ that after you complete studying, you can get a reward.

31 Each day you _____ the study time until it is adequate.

32 Alarm clocks are an example of a _____ reinforcer.

33 Contracts that provide both rewards and _____ can be powerful self-control devices.

34 By planning certain activities to occur during periods of _____, rather than deprivation, self-control can sometimes be enhanced.

35 Very often, it is more effective to get _____ _____ to cooperate with you in your change projects.

32 negative

33 punishers

34 satiation

35 someone else

discussion questions

1 How could behavioral principles be used to meet the objectives of a "free school"?

2 Describe the steps taken in using behavioral principles to help establish an open classroom.

3 Describe the steps in teaching children about the long-term consequences of their actions.

4 Summarize the research findings on the effects of self-recording on behavior changes.

5 What procedures seem to be important for making self-evaluation and self-management of reinforcers effective in maintaining responsible behavior?

6 Give an example of how to study effective self-government systems experimentally.

7 Give an example of how eliciting stimuli can be used in self-management.

8 Give an example of the use of discriminative stimuli in self-management.

9 Give an example of the use of reinforcing stimuli in self-management.

10 Give an example of the use of negative reinforcers in self-management.

11 Give an example of the use of punishing stimuli in self-management.

12 What do you see as the potential traps in programs for changing your own behavior?

13 What advice in this unit might help to avoid the traps associated with self-management?

14 What is meant by the "mutual escalation of use of coercion" as underlying marital conflict?

15 Suggest some procedures for de-escalation.

16 Why are we responsible for each other?

unit 18

Review 2

objectives

This unit reviews the material presented in units 10 through 17. For any terms or concepts that you do not understand, go back to the original material for study. Your test scores may be improved by also reviewing the exercises at the end of each unit.

review

Unit 10. Using Social and Activity Reinforcers

Using social and activity reinforcers involves a number of skills. Their full development will not occur just from reading a few pages. It will give you some ideas of what to do when, but you then need practice. A good procedure for practicing is to: (1) specify a setting, (2) specify what you are trying to do better (for example, use behavior-specific praise, make a routine task more fun, turn on a high school class), then (3) tape record a performance, (4) listen to it, and (5) record it again. Some alternatives are to practice before a mirror or team up with a friend and take turns playing teacher and student. The *out loud* practice is essential to learning new behaviors.

Social reinforcers include praise, approving facial expressions, physical nearness, and physical contact. It is important to cultivate an appropriate repertoire of such behaviors. In using praise describe the behavior you like. Be factual, not judgmental. There is a host of activity reinforcers available. The teacher should develop two lists, one related to the daily schedule and a second composed of activities that can be used any time. Contingencies are important. Use activities that the children enjoy as consequences for good work. Special activities, such as going home, to lunch, or to recess, can also be used to carefully teach appropriate group behavior at such times. Do not let a noisy class go, unless you want them to learn to be more noisy. Think carefully about the many ways you can use holiday activities to help support learning in your class.

It is also important to make teaching fun by embedding social and activity reinforcers in the instructional tasks themselves. Select material that is funny, surprising, or dramatic, and present it in a way that will get and hold the children's attention. The key is to use variations in pacing, rhythm, loudness, and pauses. This keeps reinforcement for attending on an unpredictable intermittent schedule. Some other procedures for teaching in a fun style involve making games out of drills, deliberately making mistakes, and taking a negative approach to a universal rule. The possible ways to make teaching fun as well as productive are limited only by one's imagination.

And finally, prepare well for that first day. It can make or break the school year.

Unit 11. Designing and Using Token Reinforcement Systems

Poorly motivated students sometimes need strong reinforcers. When this is the case, consider using a token or point system. Token systems are highly effective in reducing problem behavior and in increasing academic learning. But keep in mind, "Don't use it if you don't need it."

In designing a token system, the first step is to specify the behaviors that earn tokens. Chart your general goals, then get down to specifics appropriate for each child.

1 Specify quality as well as quantity.
2 Gradually increase your behavioral requirements so the children work for longer periods without reinforcement.
3 Focus on reinforcing improvement.
4 Consider writing out daily assignments for each child where appropriate.

Next, build a reinforcer menu. Consider special activities and games, foods, and play materials. With older children you might write a contract at school with reinforcers provided by parents.

In setting prices and wages, decide on an hourly wage. Then set prices: at first store items are priced at cost; each five minutes of an in-school activity costs the hourly wage; and each twenty minutes of an out-of-school activity costs the hourly wage. To specify prices in tokens, decide how many reinforcers you should give in an hour to do the job for your class. Once this is decided, the rest falls out by simple arithmetic. Adjustments can be made to your price schedule according to the law of supply and demand. Also gradually increase the work requirements for earning tokens.

"Charging" for infrequent misbehaviors (a response cost procedure) can be considered after a token system is established.

The tokens should be handy, readily given, and noninterfering. Points, electrical counters, and plastic chips may be useful, depending on the setting.

Require a work-check and corrections *before* giving tokens for academic work. The exchange should be planned to show the kids how they are coming along and how pleased you are.

Charts and records simplify the management of a token system and let both teacher and students know where things stand.

Informal token systems may be devised for a single child or a small group. A number of illustrations of such systems were given.

When it comes time to end a special reinforcement system, careful plans must be laid for the transition. If you are going to keep the kids in your class, rather than returning them to someone else, slowly fade out the components of the token system. If the children are to be returned to a regular class, follow the fade-out procedure, but also train the receiving teacher in good reinforcement procedures. Otherwise, your efforts may be wasted.

Unit 12. Point-Contract Systems for Junior High and High School Students

Point contracts are specialized token reinforcement systems in which the performance requirements and consequences are written out and agreed to. The contracts should specify responsibilities, privileges, sanctions, possible bonuses, and monitoring procedures. Three kinds of possible contracts were illustrated: the term-course contract, in which credits and grades are the consequences; the learning center contract, in which a fuller range of backup reinforcers can be used; and the home-school contract set up by counseling personnel, in which behavior and progress at school earn privileges and rewards at home.

A term-course or learning-center contract can be effective only if there is a clearly outlined program of instruction and procedures for accomplishing it. A good example is the Keller "personalized instruction" system. It requires teaching materials broken into units, a specified teaching mechanism, and specified response requirements for the students.

The research literature supports the efficacy of the Keller method over traditional lecture methods, and also establishes the importance of providing for performance practice (not just silent reading), study questions, contingent grades, and a high performance criterion. It seems likely that many of these procedures will be used in middle and high school settings in the near future.

Unit 13. Punishment: When To, How To, and Why Not To

Previous units focused on strengthening behavior; in contrast, unit 13 covered weakening it through punishment. It was shown to be an effective, though somewhat risky, method of changing behavior. Many principles about using reinforcers also apply to punishers, except the goal is to *weaken* rather than *strengthen* behavior. Usually we avoid punishment because of the potential undesirable side effects—that is, the development of escape and avoidance behavior. We teach children to hide, sneak, cheat, and lie by the improper use of punishment.

Effective punishment must do at least three things—

1 Prevent avoidance and escape from the source of punishment
2 Minimize the need for future punishment
3 Not provide a model for aggression

Prevent escape and avoidance by using punishment that consists of withdrawal of reinforcers for a period of time. This minimizes the future need for punishment by developing effective warning signals or conditioned punishers. Also, it is effective to reinforce behavior incompatible with that being punished. Effective punishment is given immediately and calmly; and it is used consistently. Two conditions when punishment might be necessary are: (1) if a behavior is so frequent that there is little incompatible behavior to reinforce; and (2) if the problem behavior is so intense that the child or someone else may be hurt.

Unit 14. Teaching Self-Confidence and Self-Esteem

The attitudes of self-confidence and self-esteem are the unseen products of successful learning experiences. What the teacher actually sees are children who *approach* learning situations and talk positively about the learning activities and their own competencies.

Each teaching instance provides an opportunity for the teacher to teach children positive attitudes about themselves and school work. There are several procedures that are likely to build confident, self-esteeming children. First, when children are praised by adults for real accomplishments, they learn to think of themselves as praiseworthy, capable individuals. Second, when the teacher presents a model of a successful, competent, self-confident person, the children are likely to imitate that model. Third, when the academic program is one in which the child can learn and can succeed, he receives daily demonstrations of his competencies.

Two specific attitudes and related behavior patterns can be taught to promote self-esteem. These attitudes are "persistence pays off" and "I know when I am right." The first is taught through a program that reinforces success following error trials and encourages trying when success is not immediate. Fooler games are used to teach "I know when I am right." The teacher makes deliberate errors that the children are trained to catch.

Self-esteem and self-confidence are products of successful teaching using reinforcement procedures. It is possible to teach these attitudes without explicitly devising a program to do so. The important thing to remember is to give praise and other reinforcers for successful performances.

Viewing self-esteem as the primary goal in instruction is likely to obscure the need for successful teaching to produce self-esteem.

Unit 15. Fears, Dependence, and Withdrawal

Respondent behavior is elicited by preceding stimuli called *unconditioned stimuli*. The responses they control involve the reactions of the smooth muscles (heart, diaphragm, blood vessels, stomach, colon, pupils, and so forth) and glands (adrenals, salivary glands, and sweat glands, for example). Emotional reactions such as fear, love, and hate involve various combinations of respondent reactions.

Neutral stimuli that consistently precede unconditioned stimuli also come to elicit reflexive actions. Social reinforcers are made effective through this reflex conditioning process. Sexual arousal that occurs simply from looking at someone you love has been conditioned in a similar way. Fears are conditioned when formerly neutral events are followed by aversive (punishing) stimuli.

A conditioned stimulus can be neutralized by repeatedly presenting the conditioned stimulus without the associated unconditioned stimulus. This process is called extinction. Fears can be extinguished if the fear-arousing stimulus is repeatedly presented and no aversive stimulus occurs.

A conditioned stimulus can also be neutralized through counter-conditioning. In this process, the conditioned stimulus precedes a response incompatible with the one now elicited. A gradual introduction of the feared stimulus while something positive is happening is an efficient procedure for eliminating a fear. Another is to reinforce closer and closer approaches to the feared stimulus.

Approaches to any emotional problem such as fear should be stated in terms of operant behavior and its consequences, since one can readily see it. It is easier to see and deal with what is happening when you focus on operant behavior rather than emotional or reflexive behavior.

Fear of school often involves emotional reactions to leaving mother, rather than a fear of school itself. The case of Karl illustrated one approach to eliminating such a fear. He was first reinforced, through doll play, for more grown-up feelings and actions; then, step by step, he was reinforced for going to school and staying there.

The key to understanding dependent behavior, such as pleading, "Help me," acting babyish, and clinging to adults for attention, is to recognize that it is maintained by social reinforcers. These can be used to teach independent behavior. When reinforcers are withdrawn from a particular behavior, the teacher should anticipate an increase in that behavior at first and some possible emotional outbursts before extinction.

A child may withdraw from adults, peers, or activities because of a conditioned fear, prior extinction of all behavior in that situation, or the failure of someone to teach the appropriate social behavior in the first place. In each case, the solution involves the reinforcement of the desired interactions.

Unit 16. Conduct Problems

Conduct problems involve intense, active, unlawful, or immoral behavior. They always have a payoff. The child learns to get reinforcement and to avoid punishment. This unit focused on the origins of such problems and approaches to changing them. There are programs for changing aggressive behavior, negativism, fighting, verbal abuse, hyperactivity, and delinquent behavior such as stealing, cheating, and lying. The basic strategy for solving these problems is to prevent the undesired behavior from paying off and to reinforce behavior incompatible with that which you wish to extinguish.

Unit 17. Self-Management

We earn various freedoms as we grow up by learning to respect the freedom of others. Responsible self-management does not come automatically; it has to be learned. We are taught to consider the long-term reinforcing and punishing consequences of our actions. This is not easy, because distal consequences are not easily connected to current behavior. The teacher, the parent, the responsible adult needs to step in and teach children the long-term consequences of their behavior when potential conflict situations arise.

In teaching long-term values, the first step is to talk about them—state a general rule about the consequences of certain kinds of behavior—so the students will learn to identify long-term consequences. Next, give practice in identifying situations where long-term consequences should be considered. Finally, give practice (in protected situations) in struggling with the consequences of different actions where values are in conflict.

The experimental study of self-management behavior is very young. One thing is clear from current research: children become responsible only if they are taught to be so. Studies have shown that when children record their own behavior, changes sometimes take place. But self-recording procedures are more effective if combined with praise from important adults. Self-recording and self-evaluation of behavior works well in token economies after the students have had training and experience. Students can also be taught to determine their own rewards in a responsible way. Current work is examining alternative designs for self-governing systems to find those that most readily foster responsible behavior with the greatest freedom from adult authority.

Another approach to self-management is through a careful understanding of behavior principles. If we can find ways to control (change) the stimulus variables that control what we do, we can change our own behavior in desired directions. We can learn to control *eliciting* stimuli that upset us by learning to relax when we start to feel upset or by learning to think about pleasant things. We can use *discriminative* and *reinforcing* stimuli to prompt a change in our own behavior and to strengthen the new behavior. The use of such procedures (as taught by behavior therapists) has been effective in relieving unhappiness, improving studying, stopping smoking, losing weight, and counselling married couples. *Negative reinforcers* can be established through the use of mechanical devices (for example, the alarm clock) to help us manage ourselves more effectively. One can also make promises or enter into contracts with others to provide *reinforcement* and *punishment* to achieve a desired change. Finally, in self-management, we should keep in mind that reinforcers vary in effectiveness with deprivation and satiation conditions. Temptation can be avoided by doing certain risky things (such as shopping when trying to diet) only under satiation conditions.

The task of self-management is not easy. It is best accomplished in cooperation with others who can help you achieve your goals.

review exercises

Unit 10

1 Give examples of how social and activity reinforcers might be used in a high school classroom. Specify a situation and what you would do.
2 For each of the following incidents in full class instruction, specify what you could say or do to handle the situation:
   a) The teacher needs papers passed out.
   b) It's time for recess. The room is noisy and the children are out of their seats.
   c) It's time for the Pledge of Allegiance.
   d) It's time to go home. The class is rowdy.
   e) The children are quietly working on an art project.
   f) The children return from recess in an orderly fashion.
   g) The bathroom group leader reports that everyone behaved well.
   h) Mary offers to help Linda finish cleaning up the paints so that Linda can go to recess on time.
   i) Bob's group works quietly on a science project while the rest of the class is seated and reading.
   j) Jimmy completes a three-minute task in arithmetic in three minutes. He has always taken twenty minutes before and needed a lot of coaxing.

k) Cedrick's arithmetic paper is neater than it has ever been.

l) Marty cleans up his messy desk without being asked.

m) Maria puts on her own boots at recess and doesn't plead for help as usual.

n) In a clear voice, John tells the class about his turtle. John usually talks softly, if at all.

3 For each of the following incidents in small group instruction specify what you could say or do:

a) Tom stays with a difficult arithmetic problem for seven minutes, without any success.

b) Five of six children are with you during a presentation. The sixth is not.

c) Charlie answers very quickly when called on in arithmetic.

d) Ann doesn't answer when called on for an individual task.

e) Bill answers when Ann is called on for an individual task.

f) A child asks to go to the bathroom in the middle of a lesson.

g) A child is on task but is displaying mildly disruptive behavior such as foot tapping or chair rocking.

h) One child announces to the group and teacher that he doesn't like the tangible reinforcement (such as raisins or cookies) that the teacher is using for the group.

i)) When asked to find something on the page, the children slap the presentation material, nearly knocking it out of the teacher's hand.

j) A child turns around and talks to visitors during the teacher's presentation.

k) Viriginia cries when she makes a mistake during her individual task.

l) The teacher calls on a child for an individual turn. The child nervously says, "I don't want a turn. I can't do it."

4 For each of the following times of the day, name three possible activity reinforcers the teacher might use:

a) Opening activities

b) Reading period

c) Seatwork or study period

5 Describe content material for children that is likely to be reinforcing or fun.

6 Describe the general procedure for embedding conditioned reinforcers in neutral material.

7 Describe a teaching style that is likely to create drama and suspense.

8 Indicate the two points in teaching a task at which it is important to use a variable pause.

9 Give an example of using the two pauses at the right places.

10 Present a teaching sequence showing the use of hinting.

11 Demonstrate the use of variable patterns of speech to make material interesting. Present the same task in a deadpan manner.

12 Demonstrate the procedure of making a drill into a race.

13 Demonstrate the procedure of making deliberate mistakes.

14 Demonstrate taking a negative approach in teaching the universality of a rule.

15 Outline how you might handle the first day of class in kindergarten, in high school geometry.

Unit 11

1 Describe the components of a token reinforcer system.

2 Indicate when such systems might be used and when they should not be used.

3 Explain why the use of special reinforcers is not bribery.

4 Describe the six main steps in designing a token system.

5 What would you do to maintain the gains of a token system while eliminating it in your own class?

6 How would you maintain gains from a token system in a special class when it comes time to return the children to their regular class?

7 Give examples of token systems existing in the business sector of our society.

8 Describe a number of places where token systems might be used to help people learn more appropriate behaviors.

Unit 12

1 State the four main features of a teacher-student contract.

2 Describe the features of a term-course contract.

3 How would a learning-center contract differ from a term-course contract? Why?

4 How would a home-school contract differ from school-based contracts?

5 Why is an explicit, effective instructional program essential to a term-course contract?

6 Describe Keller's system for "personalized instruction," and outline its essential components.

7 Give a research outcome related to study of Keller's personalized instructional system and discuss its implications for design of a contract system. (Be able to do this for each outcome mentioned).

8 Give an example of the use of a home-school contract.

9 Discuss the structure of *this* course in relation to point-contract systems.

Unit 13

1 Define two types of punishment.

2 Explain how a conditioned punisher is established.

3 What is meant by saying that a reinforcer is effective?

4 What happens when a reinforcer no longer follows a response?

5 Why did scientists think that punishment was not an effective way to weaken behavior?

6 Reinforced behavior returns to its prereinforcement strength when it is not reinforced any longer. What happens to punished behavior when it is not punished any longer?

7 Extend the principle of immediacy to punishment: why are responses that are punished immediately weakened more than those punished after a delay?

8 Explain the difference between escape behavior and avoidance behavior.

9 How is avoidance behavior learned?

10 Why should teachers avoid using punishment?

11 Analyze cheating, truancy, lying, and sneaking as effects of the use of punishment to control the behavior of children.

12 Give two key procedures involving reinforcers that are central to weakening undesired behavior.

13 Give five additional procedures for using punishment.

14 Explain what is meant by time out.

15 Is isolation always time out?

16 Give four different procedures that could be considered time out.

17 What is response cost?

18 By analogy, what would a type 2 reinforcer be?

19 Give two situations in which the use of punishment may be necessary.

20 Explain the multiple functions of stimuli such as "stop that" that have been paired with punishment.

21 What are some apparent positive benefits of the use of time out by parents?

22 What factors influence the effectiveness of time out?

23 Which is more effective, time out or response cost?

Unit 14

1 Explain why an attitude is subjective.

2 Explain how it is possible to infer attitudes from behavior.

3 Describe a procedure for teaching a child that he is a failure in school.

4 Specify three general procedures likely to produce attitudes of self-esteem and self-confidence.

5 Outline a procedure for teaching persistence.

6 Outline a procedure for teaching confidence in one's own judgment.

7 Describe the procedures used to get Robert to like himself, school, and reading.

8 Explain why those who emphasize self-esteem as a teaching goal have the cart before the horse.

Unit 15

1 Define and give an example of *operant behavior*.

2 Define and give an example of *respondent behavior*.

3 Explain what is meant by an unconditioned stimulus.

4 Explain what is meant by a conditioned stimulus.

4 Describe how Watson and Rayner conditioned a fear in a child.

6 Draw a model of respondent conditioning.

7 Illustrate how the initially neutral preceding stimuli can take on functional relations to operants and respondents at the same time.

8 Illustrate how unconditioned reinforcers can be unconditioned stimuli at the same time.

9 Explain why the teacher using good reinforcement techniques need not be concerned about emotional development in most cases.

10 Describe two ways to eliminate fears and other conditioned reactions.

11 Describe the procedures used by Patterson to eliminate a child's fear of school.

12 Explain what different types of dependent behavior have in common.

13 Give a general rule for changing dependent behavior.

14 Give three reasons why children may exhibit withdrawn behavior.

15 What is the general procedure for changing withdrawn behavior?

Unit 16

1 What kinds of behavior are covered by the term *conduct problem?*

2 What is common to the development of all conduct problems?

3 What are the common steps related to eliminating conduct problems?

4 How can a child be taught to throw tantrums?

5 Specify three ways to eliminate tantrums, and explain what is common to all these procedures.

6 Explain how negative behavior gets started and is maintained. Give an example.

7 Give one way of dealing with negative behavior.

8 Describe a study that supports the theory that reinforcement of intense response forms is critical for the development of aggressive behavior.

9 Specify one approach to eliminating swearing and name calling.

10 Define *hyperactivity*.

11 State how hyperactivity is related to brain damage.

12 Specify a procedure for dealing with hyperactivity.

13 In what way is our social system responsible for conduct problems such as stealing, lying, and cheating?

Unit 17

1 How could behavioral principles be used to meet the objectives of a "free school"?

2 Describe the steps taken in using behavioral principles to help establish an open classroom.

3 Describe the steps in teaching children about the long-term consequences of their actions.

4 Summarize the research findings on the effects of self-recording on behavior changes.

5 What procedures seem to be important for making self-evaluation and self-management of reinforcers effective in maintaining responsible behavior?

6 Give an example of how to study effective self-government systems experimentally.

7 Give an example of how eliciting stimuli can be used in self-management.

8 Give an example of the use of discriminative stimuli in self-management.

9 Give an example of the use of reinforcing stimuli in self-management.

10 Give an example of the use of negative reinforcers in self-management.

11 Give an example of the use of punishing stimuli in self-management.

12 What do you see as the potential traps in programs for changing your own behavior?

13 What advice given in this unit might be helpful in avoiding the traps associated with self-management?

14 What is meant by the "mutual escalation of use of coercion" as underlying marital conflict?

15 Suggest some procedures for de-escalation.

16 Why are we responsible for each other?

references

Unit 1

1 R. W. Malott, D. A. General, and V. B. Snapper, *Issues in the Analysis of Behavior* (Kalamazoo, Mich: Behaviordelia, 1973), p. 180. There may also be an additional issue in the Heisenberg Principle, namely the uncertainty that arises in distinguishing energy and mass in non-Newtonian physics. See: N. R. Hanson, "Philosophical implications of quantum mechanics," in P. Edwards (ed.), *Encylopedia of Philosophy*. Vol. 7 (New York: Macmillan, 1967).

2 M. Schlick, *Problems of Ethics* (New York: Prentice-Hall, 1939).

Unit 2

1 David Phillips, "Applications of Behavioral Principles to Classroom Settings," in W. C. Becker (ed.), *An Empirical Basis for Change in Education* (Palo Alto: Science Research Associates, 1971).

2 W. S. Wood, "The Lincoln Elementary School Projects: Some Results of an In-Service Training Course in Behavioral Psychology," in W. C. Becker (ed.), *An Empirical Basis for Change in Education* (Palo Alto: Science Research Associates, 1971).

Unit 3

1 R. P. Hawkins, R. F. Peterson, E. Schweid, and S. W. Bijou, "Behavior Therapy in the Home: Amelioration of Problem Parent-Child Relations with the Parent in a Therapeutic Role," *Journal of Experimental Child Psychology*, 1966, 4, 99–107.

2 W. C. Becker, C. H. Madsen, C. R. Arnold, and D. R. Thomas, "The Contingent Use of Teacher Attention and Praise in Reducing Classroom Behavior Problems," *Journal of Special Education*, 1967, 1(3), 287–307.

3 C. H. Madsen, Jr., W. C. Becker, and D. R. Thomas, "Rules, Praise, and Ignoring: Elements of Elementary Classroom Control," *Journal of Applied Behavior Analysis*, 1968, 1, 139–50.

4 C. W. Wilson and B. L. Hopkins, "The Effects of Contingent Music on the Intensity of Noise in Junior High Home Economics Classes," *Journal of Applied Behavior Analysis*, 1973, 6, 269–75.

5 N. Hauserman, S. R. Walen, and M. Behling, "Reinforced Racial Integration in the First Grade: A Study in Generalization," *Journal of Applied Behavior Analysis*, 1973, 6, 193–200.

6 J. A. Hermann, A. I. de Montes, B. Dominguez, F. Montes, and B. L. Hopkins, "Effects of Bonuses for Punctuality on the Tardiness of Industrial Workers," *Journal of Applied Behavior Analysis*, 1973, 6, 563–70.

7 R. W. Solomon and R. G. Wahler, "Peer Reinforcement Control of Classroom Problem Behavior," *Journal of Applied Behavior Analysis*, 1973, 6, 49–56.

8 J. R. Powell and N. Azrin, "The Effects of Shock as a Punisher for Cigarette Smoking," *Journal of Applied Behavior Analysis*, 1968, 1, 63–71.

Unit 4

1 C. H. Madsen, Jr., W. C. Becker, D. R. Thomas, L. Koser, and E. Plager, "An Analysis of the Reinforcing Function of 'Sit Down' Commands," in R. K. Parker (ed.), *Readings in Educational Psychology* (Boston: Allyn & Bacon, 1968) 265–78.

2 D. R. Thomas, W. C. Becker, and M. Armstrong, "Production and Elimination of Disruptive Classroom Behavior by Systematically Varying Teacher's Behavior," *Journal of Applied Behavior Analysis*, 1968, 1, 35–45.

3 E. H. Zimmerman and J. Zimmerman, "The Alteration of Behavior in a Special Classroom Situation," *Journal of the Experimental Analysis of Behavior*, 5, 1962, p. 1.

4 J. E. Hasazi and S. E. Hasazi, "Effects of Teacher Attention on Digit-Reversal Behavior in an Elementary School Child," *Journal of Applied Behavior Analysis*, 1972, 5, 157–62.

5 A. Cossairt, R. V. Hall, and B. L. Hopkins, "The Effects of Experimenter's Instructions, Feedback, and Praise on Teacher Praise and Student Attending Behavior," *Journal of Applied Behavior Analysis*, 1973, 6, 89–100.

Unit 5

1 David Premack, "Reinforcement Theory," in D. Levine (ed.), *Nebraska Symposium on Motivation* (Lincoln: University of Nebraska Press, 1965) 123–88.

2 A. E. Kazdin and J. Klock, "The Effect of Nonverbal Teacher Approval on Student Attentive Behavior," *Journal of Applied Behavior Analysis*, 1973, 6, 643–54.

3 J. Buell, P. Stoddard, F. Harris, and D. M. Baer, "Collateral Social Development Accompanying Reinforcement of Outdoor Play in a Preschool Child," *Journal of Applied Behavior Analysis*, 1968, 1, 167–73.

4 J. D. Long and R. L. Williams, "The Comparative Effectiveness of Group and Individually Contingent Free Time with Inner-City Junior High School Students," *Journal of Applied Behavior Analysis,* 1973, *6,* 465–74.

5 K. A. Lattal, "Contingency Management of Toothbrushing Behavior in a Summer Camp for Children," *Journal of Applied Behavior Analysis,* 1969, *2,* 195–98.

6 L. W. McAllister, J. G. Stachowiak, D. M. Baer, and L. Conderman, "The Application of Operant Conditioning Techniques in a Secondary School Classroom," *Journal of Applied Behavior Analysis,* 1969, *2,* 277–85.

Unit 6

1,2 These were end-of-term papers for a class in behavior modification conducted by Becker and Madsen, 1967, Urbana, Ill.

3 E. S. Geller, J. C. Farris, and D. S. Post, "Prompting a Consumer Behavior for Pollution Control," *Journal of Applied Behavior Analysis,* 1973, *6,* 367–76.

4 V. T. Mawhinney, D. E. Bostow, D. R. Laws, G. J. Blumenfeld, and B. L. Hopkins, "A Comparison of Students Studying-Behavior Produced by Daily, Weekly, and Three-week Testing Schedules," *Journal of Applied Behavior Analysis,* 1971, *4,* 257–64.

5 L. A. Doke and T. R. Risley, "The Organization of Day-Care Environments: Required *vs* Optional Activities," *Journal of Applied Behavior Analysis,* 1972, *5,* 405–20.

6 T. C. Lovitt and K. A. Curtiss, "Effects of Manipulating an Antecedent Event on Mathematics Response Rate," *Journal of Applied Behavior Analysis,* 1968, *1,* 329–33.

7 R. G. Wahler, "Setting Generality: Some Specific and General Effects of Child Behavior Therapy," *Journal of Applied Behavior Analysis,* 1969, *2,* 239–46.

Unit 7

1 T. Ayllon, "Intensive Treatment of Psychotic Behavior by Stimulus Satiation and Food Reinforcement," *Behavior Research and Therapy,* 1963, *1,* 53–61.

2 B. F. Skinner and S. Krakower, *Handwriting with Write and See,* (Chicago: Lyons and Carnahan, 1968) pp. 18, 48, 118, 119. Manuscript 2 Cursive.

3 S. Striefel and B. Wetherby, "Instruction-following

Behavior of a Retarded Child and Its Controlling Stimuli," *Journal of Applied Behavior Analysis,* 1973, *6,* 663–70.

4 O. I. Lovaas, R. Koegel, J. Q. Simmons, and J. S. Long, "Some Generalization and Follow-up Measures on Autistic Children in Behavior Therapy," *Journal of Applied Behavior Analysis,* 1973, *6,* 131–66.

5 H. M. Walker and N. K. Buckley, "The Use of Positive Reinforcement in Conditioning Attending Behavior," *Journal of Applied Behavior Analysis,* 1968, *1,* 245–50.

Unit 8

1 H. M. Walker and N. K. Buckley, *Token Reinforcement Techniques: Classroom Applications for the Hard-to-Teach Child.* (Eugene, Oregon: E-B Press, 1974), p. 24.

2 O. R. Lindsey, "Intermittent Grading," *The Clearing House: A journal for modern junior and senior high schools,* 1958, *32,* 451–54.

3 B. H. Salzberg, A. J. Wheeler, L. T. Devar, and B. L. Hopkins, "The Effect of Intermittent Feedback and Intermittent Contingent Access to Play on Printing of Kindergarten Children," *Journal of Applied Behavior Analysis,* 1971, *4,* 163–71.

4 B. F. Skinner and S. Krakower, *Handwriting with Write and See,* (Chicago: Lyons and Carnahan, 1968).

5 P. Weisberg and P. B. Waldrop, "Fixed-Interval Work Habits of Congress," *Journal of Applied Behavior Analysis,* 1972, *5,* 93–7.

6 F. D. Kirby and F. Shields, "Modification of Arithmetic Response Rate and Attending Behavior in a Seventh-Grade Student," *Journal of Applied Behavior Analysis,* 1972, *5,* 79–84.

7 S. M. Dietz and A. C. Repp, "Decreasing Classroom Misbehavior through the Use of DRL Schedules of Reinforcement," *Journal of Applied Behavior Analysis,* 1973, *6,* 457–63.

8 M. L. Schwarz and R. P. Hawkins, "Application of Delayed Reinforcement Procedures to the Behavior of an Elementary School Child, *Journal of Applied Behavior Analysis,* 1970, *3,* 85–96.

Unit 10

1 S. I. Cohen, J. M. Keyworth, R. I. Kleiner, and W. L. Brown, "Effective Behavior Change at the Anne Arundel Learning Center through   Minimum

Contact Interventions," in R. Ulrich, T. Stachnik, and J. Mabry (eds.) *Control of Human Behavior*, Vol. 3 (Glenview, Ill.: Scott, Foresman, 1974), 124–42.

2 J. S. Bailey, M. M. Wolf, and E. L. Phillips, "Homebased Reinforcement and the Modification of Pre-delinquents' Classroom Behavior," *Journal of Applied Behavior Analysis*, 1970, 3, 223–33.

Unit 11

1 M. M. Wolf, D. K. Giles, and R. V. Hall, "Experiments with Token Reinforcement in a Remedial Classroom," *Behavior Research and Therapy*, 1968, 6, 51–64.

2 K. D. O'Leary and W. C. Becker, "Behavior Modification of an Adjustment Class: a Token Reinforcement Program," *Exceptional Children*, 1967, 33, 640.

3 H. M. Walker and N. K. Buckley, *Token Reinforcement Techniques: Classroom Applications for the Hard-to-Teach Child* (Eugene, Oregon: E-B Press, 1974), 172, 177, 178.

4 H. M. Walker, R. H. Mattson, and N. K. Buckley, "The Functional Analysis of Behavior within an Experimental Class Setting," in W. C. Becker (ed.) *An Empirical Basis for Change in Education* (Chicago: Science Research Associates, 1971), 236–63.

5 H. M. Walker, W. E. Fiegenbaum, and H. Hops, "Components Analysis and Systematic Replication of a Treatment Model for Modifying Deviant Classroom Behavior," Report No. 5, Center at Oregon for Research in the Behavioral Education of Handicapped (Eugene, Oregon: University of Oregon, 1971), 1–63.

6 R. J. Ingham and G. Andrews, "An Analysis of a Token Economy in Stuttering Therapy," *Journal of Applied Behavior Analysis*, 1973, 6, 219–29.

7 J. P. Wincze, H. Leitenberg, and W. S. Agras, "The Effects of Token Reinforcement and Feedback on the Delusional Verbal Behavior of Chronic Paranoid Schizophrenics," *Journal of Applied Behavior Analysis*, 1972, 5, 247–62.

8 T. Ayllon and E. Haughton, "Modification of Symptomatic Verbal Behaviour of Mental Patients," *Behaviour Research and Therapy*, 1964, 2, 87–97.

9 D. Meichenbaum, "The Effects of Instructions and Reinforcement on Thinking and Language Behavior of Schizophrenics," *Journal of Abnormal Psychology*, 1966, 71.

10 E. L. Phillips, "Achievement Place: Token Reinforcement Procedures in a Home-style Rehabilitation Setting for Pre-delinquent Boys," *Journal of Applied Behavior Analysis*, 1968, 1, 213–23.

11 E. R. Christopherson, C. M. Arnold, D. W. Hill, and H. R. Quilitich, "The Home Point System: Token Reinforcement Procedures for Application by Parents of Children with Behavior Problems," *Journal of Applied Behavior Analysis*, 1972, 5, 485–97.

Unit 12

1 F. S. Keller, "A Programmed System of Instruction," *Behavior Modification Monographs*, Roger Ulrich (ed.) (Kalamazoo, Michigan: Behavior Development, 1970) 1, 3.

2 W. C. Sheppard and H. B. MacDermot, "Design and Evaluation of a Programmed Course in Introductory Psychology," *Journal of Applied Behavior Analysis*, 1970, 3, 5–11.

3 J. S. McMichael and J. R. Corey, "Contingency Management in an Introductory Psychology Course Produces Better Learning," *Journal of Applied Behavior Analysis*, 1969, 2, 79–83.

4 J. Farmer, G. D. Lachter, J. J. Blaustein, and B. K. Cole, "The Role of Proctoring in Personalized Instruction," *Journal of Applied Behavior Analysis*, 1972, 5, 401–404.

5 E. Alba and H. S. Pennypacker, "A Multiple Change Score Comparison of Traditional and Behavioral College Teaching Procedures," *Journal of Applied Behavior Analysis*, 1972, 5, 121–24.

6 G. Semb, B. L. Hopkins, and D. E. Hursh, "The Effects of Study Questions and Grades on Student Test Performance in a College Course," *Journal of Applied Behavior Analysis*, 1973, 6, 631–42.

7 J. M. Johnston and G. O'Neill, "The Analysis of Performance Criteria Defining Course Grades as a Determinant of College Student Academic Performance," *Journal of Applied Behavior Analysis*, 1973, 6, 261–68.

8 D. E. Bostow and R. J. O'Connor, "A Comparison of Two College Classroom Testing Procedures: Required Remediation *versus* No Remediation," *Journal of Applied Behavior Analysis*, 1973, 6, 599–607.

9 S. Engelmann, W. C. Becker, L. Carnine, L. Meyers, J. Becker, and G. Johnson, *E-B Press Corrective Reading Program* (Eugene, Oregon: E-B Press, 1974).

10 W. S. MacDonald, R. Gallimore, and G. Mac-
Donald, "Contingency Counseling by School Per-
sonnel: An Economical Model of Intervention,"
Journal of Applied Behavior Analysis, 1970, *3*, 175–82.

11 S. I. Cohen, J. M. Keyworth, R. I. Kleiner, and W.
L. Brown, "Effective Behavior Change at the Anne
Arundel Learning Center through Minimum Con-
tact Interventions," in R. Ulrich, T. Stachnik, and J.
Mabry (eds.), *Control of Human Behavior*, Vol. 3
(Glenview, Ill.: Scott, Foresman, 1974), p. 133.

Unit 13

1 N. H. Azrin and W. C. Holz, "Punishment," in W.
K. Honig (ed.) *Operant Behavior: Areas of Research
and Application*, (New York: Appleton-Century-
Crofts, 1966), 380–447.

2 G. L. Thorne, R. G. Tharp, and R. J. Wetzel, "Behavior Modification Techniques: New Tools for
Probation Officers," *Federal Probation*, 1967, *31*,
21–7.

3 O. I. Lovaas and J. Q. Simmons, M. D., "Manipulation of Self-destruction in Three Retarded Children," *Journal of Applied Behavior Analysis*, 1969, *2*,
143–57.

4 R. L. Koegel and A. Covert, "The Relationship of
Self-stimulation to Learning in Autistic Children,"
Journal of Applied Behavior Analysis, 1972, *5*, 381–87.

5 V. M. Nordquist, "The Modification of a Child's
Enuresis: Some Response-Response Relation-
ships," *Journal of Applied Behavior Analysis*, 1971, *4*,
241–47.

6 R. G. Wahler, "Oppositional Children: A Quest for
Parental Reinforcement Control," *Journal of Applied
Behavior Analysis*, 1969, *2*, 159–70.

7 L. V. McReynolds, "Application of Timeout from
Positive Reinforcement for Increasing the Effi-
ciency of Speech Training," *Journal of Applied Behavior Analysis*, 1969, *2*, 199–205.

8 J. D. Burchard and F. Barrera, "An Analysis of
Timeout and Response Cost in a Programmed Environment," *Journal of Applied Behavior Analysis*,
1972, *5*, 271–82.

Unit 14

1 A. W. Staats and W. H. Butterfield, "Treatment of
Nonreading in a Culturally-Deprived Juvenile Delinquent: An Application of Reinforcement Principles," *Child Development*, 1965, *36*, 925–42.

2 D. R. Thomas, L. J. Nielsen, D. S. Kuypers, and W.
C. Becker, "Social Reinforcement and Remedial Instruction in the Elimination of a Classroom Behavior Problem," *Journal of Special Education*, 1967,
2, 291–302.

Unit 15

1 J. B. Watson and R. Rayner, "Conditioned Emotional Reactions," *Journal of Experimental Psychology*, 1920, *3*, 1–14.

2 M. C. Jones, "A Laboratory Study of Fear: The Case
of Peter," *Pediatrics Seminar*, 1924, *31*, 308–15.

3 G. R. Patterson, "A Learning Theory Approach to
the Treatment of the School-Phobic Child," in L. P.
Ullmann and L. Krasner (eds.), *Case Studies in Behavior Modification* (New York: Holt, Rinehart &
Winston, 1965), 279–85.

4 F. R. Harris, M. K. Johnston, C. S. Kelley, and M.
M. Wolf, "Effects of Positive Social Reinforcement
on Regressed Crawling of a Nursery-School Child,"
Journal of Educational Psychology, 1964, *55*, 35–41.

5 K. E. Allen, B. Hart, J. S. Buell, F. R. Harris, and M.
M. Wolf, "Effects of Social Reinforcement on Isolate
Behavior of a Nursery-School Child," *Child De-
velopment*, 1964, *35*, 511–18.

6 H. R. Foxwell, C. L. Thomason, B. A. Coats, D. M.
Baer, and M. M. Wolf, "The Development of Social
Responsiveness to Other Children in a Nursery-
School Child through Experimental Use of Social
Reinforcement," unpublished manuscript, Univer-
sity of Kansas.

7 M. K. Johnston, C. S. Kelley, F. R. Harris, and M.
M. Wolf, "An Application of Reinforcement Princi-
ples to Development of Motor Skills of a Young
Child," *Child Development*, 1966, *37*, 379–87.

Unit 16

1 E. H. Zimmerman and J. Zimmerman, "The Alteration of Behavior in a Special Classroom Situation,"
Journal of the Experimental Analysis of Behavior,
1962, *5*, 59–60.

2 J. Dollard, L. W. Doob, N. E. Miller, O. H. Mowrer,
and R. R. Sears, *Frustration and Aggression* (New
Haven: Yale University Press, 1939).

3 R. H. Walters and M. Brown, "A Test of the
High-Magnitude Theory of Aggression," *Journal of
Experimental Child Psychology*, 1964, *1*, 376–87.

4 P. Brown and R. Elliot, "Control of Aggression in a

Nursery School Class," *Journal of Experimental Child Psychology*, 1965, 2, 103–107.

5 B. M. Hart, N. J. Reynolds, D. M. Baer, E. R. Brawley, and F. R. Harris, "Effects of Contingent and Noncontingent Social Reinforcement on the Cooperative Play of a Preschool Child," *Journal of Applied Behavior Analysis*, 1968, 1, 73–6.

6 G. R. Patterson, "An Application of Conditioning Techniques to the Control of a Hyperactive Child," in L. P. Ullmann and L. Krasner (eds.), *Case Studies in Behavior Modification* (New York: Holt, Rinehart & Winston, 1965), 370–75.

Unit 17

1 C. L. Salzberg, "Freedom and Responsibility in an Elementary School," in George Semb (ed.), *Behavior Analysis & Education* (Lawrence, Kansas: University of Kansas Support and Development Center for Follow Through, Department of Human Development, 1972), 62–77.

2 M. McNeil, S. Hasazi, A. Muller, and M. Knight, "Open Classrooms: Supporters of Applied Behavior Analysis," in George Semb (ed.), *Behavior Analysis & Education* (Lawrence, Kansas: University of Kansas Support and Development Center for Follow Through, Department of Human Development, 1972), 112–26.

3 M. Broden, R. V. Hall, and B. Mitts, "The Effect of Self-recording on the Classroom Behavior of Two Eighth-Grade Students," *Journal of Applied Behavior Analysis*, 1971, 4, 191–99.

4 D. L. Fixsen, E. L. Phillips, and M. M. Wolf, "Achievement Place: The Reliability of Self-reporting and Peer-reporting and Their Effects on Behavior," *Journal of Applied Behavior Analysis*, 1972, 5, 19–30.

5 D. A. Santogrossi, K. D. O'Leary, R. G. Romanczyk, and K. F. Kaufman, "Self-evaluation by Adolescents in a Psychiatric Hospital School Token Program," *Journal of Applied Behavior Analysis*, 1973, 6, 277–87.

6 D. R. Knapczyk and G. Livingston, "Self-recording and Student Teacher Supervision: Variables within a Token Economy Structure," *Journal of Applied Behavior Analysis*, 1973, 6, 481–86.

7 K. F. Kaufman and K. D. O'Leary, "Reward, Cost, and Self-evaluation Procedures for Disruptive Adolescents in a Psychiatric Hospital School," *Journal of Applied Behavior Analysis*, 1972, 5, 293–309.

8 T. C. Lovitt and K. Curtiss, "Academic Response Rate as a Function of Teacher- and Self-imposed Contingencies," *Journal of Applied Behavior Analysis*, 1969, 2, 49–53.

9 E. L. Glynn, "Classroom Applications of Self-determined Reinforcement," *Journal of Applied Behavior Analysis*, 1970, 3, 123–32.

10 E. L. Glynn, J. D. Thomas, and S. M. Shee, "Behavioral Self-control of On-task Behavior in an Elementary Classroom," *Journal of Applied Behavior Analysis*, 1973, 6, 105–13.

11 O. D. Bolstad and S. M. Johnson, "Self-regulation in the Modification of Disruptive Behavior," *Journal of Applied Behavior Analysis*, 1972, 5, 443–54.

12 D. L. Fixsen, E. L. Phillips, and M. M. Wolf, "Achievement Place: Experiments in Self-government with Pre-delinquents," *Journal of Applied Behavior Analysis*, 1973, 6, 31–47.

13 E. L. Phillips, E. A. Phillips, M. M. Wolf, and D. L. Fixen, "Achievement Place: Development of the Elected Manager System," *Journal of Applied Behavior Analysis*, 1973, 6, 541–61.

14 D. A. Bernstein and T. D. Berkover, *Progressive Relaxation Training. A Manual for the Helping Professions* (Champaign, Ill.: Research Press, 1973).

15 L. E. Homme, "Control of Coverants, the Operants of the Mind," *Psychological Record*, 1965, 15, 201–11.

16 N. H. Azrin and J. Powell," Behavioral Engineering: the Reduction of Smoking Behavior by a Conditioning Apparatus and Procedure," *Journal of Applied Behavior Analysis*, 1968, 1, 193–200.

17 N. H. Azrin and J. Powell, "Behavioral Engineering: The Use of Response Priming to Improve Prescribed Self-medication," *Journal of Applied Behavior Analysis*, 1969, 2, 39–42.

18 R. A. Mann, "The Behavior-Therapeutic Use of Contingency Contracting to Control an Adult Behavior Problem: Weight Control," *Journal of Applied Behavior Analysis*, 1972, 5, 99–109.

19 G. R. Patterson and J. Reid, "Reciprocity and Coercion: Two Facets of Social Systems." Paper presented at the meeting of the Institute for Research in Clinical Psychology, Lawrence, Kansas, April, 1967.

20 Richard B. Stuart, "Operant-Interpersonal Treatment for Marital Discord," *Journal of Consulting and Clinical Psychology*, 1969, 33, 675–82.

glossary

attitude The feelings one has about some class of stimulus events.

aversive stimulus A stimulus that decreases behavior when it is presented as a consequence (a punishing stimulus). A stimulus, the *contingent removal* of which increases the rate of behavior (a negative reinforcer). In common language, a painful, intensive, unpleasant stimulus.

avoidance behavior Getting away from something unpleasant by doing something to keep from getting into an unpleasant situation.

back-up reinforcer A reinforcing object or event that is received in exchange for a specific number of points or tokens.

baseline A measured behavioral performance taken over many observations against which the effects of experimental variables can be assessed (also called "base rate" or "operant level").

behavior Any observable and measureable act of an organism. A response.

behavior chain A series of alternating discriminative stimuli (S^D's) and responses. S^D's in a chain function as discriminative stimuli for responses that follow them and as conditioned reinforcers for preceding responses.

cause An antecedent event that reliably (consistently) produces an effect. If A, then B.

chain Two or more S $\rightarrow$ R sequences are combined into a longer (and fixed) behavioral sequence and followed by a terminal reinforcer (for example, S $\rightarrow$ R $\rightarrow$ S $\rightarrow$ R $\rightarrow$ S).

conditioned punisher A formerly neutral stimulus that acquires the properties of a punishing stimulus as a result of its being presented repeatedly just before another aversive stimulus.

conditioned reinforcer A formerly neutral stimulus that has repeatedly preceded a reinforcer and functions to strengthen or maintain a behavior on which it is contingent.

conduct problem A label given to intense, active, unlawful, or immoral behavior shown by children.

consequent stimulus A following stimulus which controls operant behavior by increasing or decreasing its future occurrence.

contingency A rule governing the delivery of consequent stimuli which states "if and only if response A occurs will reinforcer (or punisher) B be given."

contingent reinforcement A response is specified and a reinforcing consequence is specified to occur only after the response occurs.

continuous reinforcement Each response is reinforced.

criticism trap A situation in which critical comments seem effective because the criticized behavior often ceases, at least momentarily; however, the criticism actually functions to reinforce the behavior being attended to.

dependent variable That which is caused by a causal variable. In behavior theory, behaviors are the dependent variables.

deprivation A reduced availability of a reinforcer that increases the reinforcer's effectiveness.

determinism An empirical generalization asserting that all nature is lawful (caused), including human behavior.

differential reinforcement A process involving reinforcing some responses in the presence of some stimuli and not reinforcing others.

discrete response A response that has a clearly definable beginning and end (e.g., completing an arithmetic problem, reading a word, pushing a book off a desk).

discriminative stimulus (S^D) A preceding stimulus which sets the occasion where making a certain response is more likely to lead to reinforcement or punishment.

eliciting stimulus A preceding stimulus which controls respondent behavior (causes it).

escape behavior Getting away from an unpleasant situation that is already going on.

extinction The process whereby reinforcers are no longer presented following the response class to be weakened, but may be presented for other responses.

fading The gradual removal of a prompt. The gradual removal of components of a token system (or some special reinforcement system) to make it more like an ordinary classroom situation.

fixed-interval schedule (FI) A reinforcer is given for the first response to occur after each X minutes. The response rate is slowest just after reinforcement and highest prior to the time for next reinforcement.

fixed-ratio schedule (FR) A reinforcer is given after each X responses, producing a high response rate when in effect (more than in continuous reinforcement, less than in variable ratio).

free will Choice behavior not under coercion. Philosophically, the term also implies that choice behavior is not caused physically or divinely. This latter assumption is rejected on the basis of current knowledge of behavior.

home-school contract A contract written at school where the "payoff" comes from the parents.

incompatible behavior A behavior that cannot be performed at the same time as another behavior. For example, one cannot be studying and running around the room at the same time.

independent variable That which produces a change in a dependent variable, a cause. In behavior theory, stimulus events are the independent variables.

indeterminism A situation where events cannot be predicted; randomness, chance.

intermittent reinforcement A procedure in which only some correct responses are reinforced.

learned punisher (conditioned punisher) A formerly neutral stimulus is presented following a response, and the response occurs less frequently in the future.

learned reinforcer (conditioned reinforcer) A formerly neutral stimulus is presented following a response, and the response occurs more frequently in the future.

learning-center contract A contract which provides for reinforcers other than grades, and which may be negotiated individually as to learning requirements, points earned, and possible reinforcers.

multiple baseline design An experimental design that involves obtaining baseline measures on several dependent behaviors and applying a change procedure to each of the dependent behaviors at different points in time.

negative reinforcer The termination of a stimulus following a response, which has the effect of strengthening that response class.

operant behavior Involves the striated muscular system, is controlled by consequent stimuli, and is equivalent to voluntary or intelligent behavior.

personalized instruction A system of teaching developed by Keller where a course is broken into units and progress is checked on each unit individually. Students move through the course at their own pace. Lectures are minimized.

physical prompting The teacher physically moves the student through the response, e.g., take hand and help draw a letter.

predestination Belief that a God-like being has prearranged worldly events according to a plan.

Premack principle A higher-frequency behavior (more preferred activity) is made contingent upon a lower-frequency behavior (less preferred activity), and is likely to strengthen or increase the lower-frequency behavior.

primary reinforcers See unlearned reinforcer. Also called an unconditioned reinforcer.

prompt Previously learned discriminative stimulus which can be used to get a response to occur to a new stimulus. Prompts are eventually faded.

punisher (punishing stimulus) A following stimulus which weakens or decreases the future occurrence of the response class.

punishment The procedure of using a punisher.

reinforcement The procedure of using a reinforcer.

reinforcer (reinforcing stimulus) A following stimulus which strengthens or increases the future occurrence of the response class.

resistance to extinction Refers to how long or how often a response continues to occur in the absence of reinforcement.

respondent behavior Involves the smooth muscles and glands, is controlled by preceding stimuli (eliciting stimuli), and is reflexive in nature.

response cost Specified units of reinforcers are taken away after a response is made, and the response weakens.

reversal procedure An experimental technique that involves the removal of the change procedure in order to test the effectiveness of the procedure (an ABA design). A baseline (A) is followed by an experimental condition (B), which is followed by a return to baseline (A).

satiation The loss of effectiveness of a reinforcer when presented repeatedly (usually in a short time period).

scallop A pattern on a cumulative response record that is made up of a sequence of positively accelerating curves:

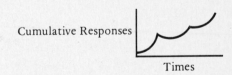

Usually associated with a fixed-interval schedule of reinforcement.

schedule of reinforcement   A rule describing which response will be reinforced.

scientific control   Demonstration of a causal relationship. Event A controls or causes event B.

self-management   Learning to manage consequences on one's own. Learning to use behavioral principles to change one's own behavior.

shaping   A behavior change procedure involving differential reinforcement and a shifting criterion for reinforcement.

shifting criterion for reinforcement   The criterion for reinforcement is initially set at a level that allows for reinforcement of behavior that is most like the target behavior. As responses closer to the target behavior are made, the criterion is again shifted. Each time the criterion is shifted, the changed criterion is a little closer to the desired target.

social reinforcer   A formerly neutral stimulus that is based on the behavior of a person is presented following a response, and the response occurs more frequently in the future.

stimulus   A physical object or event that an organism may respond to.

term-course contract   A contract specifies what must be done to earn points, how many points are required for what grade, and the sanctions for the failure to achieve a passing performance.

time out   The loss of access to all reinforcers for a period of time as a consequence of making some responses, and the response weakens.

token reinforcer   A formerly neutral stimulus that is tangible is presented following a response, and the response occurs more frequently in the future.

type 1 punishment   The presentation of events which are generally referred to as painful or aversive.

type 2 punishment   Involves the taking away or cutting off of reinforcers (includes response cost and time out).

unconditioned punisher   A stimulus that has not been previously paired with a punisher is presented following a response and decreases the frequency of the response (weakens the response).

unconditioned reinforcer   A stimulus that has not been previously paired with a reinforcer is presented following a response, and increases the frequency of the response (strengthens the response).

unlearned punisher   A stimulus that has not been previously paired with a punisher is presented following a response and decreases the frequency of the response (weakens the response.)

unlearned reinforcer   A stimulus that has not been previously paired with a reinforcer is presented following a response, and increases the frequency of the response (strengthens the response.)

variable-interval schedule (VI)   A reinforcer is given for the first response after each X minutes, on the average, producing a steady rate of responding.

variable-ratio schedule (VR)   A reinforcer is given after X responses on the average, producing very high response rates. The higher the ratio of reinforcement to responses, the higher the rate. This schedule is very resistant to extinction.

author index

subject index

ABAB experimental design, 101
Achievement Place, 194–95, 222–24, 318, 320
Activation syndrome, 285
Activity reinforcers, 97–100, 122, 184–187, 193–94
Affection, 101
Attention, 55, 69, 70
Attitudes, 272–73, 288
Aversive stimuli, 255, 259
Avoidance behavior, 58–59, 257–58, 273–74, 289–90

Back-up reinforcers, 209–12
Baseline, 53
Behavior (behavior class), 1–2, 21–25
Behavior chains, 115–16
Behavioral practice, 70, 72
"Being helpful" trap, 77–79
Bribery, 9, 206–7

Cause, 1–8
Chains. *See* Behavior chains
Change of pace, 122, 189–91
Circular explanations, 10–11
Classroom management, 2, 116–24
Concept teaching, 114–15
Conditioned punishers, 97, 100, 171, 255
Conditioned reinforcers, 95, 97, 99–100, 116, 155, 171, 207
Conditioned stimuli, 96, 285–86
Conduct problems, 301–7. *See* Problem behaviors
Consequence. *See* Consequent stimuli
Consequent stimuli, 21–23, 54–55, 96
Contingency, 100
Contingent reinforcement, 98, 100
Continuous reinforcement, 156
Continuous-stream behavior, 26
Contracts, 6–7, 211, 325–26, 326–29. *See* Point-contract systems
Control of behavior. *See* Determinism
Cost contingency. *See* Response cost
Counter-conditioning, 288–90
Criticism trap, 67–77
Cushion activity, 122, 186

DRL schedule, 163–64
Delay in reinforcement, 155, 164
Delayed auditory feedback, 219
Dependent variable, 1–3, 11
Deprivation, 322
Determinism, 1–8
Differential reinforcement, 114, 128, 136–37
Discrete response, 26
Discriminative stimuli, 22–23, 68, 113, 115, 116, 125, 128, 171, 263, 288, 321–22, 324–25
Drill, 190

Eliciting stimuli, 22, 96, 171, 284–86, 288, 320
Eliminating fears, 288–90
    counter-conditioning, 288–90
    extinction, 288
    reinforce approach behavior, 289–90
Emotional reactions, 285

Escape behavior, 257–58, 273–74
Extinction, 54–56, 114, 288

Fading, 115, 116, 216, 221–222
Fears, 285–286, 288–90
Feedback (effects of), 79–80, 219–20
Feelings, 288
First day of class, 191–92
Fixed-interval schedule (FI), 156–57, 161–63, 208
Fixed-ratio schedule (FR), 156–57
Following instructions, 122
Fooler games, 191
Free school, 313–15
Free time (effects of), 102
Free will, 6–8
Freedom of choice, 4, 312–15. *See also* Free will
Frustration, 304

Graphing, 48, 50, 74, 77, 84, 91, 152, 238

Home-school contract, 249–50
Humanistic values, 3–4

Ignore, 28, 54, 58
Immediate reinforcement, 154–55
Improvement, 155–56, 209
Incompatible behavior, 259
Independent variable, 1–3, 11
Indeterminism, 6
Individualizing instruction, 120–21, 208–10, 315–17
Instructions (effects of), 79–80
Intermittent grading, 160–61
Intermittent reinforcement, 156, 160–61, 162–63
Isolation, 260

Learned punisher, 97, 100
Learned reinforcer, 95, 97, 99–100, 116
Learning center, 193–94
Learning-center contract, 247

Medical model, 10
Models, 259, 274
Multiple-baseline design, 103

Natural lawfulness, 2–8
Natural laws, 7–8
Negative reinforcement, 255
Negative reinforcer, 55–56, 322
Neutral stimuli, 95, 96, 116, 189, 285–86

Open classroom, 315–17
Operant behavior, 2, 8–9, 21, 170–284
Operant model, 22–23, 113, 116

Peer reinforcement, 58
Persistence, 158–60, 275–76
Personalized instruction, 240–46
Physical prompting, 142
Point-contract systems, 239–250
    home-school contract, 249–50
    learning-center contract, 247
    term-course contract, 240–46
Point systems. *See* Token reinforcement systems
Positive reinforcement, 255
Positive reinforcer, 55–56

Teaching 1 is set in ten point Palatino, a fresh, graceful typeface by Hermann Zapf, 1950. Typesetting is by Holmes Typography, San Jose, California, and printing by The George Banta Co., Menasha, Wisconsin.

Sponsoring Editor: Karl Schmidt
Project Editor: Carol Harris
Designer: Paula Tuerk
Artist: Frank Remkiwicz